LIMINAL NOIR IN CLASSICAL WORLD CINEMA

Traditions in World Cinema

General Editors
Linda Badley (Middle Tennessee State University)
R. Barton Palmer (Clemson University)

Founding Editor
Steven Jay Schneider (New York University)

Titles in the series include:
Traditions in World Cinema
Linda Badley, R. Barton Palmer and Steven Jay Schneider (eds)

Post-beur Cinema: North African Émigré and Maghrebi-French Filmmaking in France since 2000
Will Higbee

New Taiwanese Cinema in Focus: Moving Within and Beyond the Frame
Flannery Wilson

International Noir
Homer B. Pettey and R. Barton Palmer (eds)

Films on Ice: Cinemas of the Arctic
Scott MacKenzie and Anna Westerståhl Stenport (eds)

Nordic Genre Film: Small Nation Film Cultures in the Global Marketplace
Tommy Gustafsson and Pietari Kääpä (eds)

Contemporary Japanese Cinema Since Hana-Bi
Adam Bingham

Chinese Martial Arts Cinema: The Wuxia Tradition (Second edition)
Stephen Teo

Slow Cinema
Tiago de Luca and Nuno Barradas Jorge

Expressionism in the Cinema
Olaf Brill and Gary D. Rhodes (eds)

French-language Road Cinema: Borders, Diasporas, Migration and 'New Europe'
Michael Gott

Transnational Film Remakes
Iain Robert Smith and Constantine Verevis

Coming-of-Age Cinema in New Zealand
Alistair Fox

New Transnationalisms in Contemporary Latin American Cinemas
Dolores Tierney

Celluloid Singapore: Cinema, Performance and the National
Edna Lim

Short Films from a Small Nation: Danish Informational Cinema 1935–1965
C. Claire Thomson

B-Movie Gothic: International Perspectives
Justin D. Edwards and Johan Höglund (eds)

Francophone Belgian Cinema
Jamie Steele

The New Romanian Cinema
Christina Stojanova (ed.) with the participation of Dana Duma

French Blockbusters: Cultural Politics of a Transnational Cinema
Charlie Michael

Nordic Film Cultures and Cinemas of Elsewhere
Anna Westerståhl Stenport and Arne Lunde (eds)

New Realism: Contemporary British Cinema
David Forrest

Contemporary Balkan Cinema: Transnational Exchanges and Global Circuits
Lydia Papadimitriou and Ana Grgić (eds)

Mapping the Rockumentary: Images of Sound and Fury
Gunnar Iversen and Scott MacKenzie (eds)

Images of Apartheid: Filmmaking on the Fringe in the Old South Africa
Calum Waddell

Greek Film Noir
Anna Poupou, Nikitas Fessas, and Maria Chalkou (eds)

Norwegian Nightmares: The Horror Cinema of a Nordic Country
Christer Bakke Andresen

Late-colonial French Cinema: Filming the Algerian War of Independence
Mani Sharpe

Australian International Pictures (1946–75)
Adrian Danks and Constantine Verevis

Film Censorship in a Cultural Context
Daniel Sacco

Liminal Noir in Classical World Cinema
Elyce Rae Helford and Christopher Weedman

Please see our website for a complete list of titles in the series
www.edinburghuniversitypress.com/series/TIWC

LIMINAL NOIR IN CLASSICAL WORLD CINEMA

Edited by
Elyce Rae Helford and
Christopher Weedman

EDINBURGH
University Press

Edinburgh University Press is one of the leading university presses in the UK.
We publish academic books and journals in our selected subject areas across the
humanities and social sciences, combining cutting-edge scholarship with high editorial
and production values to produce academic works of lasting importance. For more
information visit our website: edinburghuniversitypress.com

© editorial matter and organisation Elyce Rae Helford and Christopher Weedman, 2023, 2025
© the chapters their several authors, 2023, 2025

Edinburgh University Press Ltd
13 Infirmary Street
Edinburgh EH1 1LT

First published in hardback by Edinburgh University Press 2023

Typeset in 10/12.5 pt Sabon
by IDSUK (DataConnection) Ltd

A CIP record for this book is available from the British Library

ISBN 978 1 4744 9814 2 (hardback)
ISBN 978 1 4744 9815 9 (paperback)
ISBN 978 1 4744 9816 6 (webready PDF)
ISBN 978 1 4744 9817 3 (epub)

The right of Elyce Rae Helford and Christopher Weedman to be identified as the editors
of this work has been asserted in accordance with the Copyright, Designs and Patents
Act 1988, and the Copyright and Related Rights Regulations 2003 (SI No. 2498).

CONTENTS

List of Figures vii
Acknowledgements ix
Notes on Contributors xi
Traditions in World Cinema xv

Introduction: Liminality and the Boundaries of Film Noir 1
Elyce Rae Helford and Christopher Weedman

PART I. EXPOSING CULTURAL ANXIETIES

1. The Despair of the Noir Generation: Wajda's *Ashes and Diamonds* 11
   Alan Woolfolk

2. The Fleap Being Neither Flea nor Fly: Ida Lupino's Interrogations
   of Female Trauma in *Never Fear* 23
   Julie Grossman

3. Running Aimlessly: *Camino Cortado* and Autarkic Spain 37
   Fernando Gabriel Pagnoni Berns

4. Race and the Noir Western: Navigating *The Walking Hills* 51
   Elyce Rae Helford

PART II. RECONCEPTUALISING NATIONAL CINEMAS

5. 'My Mama Done Tol' Me': Jewish Émigré Noir, Hybridity, and Black-Jewish Relations in *Blues in the Night* — 69
   Vincent Brook

6. Expressionism, Existentialism, and Socialism in *Scars of the Past* — 87
   Milan Hain

7. The Deadly Seduction of a Rake: British Costume Melodrama, Noir, and the 'Othered' Woman in *The Gypsy and the Gentleman* — 105
   Christopher Weedman

8. Argentine Gothic-Noir Fusion in *The Black Vampire* — 131
   Osvaldo Di Paolo Harrison and Nadina Olmedo

PART III. AESTHETICS AND ANTECEDENTS

9. A 'Feeling of Suspension': Tradition and Modernity in *La Pointe Courte* — 147
   Alicia Byrnes

10. Dostoyevsky '58: Richard Brooks's *Brothers Karamazov* as Baroque Noir — 161
    Matthew Sorrento

11. Men in Black: *I Confess*, the Hitchcock Noir, and the American Gothic — 180
    David Greven

Selected Bibliography — 195
Index — 207

FIGURES

2.1	Sleep represents unawareness of women's trauma in *Never Fear*	28
2.2	Carol (Sally Forrest) foregrounded in crisis while her lover remains oblivious in *Never Fear*	29
2.3	A marginalised Carol (Sally Forrest) clings to the walls as she re-enters the world	34
3.1	Cecilia (Laya Raki) typifies the (Spanish) femme fatale	42
3.2	The most desired object in autarchic Spain: the passport	44
3.3	The gang of criminals looks for a place to rest but finds only abandoned towns	46
4.1	The noir western is a story told in hats in *The Walking Hills*	54
4.2	The earnest, sensual appeal of performer Josh White	60
5.1	Gentile versus Jewish émigré noir protagonists: Mitchum in *Out of the Past* versus Robinson in *Scarlet Street*	71
5.2	*Blues in the Night* as musical comedy and as musical noir	73
6.1	Karel Höger as the alienated mining engineer Vochoč	98
6.2	Vilma (Dana Medřická) defies many social norms and conventions, yet she comes off as a less threatening partner for Štěrba than his own wife	100

FIGURES

7.1	The rakish Deverill (Keith Michell) succumbs to the seductive Belle (Melina Mercouri)	117
8.1	A publicity poster for *El Vampiro Negro* that includes Gothic and noir imagery	132
11.1	Father Logan (Montgomery Clift) anxiously hears the murderer's confession	181
11.2	The Hitchcock cameo: the director strides across the screen atop Quebec City's 'L'escalier Casse-cou'	184

ACKNOWLEDGEMENTS

As co-editors, our first thanks go to the contributors, whose compelling studies provide the substance of this volume, illustrating whatever merit our subject and approach possess in illuminating the ongoing value of classic noir cinema for international film studies in the twenty-first century. We are grateful to have been introduced to compelling theory and new films by tremendous scholars at all stages of the profession. We appreciate and value the support of many at Edinburgh University Press, especially Gillian Leslie, Sam Johnson, Fiona Conn, and Christine Barton. A special thanks to series editors Linda Badley and R. Barton Palmer, who not only encouraged us and offered great advice that has improved the volume but also provided introductions to several of the excellent writers whose work is included herein. And cheers to MTSU graduate assistant Lis Sodl for her work on the index.

Elyce thanks her amazingly supportive spouse and son for their encouragement, patience, and reminder to take time away from academic work now and then. Sincere appreciation to Vince Brook for his friendship and helpful feedback on her chapter. And a shout-out to the #BNoirDetour crew that gathered for years on Sunday evenings for public domain noir livetweets.

Christopher is indebted to his wife Eudora and daughter Elenore for their unwavering love, patience, and good humour during the preparation of this volume. He thanks Julian Grainger for helping secure hard-to-find

ACKNOWLEDGEMENTS

British films for his chapter. He also extends his sincerest gratitude to Mary L. Bogumil, Parley Ann Boswell, Onur Duman, Susan Felleman, Christopher Hanlon, Connie Russell Hosier, Michael R. Molino, Theodore K. Quinn, and Tony Williams for their generous support and encouragement over the years.

CONTRIBUTORS

Fernando Gabriel Pagnoni Berns (PhD in Arts, PhD candidate in History) is Professor of Filosofía y Letras at the Universidad de Buenos Aires. He teaches courses on international horror film and serves as the director of *Grite*, a research group on horror cinema currently investigating horror in Baltic regions. He is author of *Historias para no Dormir* (2020) on Spanish horror television and has edited collections on the *Frankenstein* bicentennial, director James Wan (2021), and the Italian giallo film. Currently, he is editing a volume on Hammer horror and another on Wes Craven.

Vincent Brook retired as a long-time UCLA Lecturer in 2021. He has authored or edited ten books, most on Jewish issues in film and television. These include *Something Ain't Kosher Here: The Rise of the 'Jewish' Sitcom* (2003), *Driven to Darkness: Jewish Émigré Directors and the Rise of Film Noir* (2009), and *From Shtetl to Stardom: Jews and Hollywood* (2017, co-editor). He has also written *Land of Smoke and Mirrors: A Cultural History of Los Angeles* (2013) and *All About Eva: A Holocaust-Related Memoir, with a Hollywood Twist* (2021), about his German-Jewish parents' experiences in Nazi Germany and as refugees in America. Most recently, he's started a blog, babblingbrook.substack.com, on media and politics.

Alicia Byrnes is a Teaching Associate in Screen Studies at the University of Melbourne working at the intersection of women's issues in cinema and film technology. She received her PhD in Screen and Cultural Studies from Melbourne in 2021, where she was awarded the Thesis Excellence Award and the Australian Postgraduate Award. She received her MA in Cinema Studies from New York University. Her current book project, *The Matter of Absence: Female Disembodiment and Digital Cinema*, asserts the value of contemporary film technology for negotiating issues of women's representation. Her work has appeared or is forthcoming in *Film-Philosophy*, *Senses of Cinema*, and *Science Fiction Film & Television*.

Osvaldo Di Paolo Harrison is Professor of Latin American Literary and Cultural Studies at Austin Peay State University. He has published seven books related to hard-boiled literature and film noir: *Crisis del sistema capitalista en la novela negra hispana* (2022), *Femicrímenes: Femicidios en la literatura del siglo XX y XXI* (2020), *Queer Noir hispánico* (2018), *Noir Boricua: La novela negra de Puerto Rico* (2016), *Negrótico* (2015), *Gemidos y explosiones apocalípticas poshumanas: la novela negra y de ciencia ficción hispana del siglo XXI* (2013), and *Cadáveres en el armario: el policial palimpséstico en la literatura argentina contemporánea* (2011). He has also published book chapters and numerous peer-reviewed essays in national and international journals.

David Greven is Professor of English at the University of South Carolina. His books include *Intimate Violence: Hitchcock, Sex, and Queer Theory* (2017), *Queering the Terminator* (2017), and *Ghost Faces: Hollywood and Post-Millennial Masculinity* (2016). His essays on film have appeared in the journals *Screen*, *Quarterly Review of Film and Video*, *Cinema Journal*, *Genders*, *Studies in Gender and Sexuality*, *Postmodern Culture*, *The Hitchcock Annual*, *Film International*, *Flow*, *Jump Cut*, *CineAction*, and *Cineaste*, and the critical collections *The Cambridge Companion to Alfred Hitchcock*, *Close-Up: Great Cinematic Performances*, *Patricia Highsmith on Screen*, *Reading Sex and the City*, *Action Chicks*, and *Reading the Bromance: Homosocial Relationships in Film and Television*. He is currently writing a book on the Merchant-Ivory film *Maurice* (1987) for the revived 'Queer Film Classics' series.

Julie Grossman is Professor of English and Communication and Film Studies at Le Moyne College in Syracuse, New York. She is author of *Rethinking the Femme Fatale in Film Noir: Ready for Her Close-Up* (2009), *Literature, Film, and Their Hideous Progeny: Adaptation and ElasTEXTity* (2015), and *The Femme Fatale* (2020). She is co-author (with Therese Grisham) of *Ida Lupino, Director: Her Art and Resilience in Times of Transition* (2017) and co-author and co-editor with Will Scheibel (respectively) of *Twin Peaks* (2020) and *Penny Dreadful and Adaptation: Reanimating and Transforming the Monster* (2023). She is founding co-editor (with R. Barton Palmer) of the book series 'Adaptation and Visual Culture' and co-editor (with Palmer and Marc C. Conner) of *Screening Contemporary Irish Fiction and Drama* (2022). With Palmer, she co-edited the essay collection *Adaptation in Visual Culture: Images, Texts, and Their Multiple Worlds* (2017).

Milan Hain is Assistant Professor and program director of Film Studies at Palacký University in Olomouc, Czech Republic. He is the author or co-author of five books on cinema, including, most recently, *Starmaker: David O. Selznick and the Production of Stars in the Hollywood Studio System* (2023). Hain's articles have appeared in *Jewish Film and New Media*, the *Journal of Adaptation in Film and Performance*, and *Quarterly Review of Film and Video*. Recently, he was the recipient of the Visiting Research Fellowship at the University of Łódź, where he researched the representation of Czech and Polish identities in studio-era Hollywood. Since 2013, he has been a programmer at the annual Czech Noir Film Festival (www.noirfilmfestival.cz), the only event of its kind in Central Europe.

Elyce Rae Helford (www.elycehelford.com) is Professor of English, faculty in Women's and Gender Studies, and director of the Jewish and Holocaust Studies minor at Middle Tennessee State University. She is the author of *What Price Hollywood?: Gender and Sex in the Films of George Cukor* (2020) and editor or co-editor of multiple collections on gender representation in American popular media. Recent and forthcoming publications include 'Racial Darkness in *Ace in the Hole*' (*Journal of Cinema and Media Studies*, 2022), which addresses Native American and Jewish representation alongside issues of Holocaust survivor guilt in Billy Wilder's 1951 noir drama, and 'Traumatic Timescapes: Holocaust Memory in Jane Yolen's *The Devil's Arithmetic* and Nava Semel's *And the Rat Laughed*' in *Jewish Future Females*, edited by Marleen S. Barr. Helford is book reviews editor for the journal *Jewish Film and New Media* and serves on its editorial board.

Nadina Olmedo is Associate Professor of Spanish and Latin American Studies at the University of San Francisco. Her research focuses on Gothic literature, women and gender studies, and emergent horror cinemas. She is the author of *Ecos goticos en la novela del Cono Sur* (2013) and co-author of *Negrotico* (2015). She is the co-editor of the journal *Polifonia, Revista de Estudios hispanicos*.

Matthew Sorrento teaches Film Studies at Rutgers University-Camden and is editor-in-chief of *Film International*. He is the author of *The New American Crime Film* (2012) and co-editor of *David Fincher's* Zodiac: *Cinema of Investigation and (Mis)Interpretation* (2022). He has published chapters on *Full*

Metal Jacket, hybrid westerns, *The Purge* series, the crime documentary, and NBC's *Hannibal*, with entries forthcoming on Wes Craven's work in television and David Lynch and film noir. His current research focuses on noir writer David Goodis on screen, indie filmmaker Nicole Holofcener, the crime novels of W. R. Burnett, and the SyFy series *Channel Zero*. His reviews/essays have appeared in the *Los Angeles Review of Books, Film & History, The Journal of the Fantastic in the Arts, Senses of Cinema, Middle West Review,* and *Critical Studies in Television*.

Christopher Weedman is Assistant Professor of English at Middle Tennessee State University, where he serves as both director of General Education English and faculty advisor of the interdisciplinary Film Studies minor. His scholarship has appeared in *Film International, Jewish Film and New Media, Journal of Cinema and Media Studies, Quarterly Review of Film and Video, Senses of Cinema,* and the edited collections *Fifty Hollywood Directors* (2015) and *David Fincher's* Zodiac: *Cinema of Investigation and (Mis)Interpretation* (2022). He is co-editor (with Anne Etienne and Benjamin Halligan) of the collection *Adult Themes: British Cinema and the X Certificate in the Long 1960s* (2023). Currently, he is writing a critical biography of Anne Heywood, the groundbreaking British film star of *The Fox* (1967) and *I Want What I Want* (1972).

Alan Woolfolk is Vice President of Academic Affairs and Dean of the Faculty Emeritus at Flagler College. He is a scholar of social, cultural, and political theory who has published extensively on contemporary culture, public intellectuals, nationalism, literature, and film, and he has twice been a National Endowment for the Humanities Fellow. Woolfolk is currently working on the book *Dark Charisma: Agency, Authenticity, and Alien Space in Noir Film*.

TRADITIONS IN WORLD CINEMA

General editors: **Linda Badley and R. Barton Palmer**
Founding editor: **Steven Jay Schneider**

Traditions in World Cinema is a series of textbooks and monographs devoted to the analysis of currently popular and previously underexamined or undervalued film movements from around the globe. Also intended for general interest readers, the textbooks in this series offer undergraduate- and graduate-level film students accessible and comprehensive introductions to diverse traditions in world cinema. The monographs open up for advanced academic study more specialised groups of films, including those that require theoretically-oriented approaches. Both textbooks and monographs provide thorough examinations of the industrial, cultural, and socio-historical conditions of production and reception.

The flagship textbook for the series includes chapters by noted scholars on traditions of acknowledged importance (the French New Wave, German Expressionism), recent and emergent traditions (New Iranian, post-Cinema Novo), and those whose rightful claim to recognition has yet to be established (the Israeli persecution film, global found footage cinema). Other volumes concentrate on individual national, regional, or global cinema traditions. As the introductory chapter to each volume makes clear, the films under discussion form a coherent group on the basis of substantive and relatively transparent, if not always obvious, commonalities. These commonalities may be formal, stylistic or thematic, and the groupings may, although they need not, be popularly identified as genres, cycles, or movements (Japanese horror, Chinese martial arts cinema, Italian Neorealism). Indeed, in cases in which a group of films is not already commonly identified as a tradition, one purpose of the volume is to establish its claim to importance and make it visible (East Central European Magical Realist cinema, Palestinian cinema).

Textbooks and monographs include:

- An introduction that clarifies the rationale for the grouping of films under examination
- A concise history of the regional, national, or transnational cinema in question
- A summary of previous published work on the tradition
- Contextual analysis of industrial, cultural and socio-historical conditions of production and reception
- Textual analysis of specific and notable films, with clear and judicious application of relevant film theoretical approaches
- Bibliograph(ies)/filmograph(ies)

Monographs may additionally include:

- Discussion of the dynamics of cross-cultural exchange in light of current research and thinking about cultural imperialism and globalisation, as well as issues of regional/national cinema or political/aesthetic movements (such as new waves, postmodernism, or identity politics)
- Interview(s) with key filmmakers working within the tradition.

INTRODUCTION: LIMINALITY AND THE BOUNDARIES OF FILM NOIR

Elyce Rae Helford and Christopher Weedman

An appreciation of classical film noir and its importance to international cinema studies must begin with an understanding of its rich and complex history. The earliest influential studies of what has come to be identified as film noir emerged from France in the immediate post-World War II era and concentrated on a subset of Hollywood films that had previously been withheld from distribution in France during the *années noires* (dark years) of the Nazi occupation (1940–4). In their seminal 1955 study, *A Panorama of American Film Noir*, Raymond Borde and Étienne Chaumeton followed the lead of earlier critics Nino Frank and Jean-Pierre Chartier by applying the term 'film noir' to a strain of American motion pictures that French cinephiles encountered in July and August 1946.[1] These films, including John Huston's *The Maltese Falcon* (1941), Billy Wilder's *Double Indemnity* (1944), Otto Preminger's *Laura* (1944), and Edward Dmytryk's *Murder, My Sweet* (1944) were based largely on hard-boiled crime fiction written during the 1930s and 1940s (called *Série noire* by the French). Produced and distributed by various Hollywood film studios such as Warner Bros., Paramount, Twentieth Century-Fox, and RKO, these motion pictures shared 'an unusual and cruel atmosphere' as well as a 'very particular eroticism', establishing a historical 'noir series' of films by 1946. This American cycle, Borde and Chaumeton confidently announced, 'is seemingly beyond question'.[2] That this dark series of films reflected a more expansive transnational cultural mood and influence was left largely unconsidered, as was agreement on exactly what elements define film noir.

The difficulty of developing unifying or even cohesive definitions of film noir has not stopped critics from trying. Raymond Durgnat, for instance, posits the centrality of crime or criminals within an 'interbreeding' process of motifs, from 'crime as social criticism' and 'middle class murder' to 'sexual pathology' and 'psychopaths'.[3] In popular culture, noir is instead often defined by its recurring character types, such as the disillusioned private eye and the duplicitous femme fatale; by its bleak and gritty urban settings; by its subjective and, at times, complex flashback structure; or by its low-key, chiaroscuro cinematography. In this volume, we will find that the most useful definitions recognise the origins, influences, and cultural affect of noir. Paul Schrader, for example, outlines a valuable definition coming from 'the more subtle qualities of tone and mood' that are drawn from a series of 'catalytic elements', including historical ('war and post-war disillusionment'), filmic ('post-war realism' and 'German influence'), and literary ('the hard-boiled tradition').[4] These qualities – as well as Schrader's acknowledgement of 'foreign offshoots of *film noir*' from Britain and France such as Carol Reed's *The Third Man* (1949), Jean-Luc Godard's *À bout de souffle* (*Breathless*, 1959), and Jean-Pierre Melville's *Le Doulos* (1962) – illustrate what Andrew Spicer, as part of an ever-growing contemporary body of scholarship, rightly interprets as 'a transnational cultural phenomenon'.[5]

Some critics have productively made noir's definitional elusiveness the centrepiece of their analysis. James Naremore, for example, argues that film noir does not comprise a definitive genre or a unique style. Nor, he claims, can it even best be defined as 'transgeneric'. As he posits, 'Neither the film industry nor the audience follows structuralist rules, and movie conventions have always blended together in mongrelized ways.'[6] Film noir certainly involves historical and social connections; nevertheless, we cannot fully establish final boundaries or uniformity for the category.[7] As Marc Vernet, David Bordwell, Janet Staiger, Kristin Thompson, Steve Neale, and Naremore have demonstrated, the majority of films combine thematic, narrative, and stylistic elements from diverse categories and, as a result, they are, in Naremore's words, 'transgeneric or polyvalent'.[8]

In his Introduction to the Edinburgh University Press collection *Film Noir*, Homer B. Pettey openly acknowledges the problematics of 'imposing systematic, often rigid categories upon art'.[9] He recognises 'the dire need for scholars to construct a homogeneous schema for a collection of seemingly heterogeneous elements comprising film noir' as well as 'an historical evolution for film noir', but he concludes by refusing to reduce complexity for the sake of cohesiveness. Instead, Pettey's book provides a group of essays that offer 'aesthetic, thematic and interpretive strategies for opening up, expanding upon, revisiting, and re-evaluating film noir'.[10] This volume works in similar fashion.

To return to the original French critical perspective, we can understand how the creation of 'film noir' was governed and limited by its historical and cultural context. Vital is recognition that the critics who identified the original 'cycle' of noir films were ardent fans of American cinema. As R. Barton Palmer argues, 'Frank, Chartier, and others were intrigued by US productions that seemed consonant with a substantial trend within their own national cinema: the gloomy romanticism and poignant melancholia of 30s Poetic Realism.'[11] While often acknowledged alongside German expressionism as a crucial influence on film noir, poetic realism must also be recognised as having an impact on the French critics themselves, men whose affection for Hollywood led them to define noir as coming from beyond their own national borders. When explored through a broader global lens, the post-war period that brought the dark series of formerly banned Hollywood films to an appreciative French audience also saw 'the developing fashion for dark melodramas in both British and the revived German cinemas'.[12] Echoing while further nuancing contemporary scholarship, Palmer thus identifies film noir as, from its conception, 'complexly trans-national'.[13]

With similar emphasis, Pettey commences the Introduction to Edinburgh's *International Noir* with acknowledgment that 'film noir from its inception has always been a culturally diverse genre, style, sensibility and movement', adding that similar problems emerge when attempting to define or delineate the meanings of '"world", "international", or "global"' cinema.[14] Exploring film noir in such a context, he reminds us, 'requires an analytic sensitivity to aesthetic and narrative influences migrating across countries and continents'.[15]

Liminal Noir therefore begins with an appreciation of and indebtedness to a nearly 75-year history of scholarship that has defined, redefined, critiqued, and broadened the indefinite international category of film we call 'noir' to the point that it can persuasively be defined as 'one of the dominant intellectual categories of the late twentieth century' and beyond.[16] This volume proceeds from the premise that film noir theory and criticism offer a useful apparatus for reconsidering and reassessing international films from what might loosely be termed the classical era of cinema. Our purpose is not to broaden the noir canon, which, as Spicer observes, already 'remains an object of dispute and estimates of its size vary considerably'.[17] Nevertheless, we recognise that this may be one result. More central to our goals is to explore what Naremore calls more 'interesting uses' of noir.[18]

A central concern of this volume is the ways in which films linked with (though not necessarily identified as) classical noir share what Christopher Breu and Elizabeth A. Hatmaker identify as 'an affective disposition' that crosses national boundaries.[19] From such a perspective, noir is more than a category attached to a corpus; it is perhaps best considered as a way of thinking and feeling that produces texts which share particular qualities and emotional resonances.[20] Such a perspective allows us to expand the boundaries of noir study while acknowledging shared qualities, liminality in particular.

In many ways, liminality may be deemed noir's most defining feature – in areas from content and theme to style and affect. Literal borders are central to the plots of many classical noir films, for example, including contrasts between urban and rural settings (where the former symbolised corruption and the latter an innocence impossible to attain or recover) and flight across national boundaries (such as criminals in the US seeking to cross the Mexican border to escape prosecution). On the level of production, there were shifts across as well as within films from studio settings to location shooting, particularly as newsreels, wartime documentaries, and Italian neorealist cinema, alongside American noirs such as Henry Hathaway's *The House on 92nd Street* (1945), Elia Kazan's *Boomerang!* (1947), and Jules Dassin's *The Naked City* (1948), helped bring a 'semidocumentary' approach to American studio filmmaking.[21] Generic hybridity inflects noir with liminality as well, including diverse blends of established genres that achieve complex moods beyond the traditional boundaries of individual film categories.

Beyond boundaries, we can also see the liminal as related to states of transition. Grounded in the struggles of the global post-Depression and World War II era, social and psychological wellness or wholeness emerges as impossible in film noir. Noir disorients through its foregrounding of absolute states as illusory, marking true self-awareness as unreal. Cultural dictates and norms inflect and block change as they drive both obedience and resistance – often simultaneously. The petty criminal who longs for the big time or tries to go straight, the black widow who craves patriarchal power she cannot achieve, the private detective who seeks respect while shunning it: these core noir types are caught between the limitations of the real and impossible ideals. The impact of such conflicts relates directly to fragmentation, similarly central to noir. As Richard Martin argues, film noir in many aspects is 'about fragmentation, not only stylistically (the disruptive effects of lighting, mise-en-scène, and editing) and structurally (the employment of flashbacks and voice-overs) but also thematically (the dissolution of community and family, the psychological fragmentation of the protagonist)'.[22] From national and generic boundaries to fragmented narratives and divided selves, liminality offers an illuminating concept through which to explore the dark films of the classical era.

The chapters collected for this volume explore liminality, both directly and indirectly, through readings of social and psychological upheaval in films produced internationally between the 1940s and the early 1960s. We have purposely limited our focus to this cinematic period before a new generation of cultural anxieties and tensions – in part reflecting the Vietnam War and the political unrest of the late 1960s and early 1970s – brought about a more self-reflective and self-reflexive style of noir (dubbed 'neo noir') that captured these rapidly changing times. Furthermore, the films under consideration are generally not labelled noir but benefit from a focus on noir liminality in style and content. National cinemas under consideration in this book's case studies include Argentina, Czechoslovakia (now the Czech Republic), Great Britain, France, Poland, Spain, and the United States. While necessarily limited in scope, we intend these selections as representative illustrations. We hope others will expand upon this focus, taking the study of liminal noir in new directions.

The chapters in Part I of the collection, 'Exposing Cultural Anxieties', feature liminally positioned characters during moments of social and political tension within specific national contexts. For Alan Woolfolk, Andrzej Wajda's *Popiól i diament* (*Ashes and Diamonds*, 1958) uses the theme of compromised agency to address the inescapable legacy of Polish struggles against the Third Reich that were followed by violent conflict between Polish nationalists and Communists. Character and nation are inexorably bonded in this dark drama. Julie Grossman offers a study of the US gender politics of female trauma in Ida Lupino's *Never Fear* (1949), a tale of a young dancer on the verge of success who is stricken with polio. Using location shooting to particularise a modern story about desire and disability, *Never Fear* anatomises myths of completion in the contexts of domestic romance and fraught notions of health and the female body. Autarkic Spain provides the background for Fernando Gabriel Pagnoni Berns's study of Ignacio Iquino's *Camino Cortado* (*Closed Road*, 1955). Complex female characterisation, elements of melodrama, and a presentation of geographical asphyxiation result in a potent example of Francoist crime cinema that interrogates impossible hopes of escape. Finally, Elyce Rae Helford considers the racial politics of post-war America in John Sturges's little-known western-noir hybrid *The Walking Hills* (1949). Here, a Mexican border town brings together a group of treasure hunters with hidden pasts, among them an oddly placed African American performer whose diegetic songs speak directly to the film's engagement with concepts of identity.

Part II, 'Reconceptualising National Cinemas', offers case studies of films from the US, Czechoslovakia, Great Britain, and Argentina that visually and thematically explore notions of state and of national boundaries. In his study of Anatole Litvak's *Blues in the Night* (1941), Vincent Brook considers issues of hybridity in World War II-era Hollywood cinema, including the film's combination of comedic, musical, and populist elements alongside noirish violence and expressionist *mise en scène*. Through this close reading, the liminal appears in questions of generic hybridity, race relations, and the role of the Jewish émigré filmmaker. Milan Hain explores Václav Krška's *Zde jsou lvi* (*Scars of the Past*, 1958) for its subversions of prevailing ideological and aesthetic norms in Czechoslovakia of the late 1950s. Through its unconventional dark approach, the film tackles such sensitive issues as individualism and crises of conscience, making it a welcome target for a threatened Communist system. Christopher Weedman reappraises Joseph Losey's critically-neglected *The Gypsy and the Gentleman* (1958), which finds the blacklisted Hollywood director subverting the British costume melodrama by infusing it with an American noir sensibility, particularly in its dark depiction of the duplicitous femme fatale: a half-Romani, half-British travelling woman named Belle. Played by Greek cinema star Melina Mercouri in a sexually bold and aggressive manner seldom found in either British film noirs or Gainsborough-style costume melodramas during the post-World War II period, Belle embodies cultural fears of both female promiscuity and racial miscegenation and arguably serves as a harbinger of the type of sexually complex female performances that became more prevalent on British cinema screens after the emergence of the British New Wave with the release of Jack Clayton's seminal *Room at the Top* in 1959. This section concludes with Osvaldo Di Paolo Harrison and Nadina Olmedo's reading of Román Viñoly Barreto's *El vampiro negro* (*The Black Vampire*, 1953), which examines this Gothic-noir fusion against the context of national tensions over notions of civilisation vs. barbarism in Argentina of the 1950s. Generally considered a remake of Fritz Lang's *M* (1931), *The Black Vampire* combines psychological horror with the detective film to provide a problematic moral guide to national norms of citizenship.

The chapters that comprise Part III, 'Aesthetics and Antecedents', consider the ways in which noir cinematography and other artistic elements impact the meaning and affect of films that have generally been explored apart from noir. Alicia Byrnes reads Agnès Varda's debut film *La Pointe Courte* (1954) as producing an inadvertently noir aesthetic through the repurposing of a modernist novel. Varda's film offers dual narratives linked only by setting into a series of juxtapositions that generate an overall sense of uncertainty characteristic of the liminal and the porous boundaries of modernism. Matthew Sorrento's (re)consideration of Richard Brooks's *The Brothers Karamazov* (1958) focuses on noir style as it energises an adaptation of one of the most page-bound of nineteenth-century novels. While critical commentary has largely dismissed the film as tamed by the Hollywood assembly line, Sorrento illustrates how noir visuals and framing open up the screenplay's chamber-drama treatment. Lastly, David Greven brings cinema and literary history to bear on the visuals, setting, and symbolism of Alfred Hitchcock's *I Confess* (1953). In the context of the American Gothic, Greven explores the film's complex representations of male bonds and homoerotic tensions.

Ultimately, *Liminal Noir* seeks to broaden the study of classical-era international cinema through an expansive conceptualisation of liminality that is central to the original cycle and international dimensions of film noir. Contributors herein create original perspectives that reinvigorate study of a body of relatively neglected or reductively theorised motion pictures from diverse nations. Some titles will be familiar to English-speaking audiences, though usually outside the context of film noir; others will be entirely new, even unavailable outside of their country and language of origin. All reveal the benefits of study through a liminal noir lens. Of course, no single collection can be exhaustive, and our chosen focus and case-study approach has helped both to narrow our focus and to suggest the myriad possibilities of study beyond it. We hope readers learn as much from this volume and its process as we have learned in editing it.

Notes

1. Raymond Borde and Étienne Chaumeton, *A Panorama of American Film Noir: 1941–1953*, trans. Paul Hammond (San Francisco: City Lights Books, 2002), p. 1; Nino Frank, 'A New Kind of Police Drama: The Criminal Adventure' (1946), trans. Alain Silver, in *Film Noir Reader 2*, ed. Silver and James Ursini (New York: Limelight Editions, 1999), pp. 15–19; and Jean-Pierre Chartier, 'Americans Also Make Noir Films' (1946), trans. Alain Silver, in *Film Noir Reader 2*, ed. Silver and James Ursini (New York: Limelight Editions, 1999), pp. 21–3.
2. Borde and Chaumeton, *A Panorama of American Film Noir*, pp. 1–2. Traditional film noir historiographies frequently adhere to Borde and Chaumeton's assertion that the term 'film noir' was coined by Nino Frank in the socialist film journal *L'Écran Français* in August 1946. However, as Charles O'Brien demonstrates, the term's origins can instead be traced back to French newspaper film criticism, published between January 1938 and September 1939, in reference to Marcel Carné's *Quai des brumes* (*Port of Shadows*, 1938), Jean Grémillon's *L'étrange Monsieur Victor* (1938), Jeff Musso's *Le Puritain* (1938), Jean Renoir's *La Bête humaine* (1938), and other French films associated with the proto-noir style of Poetic Realism. Frank, 'A New Kind of Police Drama: The Criminal Adventure', p. 18; and Charles O'Brien, 'Film Noir in France: Before the Liberation', *Iris*, no. 21 (Spring 1996), p. 7.
3. Raymond Durgnat, 'Paint It Black: The Family Tree of the *Film Noir*' (1970), in *Film Noir Reader*, ed. Alain Silver and James Ursini (New York: Limelight Editions, 1996), pp. 37–51.
4. Paul Schrader, 'Notes on Film Noir', *Film Comment* 8, no. 1 (Spring 1972), pp. 9–10.
5. Borde and Chaumeton, *A Panorama of American Film Noir*, p. 1; Schrader, 'Notes on Film Noir', p. 9; and Andrew Spicer, 'Introduction', in *European Film Noir*, ed. Spicer (Manchester: Manchester University Press, 2007), p. 1. See also R. Barton Palmer, 'Film Noir Begins: Some Thoughts', *South Atlantic Review* 86, no. 4 (2021), pp. 1–30. Examples of this growing body of scholarship include William K. Everson, 'British Film Noir: Part I', *Films in Review* 38, no. 5 (May 1987), pp. 285–9; Everson, 'British Film Noir: Part II', *Films in Review* 38, nos. 6–7 (June/July 1987), pp. 341–7; Robin Buss, *French Film Noir* (London: Marion Boyars, 1994); Tony Williams, 'British Film Noir', in *Film Noir Reader 2*, ed. Alain Silver and James Ursini (New York: Limelight Editions, 1999), pp. 243–69; Jennifer Fay and Justus Nieland, *Film Noir: Hard-Boiled Modernity and the Cultures of Globalization* (London: Routledge, 2010); Dennis Broe, *Class, Crime and International Film Noir: Globalizing America's Dark Art* (New York: Palgrave Macmillan, 2014); Homer B. Pettey and R. Barton Palmer, eds, *International Noir* (Edinburgh: Edinburgh University Press, 2014); and Deborah Walker-Morrison, *Classic French Noir: Gender and the Cinema of Fatal Desire* (London: Bloomsbury Academic, 2020).

6. James Naremore, *More than Night: Film Noir in its Contexts* (Berkeley: University of California Press, 1998), p. 6.
7. Naremore, *More than Night*, p. 6.
8. Marc Vernet, 'Genre', *Film Reader*, no. 3 (February 1978), p. 13; David Bordwell, Janet Staiger, and Kristin Thompson, *The Classical Hollywood Cinema: Film Style and Mode of Production to 1960* (New York: Columbia University Press, 1985), pp. 16–17; Steve Neale, 'Questions of Genre', *Screen* 31, no. 1 (1990), pp. 57–8; and Naremore, *More than Night*, p. 6.
9. Homer B. Pettey, 'Introduction: The Noir Turn', in *Film Noir*, ed. Pettey and R. Barton Palmer (Edinburgh: Edinburgh University Press, 2014), p. 10.
10. Pettey, 'Introduction: The Noir Turn', pp. 11, 14.
11. Palmer, 'Film Noir Begins', p. 4.
12. Palmer, 'Film Noir Begins', p. 5.
13. Palmer, 'Film Noir Begins', p. 3.
14. Homer B. Pettey, 'Introduction: The Noir Impulse', in *International Noir*, ed. Pettey and R. Barton Palmer (Edinburgh: Edinburgh University Press, 2014), p. 1.
15. Pettey, 'Introduction: The Noir Impulse', p. 1.
16. Naremore, *More Than Night*, p. 2.
17. Spicer, 'Introduction', p. 2.
18. Naremore, *More Than Night*, p. 6.
19. Christopher Breu and Elizabeth A. Hatmaker, 'Introduction: Dark Passages', in *Noir Affect*, ed. Breu and Hatmaker (New York: Fordham University Press, 2020), p. 7. Also quoted in Palmer, "Film Noir Begins', p. 4.
20. Palmer, "Film Noir Begins', p. 4.
21. Ian Brookes, *Film Noir: A Critical Introduction* (New York: Bloomsbury Academic, 2017), pp. 42–4.
22. Richard Martin, *Mean Streets and Raging Bulls: The Legacy of Film Noir in Contemporary American Cinema* (Lanham, MD: Scarecrow Press, 1999), p. 34.

PART I

EXPOSING CULTURAL ANXIETIES

1. THE DESPAIR OF THE NOIR GENERATION: WAJDA'S *ASHES AND DIAMONDS*

Alan Woolfolk

> The determinist, the fatalist, is in despair and as one in despair has lost his self, because for him everything has become necessary.
>
> Søren Kierkegaard, *The Sickness Unto Death*[1]

The twentieth century was indelibly marked by the traumas of unprecedented wars and revolutions that exploded to the surface of history with the beginning of World War I (WWI) in 1914. Indeed, a strong and obvious case can be made for the start of WWI as the true beginning of a century that was notable for the final dissolution of political and cultural forms that had previously functioned as forms of restraint that kept the worst from happening.[2] With what George Steiner has called 'the breakdown of the European order in the "Thirty Years' War" from 1915 to 1945', successive generations born in the late decades of the nineteenth century and the early decades of the twentieth century experienced in their youth the disorder and despair of 'the dominant phenomenon of twentieth-century barbarism' that resulted in the deaths of tens of millions of human beings in Europe and Russia.[3] The first of these generations, the youngest members of whom came of age around the time of WWI, is commonly known as the 'lost generation'. It was succeeded by a generation whose births were chronologically clustered in the first quarter or so of the twentieth century. The generational consciousness of the oldest members of this cohort was shaped most deeply by WWI and the Russian Revolution, and the generational consciousness of the younger members by the youthful experiences of the Great Depression, the rise of Fascism, the Spanish Civil War, and World War II (WWII). This generation, which I shall call the 'noir generation', grew up and came of age with the experiences and legacies of a series of sustained historical traumas that culminated with the disclosure of European concentration camps and the destruction of Hiroshima and Nagasaki by atomic bombs. Just as the post-WWII generation in the United States came of age with the cultural upheavals and political assassinations of the 1960s and the Vietnam War, or later generations have grown up with the War on Terror and mass killings of students and religious congregations, every generation may be collectively marked by the transgressive events of their youth. But the noir generation may be the first and most extreme of a series of generations that experienced successive violent transgressions on a more massive scale, more directly, and with a greater sense of fatality – more directly because of the enormity of their scale and with a greater sense of fatality because the worst of the transgressions were widely perceived to be crimes of calculated brutality beyond appeal to any higher authority for justice or consolation.[4]

The Dark Past in Historical Context

The noir generation in America and especially Europe is notable for not simply widespread experiences of massive, destructive historical events across a broad range of locations and widespread exposure to symptoms of social destabilisation, but also a deep sense that transgressions were, in fact, without limit, somehow permissible, and the way of the world. The cultural narrative of this generation was prone to accepting violence, crime, and war as inevitable. This acceptance of transgression was frequently complemented by a sense that individual agency and personal responsibility were overmatched and could not prevail in the face of such massive historical disorders. As developed with great insight in what came to be called the genre of film noir, this acceptance of transgression and the abdication of agency that frequently followed were taken for granted and often linked with the notion of a 'dark past' that could not be escaped. Indeed, one of the hallmarks of film noir, as it rapidly developed during the classic noir period of 1941–58 in the United States and England (usually defined as beginning with John Huston's proto-noir *The Maltese Falcon* (1941) and ending with Orson Welles's baroque *Touch of Evil* (1958)), was the merging of space, time, and events in such a way as to give priority to time past.[5]

'Someone (or something)', R. Barton Palmer argues (with Jacques Tourneur's quintessential noir film *Out of the Past* (1947) in mind), 'is always coming "out of the past"' in film noir. This 'backward turning' may be accomplished by 'the discursive arrangement of story events, whose forward movement is interrupted by the filling in of some bypassed gap; or it may figure as . . . [a] narrator relating what has gone before and thereby demonstrating the presence of the past' within the narrator's thoughts. Or, 'a third possibility is that the present admits the return of characters who were thought to belong to the past who, it seemed, had been bypassed as the protagonist embarked on a "fresh start"'.⁶ Classic film noir defines a narrative structure, a form of cinematic modernism, which emphasises the dark pasts of its protagonists. And it is the contingent vulnerability of present life to the dark past that frequently determines the transitional, discontinuous spatial dimension of the noir world and the unstable, threatened identities of noir protagonists.⁷

All of this is not to suggest that noir films somehow simply reflect the historical reality of the noir generation. As works of art, noir films did not so much reflect reality as *refract* it to the extent that they selectively developed some of the darkest cultural motifs of the era to the exclusion of all else. In this vein, Polish director Andrzej Wajda's *Ashes and Diamonds* (*Popiół i diament*, 1958), the third film in a trilogy that includes *A Generation* (*Pokolenie*, 1955) and *Kanal* (1957), presents a synoptic chronicle of the desperation and despair of the noir generation within the historical context of WWII that American and English film noir, for the most part, only briefly references or intimates with the exception of a few films, such as Carol Reed's *The Third Man* (1949), which is an important predecessor to *Ashes and Diamonds*. As Andrew Spicer argues in his survey of European noir, 'The aspect of European film noir that emerges most strongly . . . is its *national specificity*. In each country, noir and neo-noir have individual trajectories that reflect that nation's history, its political organisation, its cultural traditions, the state of its film industry and the strength of its cinematic culture.'⁸ Although Spicer's survey does not include Poland, *Ashes and Diamonds* exemplifies his point. Opening on the last day of WWII in Europe, 8 May 1945, at the close of the Thirty Years' War, Wajda's masterpiece depicts the consequences of the transgressions that the war has unleashed in Poland. Three of the four major figures at the centre of *Ashes and Diamonds*, Maciek (Zbigniew Cybulski), Andrzej (Adam Pawlikowski), and Szczuka (Waclaw Zastrzezynski), prove incapable of escaping their respective dark pasts associated with the brutalities of WWII in Europe and, in the case of Szczuka, the Spanish Civil War. The barmaid, Krystyna (Ewa Krzyzewska), who holds the promise of a new life for Maciek, is the exception, although she frequently seems to serve more as a foil to Maciek than a character with a history in her own right (see cover image). None of the former can leave behind the legacy of the violent struggle against the Germans, as that brutal legacy is carried forward into the conflict between Polish nationalists and Communists in the film. But Maciek, whose birth year is identified as 1921 in the film, most clearly represents the despair of the noir generation as a youthful adult, who is torn between the wistfulness and promise evoked by his attraction to Krystyna and his loyalty to the cause of Polish nationalism and his comrades.

Insofar as the pivotal figures of Maciek, Andrzej, and Szczuka are trapped by the past, they resemble the traditional characters of classic film noir. But instead of the claustrophobic, transitional urban settings and deadly webs of interpersonal relations that are frequently depicted in traditional film noir, *Ashes and Diamonds* explores noir themes within the physical, psychological, and social context of massive historical events that amplify the significance and weight of characters trapped by past experiences and their own limited self-definitions. The film opens with a shot of a cross atop a Catholic chapel in a small provincial Polish town that serves to frame the assassinations of what are believed to be two Polish Communist Party officials, one at the very door to the chapel, which follow. In this scene, Wajda introduces Maciek as a youthful, nonchalant, nationalist resistance fighter working in concert with his somewhat older superior and comrade-in-arms, Andrzej. As the two prepare to assassinate who they believe to be the newly appointed local Communist Party Secretary, Szczuka, three contrasting series of personal images are developed. First, the composure of Maciek and Andrzej is contrasted with the comic panic of a third figure, Drewnowski (Bogumil Kobiela), who turns out to be the turncoat assistant to the Communist mayor of the town, Swiecki (Aleksander Sewruk). Second, the casualness of Maciek is played off against the seriousness of Andrzej. And, third, the pleas of an innocent young girl for help in placing flowers in the chapel accent the brutality of the assassinations that are about to take place in her presence.

The equanimity of Maciek and Andrzej in preparing for the assassinations reflects their experience in such matters and their lack of compunction about carrying out the killings. As the story unfolds, we learn that they are both tested veterans of the Polish Home Army and the Warsaw Uprising. Both men are habituated to killing and the brutality of war. However, Maciek's casualness in the face of brutality reveals what appears to be a youthful attempt at feigned self-control. Maciek's 'coolness' (he slowly awakens from a nap on the grass just prior to the assassinations and then becomes preoccupied with the 'ants' on his tommy gun) contrasts with the focused seriousness of Andrzej, who is clearly quite intentional in his planning and execution of the killings. Yet, it is Maciek who grows intense and ferocious once the shooting begins. In fact, Andrzej emphatically halts Maciek's frenzied shooting at the second of the dead victims, suggesting that there is something deeply enthralling about killing for Maciek.

Both men seem oblivious to the fact that the killings are carried out in front of an innocent girl and in close proximity to the chapel. Indeed, Maciek commits the second killing as the victim stands at the threshold of the chapel seeking refuge within, with his machine gun taking out the chapel door and the bullets dramatically setting the back of the victim's shirt afire. The message is clear: nothing is sacred to either battle-hardened man. Neither understands that their acts of violence are sacrilegious, that they have transgressed against the Catholic spiritual heritage of the very nation they are fighting for. Nor do they comprehend that their violence works against the acquisition of the political power that they seek. Indeed, in the next series of scenes, we learn that Maciek and Andrzej have mistakenly assassinated two innocent cement workers when the new Secretary, Szczuka, arrives, recognises that he was the intended victim, and in short order explains to a group of disturbed Polish workers on the scene that such sacrifices are the necessary price of victory for the Polish Communists: 'The end of the war isn't the end of our fight, the fight for Poland, and what kind of country it's to become has only just begun.'[9] At this point, the Polish nationalists and the Polish Communists of the noir generation begin to resemble one another in their acceptance of killing, except that the eloquent Szczuka clearly understands how to gain and hold power by winning the hearts and minds of the workers.

The similarity of the dark pasts of Maciek, Andrzej, and Szczuka becomes apparent as we learn about their respective histories. As veterans of the Polish Home Army and the Warsaw Uprising, Maciek and Andrzej share the experiences and memories of one of the most catastrophic events in Polish history, when much of the Home Army and 150,000 Warsaw civilians were decimated by the Germans in the fall of 1944. In the second bar scene with Maciek and Andrzej, as Maciek's flirtation with Krystyna advances, Maciek flamboyantly and with strained humour sets one vodka after another aflame in memory of their fallen comrades, as Hanka (Grazyna Staniszewska) sings in the background about the sacrifices of 'Polish blood' and Andrzej sullenly looks on unamused, having just learned of the death of yet another colleague, Captain Wilks. As Maciek gradually compels Andrzej to remember their fallen comrades, his unrestrained enthusiasm for the time past when they were together emerges as he exclaims, 'those were the days . . . what a life and in such company' and 'what a great crowd . . . life was better'. As Andrzej also begins to think about the past, he remembers a time when he was free of doubt, when 'we knew what we wanted . . . and what they wanted of us'. For both Maciek and Andrzej, the present is viewed in pejorative terms and comes up short of the past. Consequently, Maciek concludes with a typically cynical noir comment that 'the main thing is to find a way through this mess without being tricked or getting bored'.

This scene closely parallels another moment later in the film in which Szczuka is joined by an old Communist colleague and aide, Franek (Wiktor Grotowicz), who arrives with a bottle of Spanish wine, photographs, and a Victrola record player to reminisce about fallen comrades from the Spanish Civil War (in which the Communists suffered heavy casualties fighting the Franco regime in another losing cause) and WWII. In response to Franek's deeply felt comments about these dead comrades, Szczuka affirms that 'those were good times . . . and these will be good times too'. But Szczuka's affirmation of the present is immediately qualified when he disparagingly remarks that 'the mob down there doesn't represent Poland'. And his advice to Franek to 'learn to understand' the trials of the Polish people appears to be quickly forgotten as they proceed to discuss the killing of the two cement workers and finding the perpetrators of the killings.

Both reminiscence scenes capture what Max Weber calls 'a pathos and sentiment of community' created by war that 'makes for an unconditionally devoted and sacrificial community among the combatants'.[10] What Wajda shows us much more clearly than Weber, however, is how the pathos of a dark past created by war can lead to a dismissal of the present and override the ethos of current moral demands. Both scenes illuminate how affective attachments to the transgressive past can justify and perpetuate transgressions in what is perceived to be the degraded 'mess' of the present.

The 'mess' of the present is also depicted through a variety of mundane scenes and characters, ranging from the serious to the farcical, interspersed throughout the film. The latter include a number of scenes with the idiotic, drunken duo of Drewnowski and Pieniazek (Stanislaw Milski), the newspaper reporter, working their way up to crashing and disrupting the mayor's party; the smarmy, lecherous restaurant proprietor, Slomka (Zbigniew Skowronski), wheedling every opportunity; the pompous and pretentious impresario, Kotowicz (Artur Mlodnicki), making a regular fool of himself and initiating the ludicrous closing Polonaise; and a selection of supercilious figures, such as Mrs Staniewiczowa (Halina Kwiatkowska), Szczuka's sister-in-law, engaging in histrionics. Through them, Wajda presents a background portrait of Polish society hiding from its own emptiness and seemingly worthy of the contempt of the nationalists and Communists.

The Darkness of Agency

'What could action and agency . . . look like' in noir films, Robert Pippin asks,

> where there is almost no credible sense of any 'space of possibility' left; when the suspicion is that the very idea of someone running the show, leading his or her life, begins to look naïve or self-deceived? . . . The issue of destiny in noirs is largely framed in psychological or sociological or existential terms, and the relevant possibilities are severely constricted.[11]

Noir protagonists typically cannot escape a fate of their own making, frequently because of their attraction to a femme fatale. In the case of *Ashes and Diamonds*, there is no femme fatale, nor is there even a genuine antagonist. Rather, the *struggle* between the Polish nationalists and Communists constitutes the fatal attraction for the primary protagonist, Maciek, and the secondary protagonists, Andrzej and Szczuka. Maciek and Andrzej cannot say 'no' to the attractions of the struggle any more than Szczuka can. All act on the assumption that they are self-conscious agents intentionally implementing plans to achieve desired military and political goals. But what quickly becomes apparent is that these intentional actions frequently go awry and, even when successful, have disastrous consequences because they are carried out with moral indifference. In the opening scene, Maciek and Andrzej carry out their orders and mistakenly assassinate the wrong individuals. A short while later, when Andrzej, who is a lieutenant in the Home Army, informs his superior, Major Waga (Ignacy Machowski), that 'innocent people died needlessly', the major responds by asking Andrzej if he has suffered 'an attack of conscience', and then immediately tells him 'the war has taught us' that there must be 'no compromises', if they are to bring about a 'free Poland'. Yet, the mandate of 'no compromises' is really a mandate to morally compromise that obviates all doubts and inhibitions in the face of murderous possibilities. If one is to be loyal to the cause of a 'free Poland', then one must be prepared to ignore the dictates of conscience and act with moral impunity.

In the case of Maciek, the dictates of conscience are unexpectedly awakened by Krystyna, who moves beyond the role of what Janey Place characterises as the passive, 'nurturing', or 'redemptive' woman in film noir when, much to his surprise, she accepts his offer to come to his room, and they initiate a sexual relationship in what at the time was considered a somewhat bold bed scene.[12] The rapidly developing relationship with Krystyna opens up the possibility of a new life for Maciek. As he is faced with the prospect of once again attempting to assassinate Szczuka within a matter of hours, Maciek begins to hesitate, to develop compunctions about carrying out the killing. He tells Krystyna that he has been thinking about how 'beautiful' and 'dangerous' life is. In the pivotal scene of the film, Krystyna and Maciek visit an old crypt and read an inscription from the nineteenth-century, late-Romantic, Polish poet Cyprian Norwid. Krystyna begins by reading the inscription: 'So often, are you as a blazing torch with flames of burning hemp falling about you. Flaming, you know not if flames freedom bring or death, consuming all that you most cherish. Will only ashes remain, and chaos, whirling into the void.' At this point, Krystyna stops reading because she cannot make out the rest of the inscription. Maciek, then, with concentration, continues the quote from memory: 'Or will the ashes hold the glory of a starlike diamond, the Morning Star of everlasting triumph.' After Maciek completes Norwid's poem, Krystyna asks, 'And what are we?' to which Maciek responds: 'You are definitely a diamond.' In the stark scene that follows amidst the war rubble of what appears to be a church, Maciek comments to Krystyna with an inverted crucifix in the foreground that he would 'like to change some things and arrange my life differently', that he wants 'a normal life', remarking that he would like 'to take up my studies' and pursue a technical education. Maciek confesses: 'Until now, I didn't know what love was.' While the appropriately named Krystyna, or Christina in English (the name has the same Christian reference in both English and Polish), is clearly the inspiration for these comments, the presence of the inverted crucifix in the foreground signals that Maciek is apparently prepared to reject his identification with the downward trajectory of his transgressive life, which has led to nothing but ashes and death to this point.

Accordingly, in the next scene, Maciek unexpectedly confronts the consequences of his murderous actions when he and Krystyna enter a vestibule attached to the church to repair her shoe and are horrified to discover the bodies of the two assassinated cement workers lying in state awaiting burial. In this scene, Maciek is confronted with the clear choice of either continuing to act as an agent of transgression or rejecting the darkness of that life in favour of a crystalline life with Krystyna. Shortly thereafter, Maciek says to Krystyna that 'Perhaps I could still change everything' and embraces her in front of a white horse that wanders into the scene, which may be read as a bivalent image that is both lighthearted and humorous (given the horse's previous appearance with the foolish Drewnowski and the awkwardness of the scene) and a foreboding symbol of the apocalyptic events to follow.

Maciek's 'perhaps' (which he repeats twice) betrays his ambivalence about leaving his self-destructive life behind. In the scenes that follow, Maciek attempts unsuccessfully to evade Andrzej, who eventually catches up with him in a men's room, to press him on following through with the assassination of Szczuka. Maciek protests that Andrzej knows that he is 'not a coward', but he 'can't go on killing and hiding', that he just wants 'to live', that 'people can change'. In response, Andrzej reminds Maciek that as a soldier he must put his personal interests aside and then proceeds to invoke the camaraderie of their dark past: 'You keep forgetting . . . you're one of us and that's what counts.' A short while later, after Wajda has interspersed another farcical scene of the drunken Drewnowski spraying the mayor's dinner party with a fire extinguisher ('extinguishing' the party, in effect), Maciek relents, telling Andrzej, 'I'll do it.' As he departs, Maciek in turn asks Andrzej 'Do you believe in all of this?' With these comments, Maciek momentarily resolves his ambivalence, if not all of his doubts, and returns to the struggle. He has accepted his fate, but this time self-consciously and with barely suppressed moral compunctions.

DARKNESS AT NOON

Maciek wears dark glasses throughout much of the film because his vision has been compromised by his time in the sewers during the Warsaw Uprising (in a clear reference to Wajda's previous film *Kanal*). But the coolness of Maciek's dark glasses is also an unmistakable sign, of course, that his moral vision has been compromised. Like Andrzej and Szczuka, he finds the struggle to be strangely seductive. However, this seductiveness extends beyond the pathos of the dark past they share because the life of violence and destructiveness in the present also carries its own attractions and authority, as witnessed in the opening scene with Maciek in particular. There is a certain charisma associated with killing that ensures Maciek a status and recognition within the resistance community, that makes him 'one of us'.[13] But Maciek's return to the struggle is also fraught with complications. The first of these complications is that Szczuka has been presented to both the viewer and, to a lesser extent, Maciek as a sympathetic, even paternal, figure.

While Andrzej appears to be a member of the noir generation, Szczuka is more a member of the preceding generation, well into middle age, with a seventeen-year-old son, who has been raised by his nationalist sister-in-law, Mrs Staniewiczowa, and who has joined the Polish national resistance in his father's absence. As the film unfolds, Szczuka's narrative intersects with the narrative of Maciek to the extent that Maciek could easily be an older version of Szczuka's anti-Communist son. Twice in the film, Maciek obliges Szczuka by lighting his cigarette, but more importantly Maciek stalks Szczuka and kills him as he is on his way to see his son, who has been captured as a member of the slain Captain Wilks's Home Army unit. As Maciek shoots Szczuka four times, Szczuka stumbles into a macabre embrace of Maciek, in what could easily be construed as a last embrace of his son. The implications are clear: the conflict tearing Poland apart is highly personal and possibly intergenerational, even parricidal, as the noir generation self-destructs. At this point, Maciek no longer possesses his preternatural calmness, nor does he display his earlier intoxication with killing. Instead, Maciek panics, violently throwing down his gun and running back to his hotel room to wash and pack his few belongings before attempting to leave town. This introduces a second complication.

Maciek panics because he has been tempted by what Arthur Koestler calls 'the greatest temptation' in *Darkness at Noon*, his 1940 novel about the Communist purge trials:

> Sympathy, conscience, disgust, despair, repentance, and atonement are for us repellent debauchery ... The greatest temptation for the like of us is: to renounce violence, to repent, to make peace with oneself. Most great revolutionaries fell before this temptation, from Spartacus to Danton and Dostoevsky; they are the classical form of betrayal of the cause. The temptations of God were always more dangerous for mankind than those of Satan ... When the accursed inner voice speaks to you hold your hands over your ears.[14]

In *Ashes and Diamonds*, the temptations of the Polish nationalists and Communists mirror one another. Neither side can afford 'an attack of conscience', to recognise anything resembling an ethics of conscience. In *Darkness at Noon*, the old Bolshevik, Rubashov, sacrifices himself to the totality of the Party, while nonetheless recognising the fatal error of the Bolsheviks in the privacy of his diary: 'We have thrown overboard all conventions, our sole guiding principle is that of consequent logic; we are sailing without ethical ballast.'[15] Likewise, the Marxist revolutionary Pietro Spina in Ignazio Silone's 1936 novel *Bread and Wine* questions whether his contempt for 'moral values' as 'petit bourgeois prejudices' is the reason for the triumph of corrupt Party interests.[16] For Maciek, the recognition that his life has been morally compromised comes in an unusual fashion: he is tempted by what he calls 'a normal life'. This normal life is not a fantasy, but rather a life of possibility that Maciek has repressed, which precedes Krystyna, as witnessed by the fact that he quotes Norwid *from memory*. But Krystyna brings this repressed life of possibility to the surface of consciousness with compelling force because she acts as an agent of good who illuminates the darkness of Maciek's agency. She brings the poem and Maciek to life. Maciek instantly recognises that Krystyna is one of Norwid's diamonds amidst the ashes who is remarkable in her own right, as he remembers the lines. As a consequence, Maciek develops doubts and moral compunctions about continuing his self-destructive life that ensure he will lose his cool. Henceforth, he is in conflict with his guilt-ridden self.

Maciek's loss of composure, once he has completed the assassination, is his undoing. As he is leaving town, Maciek grows agitated and panics when Drewnowski, who has just suffered a humiliating rejection and beating from Andrzej, cries out his name. While Drewnowski had panicked in the opening assassination scene, it is now Maciek who grows frantic, but without the humorous overtones. In his frantic efforts to escape Drewnowski, Maciek clumsily collides with a small group of soldiers, attempts to flee, and is shot. In the following series of scenes, Maciek hides behind ghostlike sheets as he bleeds to death, and then eventually stumbles along mortally wounded, falling on what can only be described as an extended garbage dump, expiring in a death agony of fetal kicking racked by spasms of pain. It is a gruesome and powerful ending that draws the viewer towards a devastating conclusion: Maciek's refusal of a life of possibility with Krystyna leads to a dead end on the garbage/ash heap of history.

As a noir film, *Ashes and Diamonds* takes the determinist motifs characteristic of the genre in two directions. On the one hand, the determinism is situational. All of the film's characters are caught up in historical circumstances beyond their ability to comprehend and control. No one is even remotely a free agent, and Maciek's death is nothing less than a tragedy with the good intentions of the Polish nationalists balanced against the good intentions of the Communists. On the other hand, we are presented with the paradox of deeply flawed agents who are nonetheless responsible for their actions. Maciek is an unknowing yet knowing agent of his own fate insofar as he recognises in a moment of self-revelation that he 'can change', but then vacillates and does not change the priorities of his life. Andrzej protests that 'innocent people died needlessly' and asks if it is 'necessary to kill', and then proceeds to follow orders to kill. Szczuka speaks eloquently about the fight for Poland and 'what we are to become', but is not prepared to stop the cycle of violence. All three are opposed in their bearing and manner to the quotidian quality and ordinary vulgarity of much that is around them. All three show promise of achieving something higher. Yet, in the end, all are unable to resist the temptation of violence and are complicit in the downfall of Poland. Only Krystyna is able 'to figure a way through this mess' because she is inexplicably resistant to the corrupting influences of the disorder about her and knows how to protect herself in a world that is collapsing.

Notes

I would like to thank to Elyce Helford and Christopher Weedman for their insightful suggestions that were incorporated into the final version of this chapter.

1. Søren Kierkegaard, *The Sickness Unto Death*, ed. and trans. Howard V. Hong and Edna Hong (Princeton, NJ: Princeton University Press, 1980), p. 40.
2. See, for example, John Lukacs, *The End of the Twentieth Century and the End of the Modern Age* (New York: Ticknor and Fields, 1993).
3. George Steiner, *In Bluebeard's Castle: Some Notes Towards the Redefinition of Culture* (New Haven, CT: Yale University Press, 1971), p. 29. To place these words in context: 'The very business of rational analysis grows unsteady before the enormity of the facts. Consequently, there have been few attempts to relate the dominant phenomenon of twentieth-century barbarism to a more general theory of culture' (p. 29).
4. Reflecting on the traumas of the noir generation in 1951, Camus opened *The Rebel* with the following statement: 'There are crimes of passion and crimes of logic . . . We are living in the era of premeditation and the perfect crime.' Albert Camus, *The Rebel: An Essay on Man in Revolt*, trans. Anthony Bower (New York: Vintage Books, 1956), pp. 3–4.
5. For an analysis of *The Maltese Falcon* as a transitional, early noir film, see Alan Woolfolk, 'Hints of Modernism, Shades of Noir: Huston's *The Maltese Falcon* as Transitional Text', in *John Huston as Adaptor*, ed. Douglas McFarland and Wesley King (Albany: SUNY Press, 2017), pp. 181–96. In addition, see Alan Woolfolk, 'The Dread of Ascent: The Moral and Spiritual Topography of Hitchcock's *Vertigo*', in *Hitchcock's Moral Gaze*, ed. R. Barton Palmer, Homer Petty, and Steven Sanders (Albany: SUNY Press, 2017), pp. 237–52, for an analysis of *Vertigo* as the last of the classic film noirs.
6. R. Barton Palmer, '"Lounge Time" Reconsidered: Spatial Discontinuity and Temporal Contingency in *Out of the Past*', *Film Noir Reader 4: The Crucial Films and Themes*, ed. Alain Silver and James Ursini (New York: Limelight Editions, 2004), p. 58.

7. On the spatial dimensions of film noir, see Vivian Sobchack, 'Lounge Time: Postwar Crises and the Chronotope of Film Noir', *Refiguring American Film Genres: Theory and Method*, ed. Nick Browne (Berkeley: University of California Press. 1998), pp. 129–70. Palmer reformulates and deepens Sobchack's analysis giving priority to the temporal dimension. For a broader analysis of spatial dimensions in film noir focused on the declining spaces of urban industrial society, see Edward Dimendberg, *Film Noir and the Spaces of Modernity* (Cambridge, MA: Harvard University Press, 2004).
8. Andrew Spicer, 'Introduction', *European Film Noir*, ed. Spicer (Manchester: Manchester University Press, 2007), p. 13.
9. All quotations are from translations in The Criterion Collection DVD of *Ashes and Diamonds* (2005).
10. Max Weber, 'Religious Rejections of the World and Their Directions', in *Max Weber: Essays in Sociology*, ed. and trans. H. H. Gerth and C. Wright Mills (New York: Oxford University Press, 1978), p. 335.
11. Robert B. Pippin, *Fatalism in Film Noir: Some Cinematic Philosophy* (Charlottesville: University of Virginia Press, 2012), pp. 10–11.
12. Janey Place, 'Women in Film Noir', in *Women in Film Noir*, ed. E. Ann Kaplan (London: British Film Institute, 1998), pp. 60–3.
13. The charisma of killing becomes more explicit in neo-noir films, such as David Cronenberg's *A History of Violence* (2005), but is clearly present in classic noir films such as Robert Wise's *Born to Kill* (1947) and Edmund Goulding's *Nightmare Alley* (1947).
14. Arthur Koestler, *Darkness at Noon*, trans. Daphne Hardy (New York: The New American Library, 1961), pp. 133–4.
15. Koestler, *Darkness at Noon*, p. 210.
16. Ignazio Silone, *Bread and Wine*, trans. Eric Mosbacher (New York: Signet Classic, Penguin Group, 1986), p. 88.

2. THE FLEAP BEING NEITHER FLEA NOR FLY: IDA LUPINO'S INTERROGATIONS OF FEMALE TRAUMA IN *NEVER FEAR*

Julie Grossman

Of the many discerning observations offered by Ronnie Scheib in her sensitive writing about the films of Ida Lupino, one that stands out is about women 'not possessing their own lives'.[1] The insight is important because it helps us to see the convergence of Lupino's noir vision of post-war America and the filmmaker's emphasis in her early films on the lives and traumas of young women. In Francine Parker's retrospective on Lupino's filmmaking in 1967, Lupino described her characters aptly as 'poor bewildered people'.[2] It is this acute rendering of disappointed youth and the alienation of women that led Martin Scorsese to call Lupino's films 'a singular achievement in American cinema'.[3] For Scorsese, Lupino's films 'addressed the wounded soul and traced the slow, painful process of women trying to wrestle with despair and reclaim their lives. Her work is resilient, with a remarkable empathy for the fragile and the heartbroken. It is essential.'[4] Scheib, Parker, and Scorsese saw with clarity Lupino's searing portrait of marginalised women and a post-war society responsible for their trauma. In 1980, Carrie Rickey called Lupino's films 'Not *film noir*, but Lupino *noir*: a dimly lit low-budget world in which everyone lives sadder-but-wiser ever after.'[5]

The present chapter focuses on *Never Fear* (1949), notably the *least* obviously noir of all the films Lupino directed between 1949 and 1953 (*Not Wanted* (1949), *Never Fear*, *Outrage* (1950), *The Bigamist* (1953), and *The Hitch-Hiker* (1953) – Lupino later directed *The Trouble with Angels* in 1966). Despite *Never Fear*'s more palpably melodramatic elements, it shares important traits with the other films that constitute a distinct noir sensibility. Indeed, Lupino was a noir visionary, making films about outsider figures whose lost idealism and experiences of futility, whose confrontations with the barrenness of social conventions, and whose failed attempts to find sustenance in the institutions of marriage and family and other social organisations line her films up alongside the most trenchant of film noirs. Remarkably, Lupino channelled these noir themes into stories with female protagonists rather than the more familiar disaffected men. With her gendered twist on this series of films, Lupino explored the ordeals of marginalised and aspiring women trying desperately to navigate their lives, despite being trapped within claustrophobic and oppressive social-psychological realms.

While film noir has often embraced social outcasts, wandering individuals who do not fit into easily consumed categories for living life in wartime and post-war America, Lupino's films eschew conventional categories and endorse the value of resisting norms and labels. Her work is in fact a deliberate critique of how individuals are labelled and often imprisoned or excluded as a result of such labelling. If these 'poor bewildered people' are fortunate enough to have some around them who understand their plight, they internalise a broader social judgement on their difference and suffer nonetheless. *Never Fear*, about a young female dancer (played by Sally Forrest) who contracts polio, presents this critique of misunderstanding those who do not fit nicely into conventional roles in a metaphor invoked by one of the patients, Len (Hugh O'Brian), at the Kabat-Kaiser Institute where protagonist Carol is sent for rehabilitation. Len has a relationship with the children at the treatment centre, to whom he tells stories about an unfortunate but stalwart 'Fleap', a cross between a flea and a fly, which he draws pictures of for his audience. The fleap is an outsider, neither fish nor fowl: 'You see, he's neither a flea nor a fly and it drives him bats being nothing, so he sets out to prove to the world that someday he'll be something.' 'Flies don't like [the fleap]', Len tells the children, 'and fleas won't want to have anything to do with him. Pretty tough.'

The fleap stands in for an identity Lupino respected and empathised with, the outsider survivor figure who eludes labelling. Lupino herself was singular for her time, wanting to pursue at various moments in her life her vocation as film performer, writer, director, producer, and music composer. Lupino's hybrid films were fleap-like, too: melodramatic, they were social-problem semi-documentary critiques of post-war America, but they shared a noir sensibility with other films of the era that embraced iconoclasm and sympathy for those who had desires beyond their station and failed to acclimate to cultural norms.

Never Fear, illustrating such hybridity, had an autobiographical and semi-documentary foundation. Lupino herself had been stricken with polio as a sixteen-year-old in 1934, and when the film was released, its audience would still be vulnerable to the disease. Salk's vaccine, which helped to vanquish polio, would not be available for another half decade. The film's urgency and its realism help to account for *Never Fear*'s failure to find an audience (though the film's title was changed to *The Young Lovers* to enhance publicity). Even contemporary reviewers commented on the film's neuralgic exposure of a disease that continued to frighten Americans and threaten them with sudden and catastrophic illness. In his review for the *Los Angeles Times*, Philip K. Scheuer wrote, 'this is not a film I would ordinarily expect to patronize in my neighborhood theater'.[6] Certainly, the verisimilitude – especially the scenes at the actual Kabat-Kaiser Rehabilitation Institute in Santa Monica – bore out Scheuer's perplexity about the film having been made.

Never Fear was officially the first imprint of The Filmakers, Lupino's independent film company founded with her then-husband Collier Young and Malvin Wald; the earlier 1949 film *Not Wanted* had been made by The Filmakers' precursor organisation, Emerald Pictures (named after Lupino's mother Connie Emerald), run by Lupino, Young, and Anson Bond. Lupino was the uncredited director of that film, having replaced Elmer Clifton when he became ill just as production began. So *Never Fear* was Lupino's first credited directing work, and it was released alongside some impressive manifestos explaining her new role as a leader at The Filmakers. Because Lupino was well known as a performer, The Filmakers' promotional ads were able to trade on her fame. In early 1950, an ad called 'Why I Made "Never Fear" by Ida Lupino' appeared in the *Citizen News*.[7] Lupino touts the film's exploration of courage and heroism, but there are two more interesting points made in the ad. First, Lupino claims that she 'saw this story happen', which presumably refers to her having experienced polio herself but also to her status as a 'visionary' filmmaker; she repeats the words that open the film itself, that *Never Fear* was 'photographed where it happened', reinforcing additionally that the truth of the story lies in its relevance to a society in the throes of a polio pandemic. Second, Lupino follows this credentialing of the film's realism by referring to her own credentials, earned with the success of *Not Wanted* about an unwed mother. She says that the 'support the American public gave to "NOT WANTED" . . . proved to me that most people do want something different out of Hollywood'. Days later, The Filmakers published a full-page ad in *Variety* that echoes this language. In their 'Declaration of Independents', The Filmakers laud producer-writer-directors committed to realism and to social-problem films that avoid an escapist feel-good Hollywoodism with conventional characters and story arcs:

> We are deep in admiration for our fellow independent producers – men like Stanley Kramer, Robert Rossen and Louis de Rochemont. They are bringing a new power and excitement to the screen. We like independence. It's tough sometimes, but it's good for the initiative. The struggle to do something different is healthy in itself. We think it is healthy for our

industry as well. That is why we independent producers must continue to explore new themes, try new ideas, discover new creative talents in all departments. When any one of us profits by these methods, there is bounty for us all – major or independent. We trust that our new Filmakers Production, NEVER FEAR, is worthy of the responsibilities, which we have assumed as independent producers.[8]

Lupino and her colleagues wished to cast non-stars as performers and to shoot on location to present stories 'where they happened'. By this time, Malvin Wald had joined Young and Lupino as one of the executives to form The Filmakers; Wald had co-written (with Paul Jarrico) the story on which *Not Wanted* was based; he had also written the original story and co-wrote the screenplay for *The Naked City* (1948), Jules Dassin's semi-documentary noir that ends with the iconic line, 'There are eight million stories in the naked city. This has been one of them.' *Never Fear* continues *The Naked City*'s bid for authenticity, an attempt to tap the 'signifying potential of real space', as R. Barton Palmer describes post-war realist filmmaking in *Shot on Location*.[9] Anne Morra has observed that, throughout her career, Lupino objected to 'the artificiality of being in a studio movie. When she was ready to make her own films, that's what she took out of the equation, to have as much realism as possible.'[10]

Not only does *Never Fear* announce its intention to present the film 'where it happened', but as Scheib notes, with its low-key inclusion of real patients at the Kabat-Kaiser, 'one always has the sense that there are other "stories" in *Never Fear*'.[11] At the end of the film, as Carol leaves the rehab centre, other patients are marshalled in to visit her doctor, suggesting in a narrative ellipsis that Carol's experience is part of a larger social dynamic. Tapping into the semi-documentary strain of film noir in films such as *The House on 92nd Street* (Henry Hathaway, 1945) and *The Naked City*, and also the fatalism and unmasking of post-war optimism endemic to the series, *Never Fear* resists ameliorative filmmaking and captures an artistically activist desire to tell stories about subjects that mattered to viewers in their real lives. Further, like much of Lupino's work as a performer and a filmmaker, *Never Fear* expresses that paradox embodied in the noir corpus that earnest humanist values sit directly beside a powerful sense of loss and futility.

Perhaps the most identifiably noir trappings of *Never Fear* appear in the 'Happy Homes' sequences of the film and the scene in which Carol's former dance partner fiancé Guy (Keefe Brasselle) drowns his sorrows on a date with Phyllis Townsend (Eve Miller), an office worker at a real-estate company run by a blustering hypocrite called Mr Brownlee (Jerry Hausner). In these office scenes, the youthful Guy collides with a cynical world of post-war exploitation, Lupino's send-up of the housing boom following the war's end. Mr Brownlee pitches the American dream to aspiring homeowners, intoning about war vets and 'what those boys did for us over there. I didn't get into the struggle, punctured ear drum, you know, but *c'est la guerre*.' Brownlee takes people's money to purchase a 'Happy Home', their share of the American dream, but when they miss their payments, he evicts the 'deadbeats': 'Friday is e-day. E is for eviction – out in the street. Out!'

It is not only the greedy Mr Brownlee who develops the film's scathing critique of failed post-war idealism. More interesting still, in Lupino's portrait of American angst and alienation, is the presence of Brownlee's knowing receptionist Phyllis, who eyes her boss's sleazy doings and, when Guy is rejected by a self-pitying Carol, telling him bitterly to find another dance partner, dining with him and inviting him to her apartment. Lupino's camera takes ample notice of Phyllis, whose quiet observation of Brownlee's tactics registers a knowledge of his corruption. The film seeds its commentary on post-war US culture in Phyllis, suggesting in particular a disappointing aftermath to the war for women. In this way, Phyllis's traumas may be different from but are parallel to Carol's devastation, adding another female perspective. Phyllis has withstood, she tells Guy, a 'hasty wartime marriage', and this has left her divorced, sad, and alone. Eve Miller's performance style contrasts markedly with Sally Forrest's, advancing the film's melancholic tone. Instead of a traditional roster of women characters (good/bad girl), *Never Fear* deepens the film's female noir by adding Phyllis's darkened point of view to Carol's. At the same time, these performers' affect and acting styles are distinct. Forrest plays Carol at certain points quite melodramatically, insisting, for example, 'I'll never walk or dance again. I'm no good to anyone anymore . . . Can't you understand? I just want to be left alone.' At other moments, Carol is sarcastic, telling Len at the rehab centre, 'Oh, I'm having the time of my life.'

In *The Men* (1950), Stanley Kramer's production directed by Fred Zinnemann that was released months after *Never Fear*, Marlon Brando's Ken Wilacek would resort to sarcasm in his beginning voice-over, but the cynical detachment of a disabled war vet would affect viewers differently in 1950 than would a woman's self-pitying irony. *Never Fear* explores layers of female dissatisfaction expressed in sarcasm and irony. Phyllis's words are also dry, her delivery more in line with an understated noir than Carol's caustic satire. 'What's wrong?' Guy asks her. 'Just about everything', she answers. Played by Eve Miller with a plaintive world-weariness, especially touching to watch now, given the performer's suicide in 1973 at the age of fifty, Phyllis's deportment and delivery communicate a noir tone of disappointment and loneliness. As Scheib notes, her 'time-arresting, other-dimensional face haunts the film beyond all story functionalism [. . .] . It measures a lost potential the film never quite admits to tracing.'[12] More recently, Manohla Dargis observes a similar *weltschmerz* in Miller's performance of Phyllis, describing the sequence as 'a would-be fling [. . . that] condenses a movie's worth of adult desire and regret into the melancholy that settles in her face'.[13] Carol's affect spans beyond the melancholic noir of Phyllis, as the former dancer is torn between an earnest desire to adapt and a self-defeating wish to give in to cynicism.

Francine Parker has remarked that *Never Fear* is consistent with Lupino's narrative preoccupation with female trauma: 'A woman's world is once more the movie's base, a world again characterised as a struggle to overcome the attack of an unseen, brutalizing enemy.'[14] Part of this gendered landscape is male imperviousness to women's suffering, notably seen in Lupino's next film *Outrage*, when the protagonist's fiancé becomes impatient following her rape; he insists that the two should marry, and when she shows a bewildered resistance, he tries literally to shake her out of her recalcitrance. In *Never Fear*, Guy is, as his name suggests, an average nice guy. But he, too, brings a cluelessness to his scenes. Scheib points out that while Guy and Carol cuddle at the picnic at the Kabat-Kaiser, Guy finds the gathered community 'a mild source of annoyance'.[15] In the date scene referred to above, Guy is drunk at Phyllis's apartment. He falls asleep, and the scene ends with the mature and wiser Phyllis clenching her fist with frustration and repressed sadness, while Guy nods off (see Figure 2.1). He is thus the same figure of passivity Lupino already associated with actor Keefe Brasselle in *Not Wanted*, when his character is

Figure 2.1 Sleep represents unawareness of women's trauma in *Never Fear*. [frame capture]

first seen sleeping on the bus, letting his head droop on Sally Kelton's (also Sally Forrest) shoulder beside him. Sleep denoting passivity in these cases, Brasselle's men are not awake to women's trauma.

The most notable instance of this imperviousness in *Never Fear* occurs in the key scene in which Carol first shows symptoms of illness: suffering in desperation, as her fever rages and she clutches onto a rope for ballast, Carol is pictured pointedly behind Guy's ebullient piano playing. Lupino's characteristically ironic shot composition places Carol in crisis in the foreground while her lover remains oblivious, facing away from her, emphasising a noir window into a woman's experience of alienation and aloneness (see Figure 2.2).

Carol's isolation has a noir fatalism to it, catastrophic illness striking just as the dancers are on the cusp of success. In the image, the arrangement of ropes she clutches also makes it appear as if Carol is behind bars, imprisoned and alone in her suffering. The suddenness with which Carol is struck with polio repeats the noir trope that catastrophe may reach out to claim individuals when they are least expecting it. Everyone is vulnerable to, and no one is safe from, unforeseen crisis. In the years before *Never Fear* was released, *Out of the Past* (Jacques Tourneur, 1947) showed urban iniquity seeping into the country spaces of Bridgeport, California and *Shadow of a Doubt* (Alfred Hitchcock, 1943) cast a shadow not only on middle American suburban life but on a good

Figure 2.2   Carol (Sally Forrest), foregrounded in crisis while her lover remains oblivious in *Never Fear*. [frame capture]

girl who is enveloped in darkness and initiated into a hellish inversion of the American dream. The 'this could happen to you' elements of film noir – its insistence that no good boy or good girl is free from the taint of evil or threat of catastrophe – is a theme emphasised by Lupino. Consider the fairly blunt presentation of this idea in the beginning titles of Lupino's *The Hitch-Hiker*, the only classic film noir directed by a woman:

> This is the true story of a man and a gun and a car. The gun belonged to the man. The car might have been yours – or that young couple across the aisle. What you will see in the next seventy minutes could have happened to you. For the facts are actual.

The first thing we learn about the film is that its terror applies to the viewer. *The Hitch-Hiker* declares its relevance to audiences and its intention to unsettle viewers about their own exposure to danger and violence. This is a noir post-war universe in which the supposed safe realms of America may be under assault by 'a man and a gun and a car'. The effectiveness of Lupino's reach was borne out by complaints following the release of the film by those thumbing rides, who lobbied, 'Some people are happy to help, to give a guy a lift. But you point the finger at them, and scream, "When was the last time you invited death into your car?"'[16] The film sufficiently scared drivers that they were at risk from serial killers wandering the open American roads.

The precariousness of mundane daily life is a clear preoccupation in all of Lupino's films. Even the original title of Lupino's next film after *Never Fear*, *Outrage*, reinforces this idea. In *Outrage*, Ann Walton (Mala Powers)'s rape occurs one evening after she leaves her office, days before she is poised to marry. This film's stalking sequence features some stunning noir composition, including expressionist shadows and a terrifying symbolic use of visual images and sound. But the original title of *Outrage* (written by Malvin Wald) was 'Nobody's Safe', a direct assault on audiences' post-war quietude and sense of safety. In Lupino's America, no one is free from the threat and contamination of violence, including an internalisation of guilt and self-pity, as happens with Ann, the rape victim in *Outrage*, as well as in *Never Fear*, in which Carol's noired subjective life becomes a major focus of the film. *Never Fear* presents a unique case in which the idea of fatalism has not only a filmic reference point in noir representations of the fatalist underside of post-war America but also a documentary version of the same idea in its depiction of the sudden onset of polio. In 1949 and 1950, polio could strike anyone. Its victims were blindsided, like noir protagonists, but in this case by terrifying illness, the rug pulled out from under their normal and happy life. As melodramatic as some of the scenes are in *Never Fear*, this medico-fatalistic aspect of the film has an uncanny relevance to our present moment. Polio may not be a concern in 2020–1, but the virus that is overwhelming the globe has a similar profile in that its effects are radically variable. At the time of this writing, COVID-19, like polio, strikes individuals dramatically differently. Lupino was fortunate in that her bout with polio was short-lived (though she carried a numbness in one of her hands for years after).[17]

Noir inevitability and fatalism – as Tom Neal's Al Roberts says straightforwardly in *Detour* (Edgar G. Ulmer, 1945), 'No matter what you do, no matter where you turn, fate sticks out its foot to trip you' – describe Lupino's tone throughout her early films, including *Never Fear*. Lupino consistently deploys a powerful sense of irony in acknowledging that human effort and idealism might be futile in a world constructed philosophically, as well as culturally, to thwart individual desire. Thus, *Never Fear* takes pains to emphasise Carol's vibrancy in early scenes: her energetic dance routine, her verve, and her excitement at the film's start about being on the cusp of 'making it' in the ever-elusive field of performance and entertainment. The swordplay dance routine at the beginning of the film functions as an ironic counterpoint to a later wheelchair square dance scene, whose poignancy and grace are enhanced by its parallel with the earlier performance.

At the Kabat-Kaiser, Carol reluctantly goes with Len to the square dance. The scene is riveting, wheelchairs moving towards the camera, then synchronously turning a corner away from one another to meet again at the far end, before a do-si-do, all the while avoiding the awkwardness of wheels locking. As the wheelchairs approach the viewer, the camera is positioned with a low angle, recording the grace and strength of the dancers and the ingenuity of the choreography. The square dance caller, as well as child observers, is rendered naturalistically.

As with Carol's emotion contrasting with Phyllis's understated demeanour, the film's representation of disability includes an active tension between melodrama and realism. We wince at Carol's self-pity ('I'm a cripple!'), but we also see carefully filmed scenes like the square dance, in which the efforts and pleasures of the participants are shown without any dramatic excess. Similarly, the montage presentation of Carol's hydrotherapy, with multiple patients working in the pool, and the documentary style with which Lupino records Carol's other physical therapy sessions create a routine workaday quality to the environment and demonstrate a respect for the slow but marked achievements of ordinary patients and medical personnel. In combining melancholic disappointment with the quotidian, Lupino emulates the dual perspectives of critique-oriented melodrama and realism in film noir. The criminality that typically characterises classic film noir appears here as a subdued appraisal of post-war exploitation and loss in the 'Happy Homes' narrative, and the film's documentary realism reveals the unromanticised details of Carol's life at the Kabat-Kaiser Institute.

Moreover, *Never Fear* dramatises its realistic portrayal of a medical setting alongside noir melodrama in a gendered presentation of Carol's guilt about her stricken body. This attention to a woman's self-consciousness about her identity being compromised because her body is afflicted can be seen more starkly when we compare *Never Fear* with several other films of the period, including *The Men*. Less invested in patriotic melodrama than an earlier film like *The Best Years of Our Lives* (William Wyler, 1946), *The Men* – about a paraplegic war veteran – nevertheless made use of a familiar figure, the angsty male protagonist. The tone of Brando's persona had already been established in his earlier star turn as Stanley Kowalski on the Broadway stage.

Both *The Men*'s Ken Wilacek and Carol Williams are defined by their strong bodies, which makes their afflictions more painful. Brando's character Ken was noted for his physicality – 'he was quite an athlete', Ellen (Teresa Wright) remarks; in *Never Fear*, Carol's athleticism and physical prowess are also emphasised at the beginning of the film in the extended dance sequence referenced above. In both of these films, gender plays a strong role, with Ken's doctor telling his fiancée that Ken is 'depressed. He feels himself totally dependent on others. He says to himself, "I'm not a man any longer. I can't make a woman happy". Is it any wonder he finds it difficult to adjust to the situation?' *The Men* explored masculinity and disability, but it was also channelling a patriotism that recognised the sacrifice 'The Men' made in serving in the war. *Never Fear* is different because the agony of the protagonist does not tap into that larger redemptive context of masculine heroism.

Another useful contrast with Lupino's film can be seen in the later biopic *Interrupted Melody* (Curtis Bernhardt, 1955), based on the autobiography of opera singer Marjorie Lawrence, who contracted polio in 1941. Notably, the film's release in 1955 coincided with the year in which Salk's vaccine was first available, adding to the film's tone of affirmation. Suddenly afflicted with the disease, both Carol Williams and Lawrence (Eleanor Parker) battle feelings of unworthiness based on gender, though Lupino makes the fictional Carol a dancer to underscore the starker limitations she would face returning to her art and profession. While addressing the struggles of Lawrence to overcome depression following her paralysis, *Interrupted Melody*'s CinemaScope rendering of the singer's comeback differs from the understated intimations of Carol's future in *Never Fear*. In keeping with the principles of ameliorative cinema and classic Hollywood melodrama, the MGM film depicts Lawrence's triumphant return to performing, which is linked – as in *The Men* – to the self-sacrifice of WWII soldiers. As she traverses the space of a veteran hospital ward in her wheelchair, Lawrence serenades wounded soldiers with 'Somewhere Over the Rainbow', symbolising an active rejection of her previous defeatism. Lawrence then goes on tour overseas with the military, which the film captures in a celebratory montage sequence. The final scene of the film takes place on the Metropolitan Opera Stage. Performing as Iseult in a climactic moment, Lawrence stands up unexpectedly and for the first time since the onset of her illness. Her transcendence of her disability is figured literally as operatic.[18]

In making the protagonist in *Never Fear* a female survivor of what was at that time a disease that struck ordinary citizens rather than heroic soldiers or famed divas, *Never Fear* was not so typical; it was in fact quite a radical story about women, disability, stifling gender roles, and a broader social environment that would not offer redemption. Earlier representations of a woman with a disability, in a film like *Johnny Belinda* (Jean Negulesco, 1948), also gave an idealised view of female disability (interestingly, this film's representation of rape as less important than the healing power of romance contrasts with Lupino's bold depiction of rape and its impact in *Outrage*).

In *Never Fear*, Carol worries that her disability makes her 'incomplete', not a real or fully realised woman, her self-loathing reaching a peak when she lacerates the sculpted head of a woman who is part of a pair of clay figures. Carol also mourns a conception of eroticised femininity signified in the nightgown Guy gives her as a present at the Kabat-Kaiser that her paralysis and illness render obsolete. Lupino emphasises Carol's self-pity while showing the destructiveness of her turning on herself, but her internalisation of guilt and failure are fully a product of gendered ideals of femininity that see her bravura dancing at the beginning of the film as having more value than her participation in an intricate wheelchair dance at the Institute.

In his analysis of the representation of disability in film noir, Michael Davidson shows how characters with disability mark the male protagonist's impairment and also how a post-war image of productive masculinity is weakened or threatened by disability or 'the phantom limb' in classic film noir; Arthur Bannister's polio, for example, in *The Lady from Shanghai* (Orson Welles, 1947) suggests 'impotence and physical wastage'.[19] While acknowledging that these films provide a 'venue for representing otherness in a culture of the same',[20] Davidson shows the exploitative practices of these films' use of disability in supporting characters who exist in part to symbolise 'the hero's psychic wounds'. But *Never Fear* presents a different kind of case where the representation of disability is accompanied by gender critique. In Davidson's terms, disability becomes in other film noirs a metaphor for feminised or weakened men; in *Never Fear*, disability threatens femininity, Carol thinking that her paralysis renders her an impossible mate for Guy. In Carol's self-loathing, Lupino anatomises the damaging influence of an idealised femininity. Carol's self-pity is directly tied to her feelings of failure as a woman. Feeling she is robbed of a conventional definition of feminine allure, Carol struggles most because of the oppressive gender attributes that labelled her attractive before and undesirable after she is afflicted by polio. Carol's slowness to adapt to her disability underscores the damage of oppressive gender categories that cause suffering beyond the physical pain resulting from illness. *Never Fear* does not use disability to point to or symbolise something else; it depicts the sudden onset of the disease and honours the real trials and challenges faced by polio victims. Alongside the facts of polio, *Never Fear* shows how Carol's disability reveals the severe constraints of gender norms.

Especially in *Never Fear* and the powerful film that followed, *Outrage*, Lupino displayed an uncanny understanding of how women internalise social and gender roles, adding to their sense of hopelessness and loss. Finding the integrity in women's hard work and attempts at independence, Lupino's noir vision honours their suffering and their survival. 'Keep your hands off the rails', Carol is told by Dr Middleton, as she exits the Kabat-Kaiser at the end of *Never Fear*.

At the film's conclusion, Lupino's shot composition has Carol scaling the walls on the street as she re-enters the world, suggesting her continued struggles on the margins of mainstream culture (see Figure 2.3). But we are reminded throughout her impressive oeuvre that Lupino stands very strongly on the side of the fleap, seeing thresholds and liminality as sites resistant to objectification. The fleap's difference marks the fleap's value, even as this figure bears the brunt of how narrowly difference is conceived in a forbidding social world.

Never Fear reveals the generic elasticity of film noir, and film noir makes more legible *Never Fear*'s mid-twentieth-century analysis of an illusory American

Figure 2.3 A marginalised Carol (Sally Forrest) clings to the walls as she re-enters the world. [frame capture]

dream. Lupino's film refocuses a classic noir perspective on female desire, loss, and disappointment, clarifying the insufficiency of cliched character patterns, such as the good girl, or the femme fatale. Instead, *Never Fear* combines film noir's fatalism, spotlight on desire, and strains of documentary realism into a female-centred view of disability and the jaded promises of post-war America. Lupino's independent filmmaking highlights women grappling with female trauma and thwarted desires, while marking their feat, like the outsider fleap, of surviving.

Notes

1. Ronnie Scheib, 'Ida Lupino, Auteuress', *Film Comment* 16, no. 1 (January/February 1980), pp. 54–64, 80.
2. Francine Parker, 'Discovering Ida Lupino', *Action* 2, no. 3 (May/June 1967), p. 22.
3. Martin Scorsese, 'The Lives They Lived: Ida Lupino; Behind the Camera, a Feminist' (obituary on Ida Lupino), *New York Times Magazine*, 31 December 1995, p. 43.
4. Scorsese, 'The Lives They Lived', p. 43.
5. Carrie Rickey, 'Lupino Noir', *Village Voice*, 29 October 1980, p. 43.
6. Philip K. Scheuer, 'Lupino's "Never Fear" Turns Light on Polio', *Los Angeles Times* 20 (February 1950). Press Clippings, the Margaret Herrick Library of the Academy of Motion Picture Arts and Sciences, Los Angeles.
7. Ida Lupino, 'Why I Made *Never Fear*', Advertisement in the *Citizen News*, 17 February 1950. Press Clippings, the Margaret Herrick Library of the Academy of Motion Picture Arts and Sciences, Los Angeles.
8. 'Declaration of Independents', *Variety*, 20 February 1950, p. 12.
9. R. Barton Palmer, *Shot on Location: Postwar American Cinema and the Exploration of Real Place* (New Brunswick, NJ: Rutgers University Press, 2016), p. 51.
10. Anne Morra and Isabel Custodio, 'Her Way: Anne Morra Presents Lupino's *Never Fear* and Discusses the Director's Place in Film History', *MoMA Magazine*, 2 August 2019, https://www.moma.org/magazine/articles/130.
11. Ronnie Scheib, '"Never Fear" (1950) [sic]', in *Queen of the B's: Ida Lupino Behind the Camera*, ed. Annette Kuhn (Westport, CT: Greenwood Press, 1995), p. 49.
12. Scheib, '*Never Fear*', p. 53.
13. Manohla Dargis, 'Revisiting a Film from Ida Lupino, Hollywood Star Turned Director', *New York Times* (24 January 2019), https://www.nytimes.com/2019/01/24/movies/never-fear-the-young-lovers-review.html.
14. Parker, 'Discovering Ida Lupino', p. 22.
15. Scheib, '*Never Fear*', p. 52.
16. 'RKO Refuses to Blunt Its "Hitch-Hiker" Blurbs Tho Ride-Thumbers Beef', *Variety*, 17 April 1953. Press Clippings, the Margaret Herrick Library of the Academy of Motion Picture Arts and Sciences, Los Angeles.
17. See Therese Grisham and Julie Grossman, *Ida Lupino, Director: Her Art and Resilience in Times of Transition* (New Brunswick, NJ: Rutgers University Press, 2017).
18. In the Kino Lorber audio commentary of *Never Fear*, Alexandra Heller-Nicholas points out that the film is 'massively important, it's massively relevant' because of its reminder – given the bewildering present-day anti-vaccination fervour – of

the historical significance of vaccinations that have stopped the spread of deadly diseases (*Ida Lupino: Filmmaker Collection* (*Not Wanted / Never Fear / The Hitch-Hiker / The Bigamist*). Kino Lorber Blu-Ray/DVD).
19. Michael Davidson, 'Phantom Limbs: Film Noir and the Disabled Body', in *The Problem Body: Projecting Disability on Film*, ed. Sally Chivers and Nicole Markotic (Columbus: The Ohio State University Press, 2010), p. 56.
20. Davidson, 'Phantom Limbs', p. 62.

3. RUNNING AIMLESSLY: *CAMINO CORTADO* AND AUTARKIC SPAIN

Fernando Gabriel Pagnoni Berns

The noir film is predicated upon the spaces of modernity, its fractured narrative symptomatic 'to the violently fragmented spaces and times of the late-modern world'[1] where the American dream is shattered 'by the realities of daily existence'.[2] Lighting rich in shadows, voice-over narrations, flashbacks, paranoia, and femme fatales are markers of noir and consequences of the anxieties produced by modern dislocation and urban life. 'Indeed, the true domain of the noir is night, just as the inescapable terrain of the noir is the city.'[3] In this scenario, rural settings 'seem few and far between'.[4]

The latter is true for the US, where modernity seemed both a dynamic force of change and a threat to civilisation.[5] Other geographical spaces, however, engaged with the noir tropes in different ways, according to their own social and cultural contexts. Spain, for example, only reached modernity in dates as late as the mid-1960s. The brutal dictatorship of Francisco Franco, which ran from 1939 to 1975, kept Spain in a state of isolation and autarchy, especially in the first years. Class mobility, urbanisation, and consumerism came only when Spain became open to the world in the 1960s. In fact, Franco advocated for a crusade against modernity and, as a result, Spain 'was the last European country to undergo industrialization'.[6] As a result, Spanish noir cinema, a popular vernacular cycle in the 1950s, was informed by non-modernist sensibilities.

For example, the femme fatale, in Spanish noir, is a nuanced creature where the 'whore' and the 'virgin' cohabit together rather than being two distinctive characters. The femme fatale of classic noir cinema was a warning sign amidst the gender shifts taking place in the aftermath of World War II. The trope was 'a projection of male desire and anxiety',[7] one of the ways men 'control women's sexuality in order not to be destroyed by it'.[8] Unlike the US and other European regions, Spain did not see extreme gender shifts after the Spanish Civil War (1936–9) and World War II, as citizens were taught 'that not only were women and men different but that women had to obey their fathers and husbands, and could never aspire to be equal to their brothers'.[9] As a result, crime films such as *Camino Cortado* (*Closed Road*, Ignacio Iquino, 1955), *Los Peces Rojos* (*The Red Fishes*, José Antonio Nieves Conde, 1955) or *Manos Sucias* (*Dirty Hands*, José Antonio de la Loma, 1957) are led by femme fatales who are capable of cruelty and greed to become, in the next second, sacrificial heroines. They are, in fact, the product of noir mixed with melodrama, the 'feminine' film genre par excellence in Spain.

Criminal men, in turn, were not the pawns of women's greed, as there was little to lust for in the obscurantist, rural Spain of the 1950s. Thus, the rationale behind their criminal acts is mostly secondary in Spanish noir. What remains is hopelessness materialised in the forms of barren spaces (in contrast with the urban spaces of American noir cinema) that haunt the male characters, imprisoning them. In films such as *Manos Sucias* and *Camino Cortado*, the empty, rural, beautiful, and haunting Spanish countryside is as important a character as the male criminals.

In this chapter, I provide a close reading of *Camino Cortado*, a film symptomatic of the many issues shaping Spanish noir cinema and the social and cultural context of autarky bounding Spain at the time. The film revolves around fugitive criminals fleeing from the police. Soon, they are running aimlessly through a small town at the brink of being flooded. This film offers the perfect concentration of elements dominating Spanish Francoist noir cinema (1950–60), including the mix of noir sensibilities with melodrama and geographical asphyxiation within a context of national isolation.

Spain in the 1950s: Autarchy and Social Asphyxia

In *Camino Cortado*, a group of criminals steal and kill with a goal in their mind: escaping Spain. Yet, the film taps into historical and societal concerns about the obscurantism and stagnation dominating Spain through its autarkic era. Thus, the criminals end running aimlessly through the country without any possibility of getting abroad. Spain was, basically, an asphyxiating fatherland.

Francoist Spain can be divided, broadly speaking, into three main stages after the Civil War (1936–9), stages that devastated the country and provoked the collapse of the Spanish Republic. The first was fascism, right up until the end of World War II. Those were years in which Franco tried to graft onto Spain the fascist governments of Adolf Hitler and Benito Mussolini, even if the dictator 'never fully adopted the entire core fascist revolutionary ideology'.[10] Oppression took on a predominantly violent form in the cities and little towns, as any form of resistance or sympathy with the 'reds' (communists) or the left met with imprisonment without proper trial, executions, and physical disappearances of persons. After the fall of the fascist regimes in Europe, Franco felt obliged to change his philosophy and adopted an autarkic economy and international isolation until 1959. Finally, after the complete failure of this autarkic stage, Spain embraced modernity, dominated by a sense of 'peace and progress', which lasted until the death of the military leader in 1975.

According to Antonio Cazorla Sánchez, a scholar who dedicated many works to tracing the history of Spain and the lives of the common citizens under Francoism, autarky 'was an economic policy adopted by the regime that included massive state intervention in the economy and was intended to enable the country to attain full economic independence from world markets'.[11] That period saw how 'the Francoist state massively intervened in the economy, regulating both trade and the supply system. It also manipulated markets, imposed import substitution, and forced industrialisation. The result was an unmitigated economic and human disaster' characterised by serious 'food shortages which caused widespread famine among the poor'.[12]

Numerous factors guided Franco to adopt autarky as the main economic and cultural philosophy of his government right up until the 1960s. The regime itself 'stressed that the country was affected by world war within months of the end of the Civil War and was then "ostracized" by the international powers'.[13] Not only did the world conflict make trade difficult, but 'the Allies were reluctant to provide Spain with food and other material when Franco's sympathy for Nazi Germany was so manifest'.[14]

The ideological base for Franco's politics of autarky was predicated on the leader's desire for

> extreme nationalism, a rejection of liberalism, a desire for national industrialization, a sympathy for fascist ideas, and a readiness to enter the war on the side of the Axis. Moreover, autarky fitted very well with a broader ideological belief in the need to seal Spain off culturally from the outside world. The making of the Francoist 'New State' was seen as being dependent upon a Catholic 'moral reeducation' based upon the 'essential values of Spanishness'.[15]

Rather than just a matter of economic policies, autarky was a nationalist ideal. The commitment to Catholic values, such as the enthroning of the family and conservative gender roles, brought Franco the support of the Catholic Church, all of them (Franco, the political right, and the Church) affirming the creation of the 'authentic' Spain. Franco, thus, governed Spain 'por la gracia de Dios' (for God's will).[16] To some point, people supported Franco's ideals, as the effects of the extreme violence suffered through the Civil War was still too present. After years of war between neighbours and friends (the Spanish Civil War), people embraced the 'peace' that Franco offered, one that allowed a common citizen to go outside to buy bread without the fear of being killed by a stray bullet. As such:

> part of the legitimation of Franco's power rested on the memory of the mayhem of the Civil War, and the desire to gain and preserve peace. Even if Franco promised union when he assumed the government in 1939, he took good care to evoke the dangers of the past: loosening the grip could allow violence to erupt again.[17]

The consequences of autarky, rather than fruitful, were disastrous to Spaniards, hurting the country and furthering the problems initiated during the Spanish Civil War. Autarky leads 'to problems such as the development of the black market (*el estraperlo*), hunger, unemployment, and increased prostitution'.[18] For example, 'the attempt to achieve autarky in the wheat production sector was disastrous and, ironically, the country became dependent upon imports'.[19] In consequence, the hunger produced by the Spanish Civil War was increased, rather than diminished, with Franco's autarkic project. 'So dire was the situation that the postwar decade was and still is commonly referred to as "the years of hunger" (*los años de hambre*).'[20] In retrospective, Franco's project of national autarky was called 'suicidal',[21] a decision that depressed 'triggers for modernization, since external impulses were non-existent'.[22]

In 1959, the Francoist regime finally discarded autarky in favour of a plan of economic liberalisation. The so-called Stabilisation Plan was a turning point in the history of Spain and brought the country to a late modernisation through the 1960s. The plan was supported by the IMF, 'which imposed conditions for Spain's economic development, including currency devaluation and other measures to attract foreign investment'.[23] Devaluation, exports, and the freezing of salaries gave impulse, indeed, to foreign economic investments. The immediate effects, however, were impoverishment and migration of many Spaniards; nonetheless, the Stabilisation Plan – slowly – brought the first airs of modernisation. The '*España es diferente*' ('Spain is different') slogan was the 1960s' campaign to open the nation to the rest of the world and bring in the necessary dollars to start the path to modernity. Spain, during the 1960s, was sold abroad as a picturesque, affable, and carefree country where modernity and ancient cities and castles cohabited together, bringing tourism in huge waves and putting the country, finally, on the map of modern Europe.

Spanish noir, however, was a cycle made only through the 1950s, when Spain was under the autarkic umbrella. It was appropriate that the genre flourished in that era, as the lack of hope, the feeling of entrapment, and a pitch-black present fitted perfectly to the noir mold of chiaroscuros and paranoia.[24]

As stated by Tatjana Pavlović, 'Francoist cinematographic politics reflected a more general climate of political repression.'[25] The Francoist regime paid great attention to the themes brought to the screen, since, according their policies, nothing related with criminality or horror should be exhibited as happening within Spanish territories.[26] The National Department of Cinematography (*Departamento Nacional de Cinematografía*), created in May 1938, was an offshoot of the Delegation of Press and Propaganda (*la Delegación de Prensa y Propaganda*) and, as such, film was considered as part of official propaganda, a form of national projection upon the world.

Noir existed even in this context of extreme censorship and restriction. 'Censorship included supervision and approval of film scripts, prohibition of particular scenes, requests for modifications of particular scenes, issuing of filming permits, and issuing of permits allowing for the exhibition of Spanish and foreign films on national territory.'[27] It may be baffling that noir (and, later, the horror genre) existed at all in such a repressive climate dominated by dictatorship. But as Pavlović rightly explains, 'despite the strong political and moral motivation behind censorship, the censorial apparatus was surprisingly arbitrary and ambiguous'.[28] Indeed, censorship was mostly sustained by the capricious subjectivity of the censors than based on some logical set of norms and rules. As such, noir flourished in a repressive landscape, providing viewers with glass darkly glimpses of life within the walls of autarkic Spain.

Jo Labanyi, Antonio Lázaro-Reboll, and Vicente Rodríguez Ortega argue that Spanish noir was 'clearly derivative' of the American in its tropes and narratives.[29] For the authors, this should not be 'interpreted as a failure of creative imagination but rather as an attempt to situate Spanish cinema within the contours of a transnational cinematic mode of address that was swiftly expanding from the United States to Europe and East Asia'.[30] However, this connection between Spanish noir and its American counterpart may be overstated, with Spain preferring for its crime stories open spaces and common citizens rather than detectives or cops. I agree more with the next statement: '[B]eing made during the dictatorship, Spanish *noir* [. . .] walked a thin line since it focused on the dark underbelly of society, revealing the moral rot of postwar Spanish society, contradicting the illusion of wellbeing that Francoism attempted to instill into its citizens.'[31] As we shall see, *Camino Cortado* is an exemplary representation of Francoist noir made during the autarkic era. Characters running aimlessly, trying to escape without any exit sign in sight are typical of Spanish noir of the 1950s. With a country completely closed to foreign interaction, Spaniards were, like the characters of *Camino Cortado*, trapped within a situation outside their control and with only a bleak end of the road ahead of them.

Camino Cortado: Trapped Within

Iquino's film starts with the opening credits superimposed on a wall of strong rocks, anticipating the film's thesis: the way out is completely blocked; Spain is trapped within heavy walls. The film's first sequence, however, evokes the narrative and setting of the traditional American noir: a seedy nightclub where Cecilia (Laya Raki) works as an exotic performer. She is typified as the femme fatale: she dances wearing a brief dress while playfully flirting with the all-male clientele. In concordance with the narratives of the American noir film, the nightclub attracts criminals who use the place to concoct their criminal plans, among them Juan (Viktor Staal), Cecilia's boyfriend (see Figure 3.1).

Their plan is simple: steal money from a rich rancher and run away 'to France', a country that Juan illustrates as the opposite of Spain. The nightclubs are luxurious and the women dancing there only wear diamond earrings. The imagery of France works in sharp contrast with the sad state of the nightclub where Cecilia worked and, by extension, with Spain. The reference to women dancing almost naked refers to the moral obscurantism that dominated autarkic Spain during the Francoist era. The lack of modernity existed in a vis-à-vis relationship with lack of moral freedom, with Franco sustaining strong Catholic values as the 'real' Spain. Unlike the obscurantist Catholic Spain, liberal France is the geographical locus of social mobility, sexual freedom, and progressive ethos.

Figure 3.1 Cecilia (Laya Raki) typifies the (Spanish) femme fatale. [frame capture]

The selection of France as the perfect destination was not casual. France is a neighbouring country that received, in the early years of Franco and just after the Civil War, a 'mass' of Spanish expatriates fleeing the dictatorship.[32] In France, left-wing groups and other social organisations – like the newspaper *Le Socialiste*, published in France since 1961 – sought, in a daily struggle against Franco in the ideological field, to return democracy to Spain.[33] No wonder, then, that France is coded as the ideal geographical destination for the gang of crooks planning a big robbery. In a sense, what the gang of criminals – Juan, Cecilia, Miguel (Armando Moreno), and Antonio (Eugenio Domingo) – want is to get some money to flee to France, an idea of escape that surely resounded in the mind of many Spaniards watching the film. By 1955, the year in which Iquino's film opened, the autarkic plans were already a complete failure.

The subtle references to misery and lack of economic resources appear in the film's first minutes: talking to the bartender, Juan asks for a bottle of alcohol and some sandwiches. The bartender, however, has his doubts; it is clear that Juan has no money nor much credit left at the nightclub. Unlike classical noir, where money is mostly used by men as the path to social mobility, heterosexual desire, or tough male prowess,[34] here the main reason behind the robbery seems to be poverty and hunger. In a key scene, Juan tries to convince Cecilia to break her contract with the place and run away with him to France. The owner of the nightclub angrily asks Juan to leave.[35] After a fist fight, the owner resentfully spits to Juan that the only thing he has to offer to Cecilia 'is hunger'.

To enhance the image of immigration as an ideal, the scene cuts to a close-up of one of the most desired items in any country under dictatorship: the passport. Cecilia is happy with the idea of fleeing Spain. She even addresses one of the most important issues for those seeking to immigrate: employment in a foreign country. Cecilia hopes to work as a Spanish dancer, since friends living in France told her that people with this skill find good jobs there. Thinking about her future as an employed woman in a foreign country – rather than how to manipulate men – downplays her status as erotic icon (built in the previous dancing scene) and links her to the struggles of the autarkic era. As such, she is closer to real Spanish women in the audiences than to the American trope of the femme fatale. Cecilia is not looking for money, but for a job. Money is her way out of Spain to get that job. Thus, the film inserts itself within an imaginary that was prevalent in Francoist Spain: social oppression, poverty, and the desire of immigration.

Social asphyxiation is also mentioned in the opening scene at the bar. Antonio, the youngest of the criminals, wants to flee Spain because he works on a ranch owned by his uncle, a man depicted as a tyrant. The uncle got his power illegitimately, by stealing the place from Antonio's mother. This lack of legitimate power connects Antonio's uncle with the figure of Francisco Franco, who usurped power after a military coup.[36]

The plan goes right, to some point, as agreed. The gang steals a car from a middle-class man who is 'in Germany' for a few days. The stolen car has a sticker on the windshield which says '*en visita turística*' ('on tourist visit'). The film reaffirms the value of money to flee the country; yet, while upper-class and rich people can do so through tourism, the criminals, all belonging to the lowest classes, need to immigrate permanently and furtively. It is interesting to note that the film does not address why the criminals need to pass the frontier unnoticed, when they could immigrate openly if they had the money. It is also assumed that no one will know that the money the gang owns is stolen; thus, dealing with the local authorities should not be a problem. Immigration by all means resides at the core of Iquino's film as a source of anxieties and dread. It seems that just the idea of immigration is criminal somehow. Cecilia even makes her case: she has a legit passport, so she does not need to cross the frontier through subterfuge as does the rest of the gang. The passport is recurrently turned into a fetish object that symbolises freedom from both poverty and oppression. This image follows the reality of the era: 'It was very difficult to get a passport – the Francoist authorities demanded good reasons, or good contacts, before handing such documents to ordinary citizens.'[37] The pride Cecilia feels at having a passport illustrates the importance of those documents through the whole Francoist era, especially in the first half, when fascism and poverty were a daily pressure and the country celebrated isolationism (see Figure 3.2).

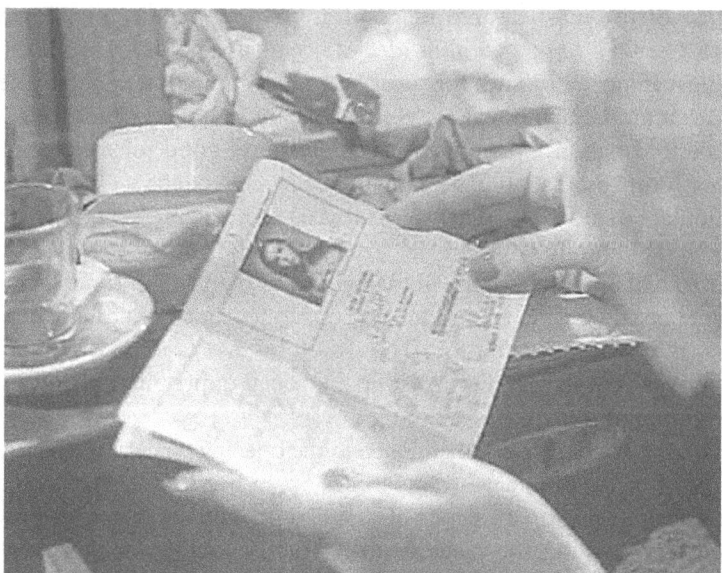

Figure 3.2 The most desired object in autarchic Spain: the passport. [frame capture]

The crime itself occupies little screen time, differentiating the film significantly from US noir. Even the sequence depicting the gang travelling to the ranch takes more time that the robbery. During this lengthy sequence, the characters ride in silence, drinking alcohol, smoking, or sleeping. When the gang reaches the ranch, a close-up reveals a stone with an inscription: '*camino particular*' ('private road'), signalling the beginning of the road that takes them to the ranch. The image of a 'private road' takes viewers to a 'healthy' economy (that of the ranch's owner) in sharp contrast with the 'closed road' of the title, and which, arguably, symbolises autarkic Spain.

The crime takes place out of sight. Viewers are obliged to wait patiently with Cecilia in the car while the criminals assault (and accidently kill) Antonio's uncle. While Cecilia gets close to a nervous breakdown waiting in the car for some news, a poor man cuts through the road with his flock of (slowly) passing sheep, thus prefiguring the film's main theme: the closed road. It is interesting how Cecilia is depicted through the film and how she differs from the traditional femme fatale of noir. In a previous scene in the nightclub, one of her friends asks Cecilia if she is taking money from Juan: she laughs and denies this. As she states, she is incapable of doing such a thing. Later in the film, she flirts with both Juan and Miguel, a narrative choice that codifies her, together with her silent complicity in murder (she accepts to follow the plan even after murder has taken place), as a femme fatale. Yet, the rhetorical figure of the traditional femme fatale is inextricably linked to modernity, a stage still to come to Spain. 'In what does the deadliness of the femme fatale consist and why is she so insistently a figure of fascination in the texts of modernity?' asks Mary Ann Doane. The answer is univocal: 'she is not the subject of feminism but a symptom of male fears about feminism'.[38] Feminism, sweeping Europe and America in the 1960s, was practically absent in Francoist Spain, with women and femininity still linked with traditional roles and spaces.

Conservative newspapers responding to Franco were quick to disseminate the idea that Spanish women were 'healthy' and only wanted to be married and have children.[39] Feminism or, at least, the female mobility taking place in America in the second post-war period, was something practically absent in the Spain of Francisco Franco, as women were fitted into morally appropriate roles and practices in the autarkic Spain. Women actually lost some of the rights gained during the democratic Republic. For example, women under Franco's regime were only able to work outside home with their husbands' authorisation.[40] Neither could they 'hold a passport or a bank account without their husbands' permission'.[41] Following the norms of the conservative filmmaking of the era, Cecilia slowly shifts from her femme fatale persona to the maternal. As the gang of crooks gets into increasingly dire situations, the relationships get more and more tense, with young Antonio, filled with guilt and doubts, being the target of Juan's ire. Cecilia cares for and protects Antonio the best she can, even if her actions attract Juan's fury. This act of self-sacrifice takes Cecilia closer to the traditional feminine role as imposed by Spanish melodrama.

Similarly, masculine roles, while remaining mostly rooted in patriarchal fantasies of superiority, also experiment with some ambiguity that produces a small dislocation of the American noir counterpart. Juan is the quintessential noir tragic figure, his plans doomed to fail. However, while travelling to France, Juan mentions that he wants to marry Cecilia and live a happy, homely life, far from crime, thus complying with the Francoist ideals of family values.

Yet, the immigration is impossible. The film's last hour depicts the increasingly desperate attempts of the gang fleeing Spain to access France. Like in real Spain, fleeing to another country proves to be a problematic affair. Policemen block the road to the national border, obliging the gang to search desperately for alternative roads. Unknown to them, the police are blocking off the roads because an old dam will be demolished with dynamite and the town and the roads will be flood with water. The officials are there to keep the streets empty and not, as the gang suspects, to chase them. Running away from the cops, however, the criminals get deeper into the obscurantist heart of autarkic Spain. Their momentary shelter is an abandoned town, one of the many villages that were literally asphyxiated by autarky and declining economies. Juan and the others believe that the signs indicating 'bar' or 'food' will take them to lively places, but the only thing they find are ruined buildings at the brink of collapse, their owners and customers long gone. By the mid-1950s, 'the government tried to stem the tide of rural depopulation by offering monetary incentives to remain, but later conceded its inevitability'.[42] Smalls towns were doomed to disappear through the autarkic years, where the scarce jobs still existing can only be found in cities. Before leaving the abandoned town, the criminals must resort to drinking water from a river, their only real provider of resources in this severely impoverished landscape (see Figures 3.3).

Figures 3.3a & 3.3b   The gang of criminals looks for a place to rest but finds only abandoned towns. [frame capture]

The situation worsens when Juan kills a cop after their car gets stuck in mud. Ironically, the officer only wants to help, not arrest them. Again, the impossibility of fleeing Spain is highlighted: not only are the roads blocked, but the lack of asphalt and proper infrastructures (a debt that would wait until modernisation in the 1960s) enhances the sense of entrapment. Escaping from impoverished Spain is proved futile. Like many citizens stuck in a country isolated from modernity, Juan, Cecilia, Antonio, and Miguel are trapped within the economic and cultural walls of fascism and autarky. Soon, they are chased not only by police trying to arrest them for killing their partner, but also by intense heat (the story takes place through a hot summer) and a complete lack of resources. Wherever they go, they find only abandoned towns.

At the film's climax, tensions have peaked within the gang, with Cecilia and Antonio preferring to give themselves up to the authorities, Juan getting increasingly cruel, and Miguel remaining somehow stuck in the middle. Fittingly, the final showdown between the gang and the police takes place in an abandoned small town, all the houses in a poor state, little more than precarious walls and ceilings on the brink of collapse. It is clear that the habitants abandoned the rural town many years ago. At the end, a policeman kills Antonio and, sick of running around without finding any exit from Spain, Miguel confronts Juan. The film ends with another officer killing Juan, while Cecilia and Miguel give themselves up to the authorities, the only way they could find to stop the spiral of running around without any exit in sight. The film's last shot depicts the dam being demolished and the waters sweeping the ruined ghost towns. Indeed, there was no way to escape from Spain and its autarkic philosophy that traps citizens within misery, mud, and the wreckage of the old Republic.

Conclusion

The sinister geography prepares viewers for the climactic moment when Cecilia and Miguel abandon all hope. Here again *Camino Cortado* invites comparison with the reality of Spain and the somewhat joyless conclusions. In 1959, four years after Iquino's film, Spain would definitively abandon the autarkic circle/cycle of entrapment and isolation to open the country to the world.

With the Stabilisation Plan, Spain made investments in new high-capacity roads, rails, bridges, and general infrastructure.[43] Towns swept away by water may be read as exaggeration, but the flushing out of the old and cleansing the nation would ring true as modernity and openness came to Spain: the celebration of modernity and the coming of change to the traditional Spanish geography. The climax of *Camino Cortado* illustrates the anxieties not only towards the autarkic philosophy, but to the inevitability of modernity arriving. Water comes to obliterate what has been already obscured: the fate of all the habitants of all those small towns that the autarkic policies previously destroyed.

Faithful to the noir tropes, *Camino Cortado* offers a reading of national entrapment; Juan, Cecilia, Antonio, and Miguel run around aimlessly, finding cop enemies, misery, and economic devastation wherever they go. As such, Iquino's film reveals deep-seated anxieties regarding Francisco Franco's autarkic world where citizens want to escape but were doomed to keep running without being able to find the exit of an asphyxiating country dominated by precariousness.

Notes

1. Edward Dimendberg, *Film Noir and the Spaces of Modernity* (Cambridge, MA: Harvard University Press, 2004), p. 6.
2. Wheeler Winston Dixon, *Film Noir and the Cinema of Paranoia* (Edinburgh: Edinburgh University Press, 2009), p. 10.
3. Dixon, *Film Noir and the Cinema of Paranoia*, p. 3.
4. Dixon, *Film Noir and the Cinema of Paranoia*, p. 4.
5. James Naremore, *More than Night: Film Noir in its Context* (Los Angeles: University of California Press, 2008), p. 42.
6. Susan Gay Drummond, *Mapping Marriage Law in Spanish Gitano Communities* (Vancouver: UBC Press, 2006), p. 48.
7. Julie Grossman, *Rethinking the Femme Fatale in Film Noir: Ready for Her Close-Up* (New York: Palgrave Macmillan, 2009), p. 2.
8. Janey Place, 'Women in Film Noir', in *Women in Film Noir*, ed. E. Ann Kaplan (London: British Film Institute, 1998), p. 49.
9. Antonio Cazorla Sánchez, *Fear and Progress: Ordinary Lives in Franco's Spain 1939–1975* (Malden, MA: Blackwell, 2010), p. 92.
10. Stanley Payne, *Fascism in Spain, 1923–1977* (Madison: University of Wisconsin Press, 1999), p. 326.
11. Cazorla Sánchez, *Fear and Progress*, p. x.
12. Cazorla Sánchez, *Fear and Progress*, p. 6.
13. Michael Richards, 'Autarky', in *Encyclopedia of Contemporary Spanish Culture*, ed. Eamonn Rodgers (New York: Routledge, 1999), p. 37.
14. Richards, 'Autarky', p. 37.
15. Richards, 'Autarky', p. 37.
16. Sima Lieberman, *Growth and Crisis in the Spanish Economy: 1940–1993* (New York: Routledge, 2005), p. 27.
17. Fernando Gabriel Pagnoni Berns, 'Stories to Make You Think: The Horror of Daily Life under Francisco Franco's Regime in *Historias para No Dormir*', in *Global TV Horror*, ed. Stacey Abbott and Lorna Jowett (Cardiff: University of Wales Press, 2021), p. 73.
18. Tatjana Pavlović et al., *100 Years of Spanish Cinema* (Malden, MA: Blackwell, 2009), p. 61.
19. Richards, 'Autarky', p. 37.
20. Pavlović et al., *100 Years of Spanish Cinema*, p. 61.
21. Juan Díez Medrano, *Framing Europe: Attitudes to European Integration in Germany, Spain, and the United Kingdom* (Princeton: Princeton University Press, 2003), p. 163.

22. S. P. Mangen, *Spanish Society After Franco: Regime Transition and the Welfare State* (New York: Routledge, 2001), p. 32.
23. Sharryn Kasmir, *The Myth of Mondragon: Cooperatives, Politics, and Working-Class Life in a Basque Town* (New York: State University of New York Press, 1996), p. 77.
24. Thereafter, modern Spain basically discarded the noir genre; instead, the 1960s and 1970s became the golden age of Spanish horror, a new form of materialising the repressive state into film fiction.
25. Pavlović et al., *100 Years of Spanish Cinema*, p. 62.
26. Xavier Aldana Reyes, 'The Curious Case of the Spanish Televisual Vampire', *Horror Studies* 8, no. 2 (2017); Rubén Sánchez Trigos, *La Orgía de los Muertos: Historia del Cine de Zombis Español* (Madrid: Shangrila, 2019), p. 159; Fernando Gabriel Pagnoni Berns, *Alegorías Televisivas del Franquismo: Narciso Ibáñez Serrador y las Historias para no Dormir (1966–1982)* (Cádiz: Universidad de Cádiz, 2020), p. 51.
27. Pavlović et al., *100 Years of Spanish Cinema*, p. 62.
28. Pavlović et al., *100 Years of Spanish Cinema*, p. 62.
29. Jo Labanyi, Antonio Lázaro-Reboll, and Vicente Rodríguez Ortega, 'Film Noir, the Thriller, and Horror', in *A Companion to Spanish Cinema*, ed. Jo Labanyi and Tatjana Pavlović (Malden, MA: Blackwell, 2013), p. 261.
30. Labanyi et al., 'Film Noir, the Thriller, and Horror', p. 261.
31. Labanyi et al., 'Film Noir, the Thriller, and Horror', p. 261.
32. Anatoly Krasikov, *From Dictatorship to Democracy: Spanish Reportage* (Oxford: Pergamon Press, 1984), p. 6.
33. The newspaper, in fact, had existed since 1944, but was obliged to change its name due to Francoist pressures on the French government. See Andreu Claret Serra, 'Prensa Clandestina y del Exilio bajo el Franquismo', *Asociación de la Prensa de Madrid* (November 1986), p. 31.
34. Steve Cohan, *Masked Men: Masculinity and the Movies in the Fifties* (Bloomington: Indiana University Press, 1997), p. 42.
35. Interesting is how the owner of the place is depicted: wearing a dirty, sweaty shirt, and dishevelled hair, he is closer to the image of hunger and disempowerment than that of the owner of a nightclub.
36. The Spanish Civil War ended on 31 March 1939, with the victory of the rebel and pro-fascist advance over those who defended the legit Republic. Franco usurped the government rather than being elected, a fact that brought to the population the same feel of oppression Antonio feels in the ranch where he works.
37. Jason Webster, *The Spy with 29 Names: The Story of the Second World War's Most Audacious Double Agent* (London: Chatto & Windus, 2014), p. 42.
38. Mary Ann Doane, *Femmes Fatales: Feminism, Film Theory, and Psychoanalysis* (New York: Routledge, 1991), p. 2.
39. Pagnoni Berns, *Alegorías Televisivas del Franquismo*, pp. 122–4.
40. Pagnoni Berns, *Alegorías Televisivas del Franquismo*, p. 135.
41. Jo Labanyi, 'Feminizing the Nation: Women, Subordination and Subversion in Post-Civil War Spanish Cinema', in *Heroines without Heroes: Reconstructing Female*

and National Identities in European Cinema, 1945–1951, ed. Ulrike Sieglohr (London: Bloomsbury, 2016), p. 168. Cecilia's passport, in this scenario, is a double element of pride: it marks the possibility of fleeing and, on the other hand, some female empowerment.
42. Mangen, *Spanish Society After Franco*, p. 39.
43. Sasha David Pack, *Spain in the Age of Mass Tourism, Modernization, and Dictatorship, 1945–1975* (Madison: University of Wisconsin, 2004), p. 17.

4. RACE AND THE NOIR WESTERN: NAVIGATING *THE WALKING HILLS*

Elyce Rae Helford

The tagline in the trade ad for *The Walking Hills* (John Sturges, 1949) tempts the moviegoer with a dark adventure: 'Alone in the desert . . . nine men and a woman . . . seeking fabulous treasure and escape from their pasts.' Filmed in black and white, with all but an opening scene and flashbacks shot on location in Death Valley, the picture sets itself apart from the optimism and wide-open spaces of the classic American western, even as its conclusion is less bleak than classic noir. Instead, *The Walking Hills* typifies an early contribution to the subgenre of the darker, more psychologically complex 'noir western'.

The western and film noir may at first seem dissimilar, even at odds in terms of their objectives. Forming a hybrid would seem to require an implausible reconciliation of grandeur and claustrophobia, of moral clarity and troubling ambivalence, of a hopeful outlook and a deeply cynical one. Within the US, these binaries further rest on an opposition between a fundamentally patriotic vision and a harshly critical social perspective. Despite this, as Imogen Sara Smith argues, film noir 'infected' westerns with its murkier view without difficulty. Smith accuses noir darkness of 'staining pioneer myths with themes of psychological disturbance, betrayal, corruption, and the illusiveness of freedom in a society predicated on it'.[1] Yet, she continues, darkness and the western were never far apart, for a 'frontier where land and resources are free to be grabbed by all takers is a recipe for instability and conflict'.[2] Such tensions are the heart of *The Walking Hills*, a film in which a loose band of friends and strangers find themselves bonded in secrecy in a search for a one-hundred-year-old treasure buried in the desert.

Exactly when the Hollywood western took on noir elements is difficult to pin down. David Meuel is comfortable giving some precise dates in the subtitle to his book *The Noir Western: Darkness on the Range, 1943–1962*. He argues that an infusion of noir led to a 'Golden Age of westerns from the late 1940s to the early 1960s' that would 'change the western forever'.[3] Rather than a linear generic evolution, Smith, by contrast, prefers not to 'mark off the exact boundaries of the "noir western" within [a] gradual darkening and deepening of the genre'.[4] Instead, she identifies a small group of post-World War II westerns that 'exhibited distinctive aspects of film noir: chiaroscuro lighting, haunted heroes, dangerous women, confusing plots driven by secrets from the past, and a pervasive sense of anomie'.[5] Such elements all play a part in *The Walking Hills*.

Generally considered a lesser imitation of *The Treasure of the Sierra Madre* (John Huston, 1948), *The Walking Hills* received only brief, superficial reviews at its opening in March 1949 and almost no critical attention since. Typical are dismissive assessments, such as 'It's a routine yarn, but with interesting sidelights'.[6] Even when there is praise, such as one anonymous reviewer's appreciation of the 'touching love story' and 'slashing action sequences', most reviewers are less kind.[7] Darr Smith, for the *Los Angeles Daily News*, is particularly harsh:

> No doubt about it, screenwriter Alan Le May had one whopping idea when he started out to write this one. But it died somewhere between the performances and the direction. Best performers in the pictures [*sic*] were the technicians behind the wind machine. They made the sandstorm really terrifying.[8]

Beyond the climactic tempest, only one other highlight appears in multiple reviews: the diegetic performances of folk-blues musician Josh White.[9]

Glenn Lovell's biography of director John Sturges nuances such reviews by offering a bit of historical and production context for the film, including that it 'became Columbia's top-grossing release of the year, and the first indication that Sturges could be commercial'.[10] Lovell notes that the film may lack the 'psychological complexity or savage irony' of *Treasure of the Sierra Madre*, but he praises *The Walking Hills*, conversely, for its relative freedom from 'the ethnocentrism that characterised studio action pictures of the period', identifying the film's Black and Native American characters as 'the conscience of the group'.[11]

Beyond reviews and biographies, the film has gone without academic study. Smith, for instance, does not discuss it in her chapter-length analysis of noir westerns. Meuel mentions it only once in his book, identifying it as #9 in his appendix of 'Fifty Additional Noir-ish Postwar Westerns Worth Seeing', without further comment. And Gene Blottner identifies the film as a noir western in his 1940–62 Columbia filmography.[12] In such context, this chapter proposes a purposeful – if necessarily partial – rectification of scholarly neglect. The following paragraphs read the film's relationship to its era of production, considering it primarily through liminal noirish elements and their impact on its presentation of race in early post-World War II America.

Film Noir and the Western

The Walking Hills opens with a title card to establish the film's resonant setting. Filmed almost exclusively in Death Valley, we read (to the accompaniment of traditional Hollywood-style upbeat 'Mexican' music) that the film is set in the present day of a US border town: 'Calexico in America and Mexicali on the Mexican side.' When this post-credits title card fades, we are in the hot midday of a city street, following a furtive young man, making his way down a sidewalk. He comes upon a diner, through the window of which he catches the eye of a dark-haired waitress, who glares at him then turns away. As he passes, we see he is being tailed by two men, an old gentleman in a striped suit, and a dark, sharp-eyed, younger man, sporting a fedora instead of the more prevalent cowboy hats, clearly marking him as an outsider. We will soon come to learn that he is a private detective. The stage is set for conflicts over boundaries, both literal and figurative.

In classic westerns, the Mexican border – always depicted from a North American viewpoint – reflects a mythic space of freedom and adventure. In westerns of the pre-World War II era, going south of the border offers an open opportunity for the white American man, frequently bringing a chance for excitement and rarely causing complications for a safe return home.[13] Thus, the classic western is, according to José Limón, 'fundamentally a genre of imperialism'.[14] Later examples, including the noir western of the postwar era, continue reliance on such symbolism, but expand critique, including contestation of colonising fantasies through commentary on gendered and racialised space. Changes to social institutions, including middle-class women's movement into the workforce and African American men's advancement through the GI Bill, reveal limited American confidence in cultural absolutes, and we see this in the anxiety produced by and reflected within film noir.[15] Thus, from pre- to post-war, the border shifts in meaning and focus. As Smith argues, 'The Mexican border is an essential noir locale: a no-man's land populated by fugitives, illegal immigrants, and those who prey on them.'[16] At its bleakest, noir renders Mexico a 'lawless land for Americans, easygoing but treacherous, rife with smugglers, drug dealers, exiled gangsters, lone murderous bandits, and egregious tourists'.[17] Perhaps nowhere is this illustrated more clearly than in *Touch of Evil* (Orson Welles, 1958), in which Welles's corrupt police captain Quinlan exits the Mexican side of town with the line

'Let's go back to civilisation', and Mexican officer Mike Vargas (Charlton Heston, in brownface) tells his white American wife (Janet Leigh) that border towns bring out the worst in a country.

Produced within the middle years of the classic film noir cycle but during the early days of the darker western, *The Walking Hills* is relatively tame in its assessment of the Mexico border. The film's entirely American central cast of characters move with relative ease across the border in search of treasure. Furthermore, while riches beckon the adventurers (as well as those forced along, having overheard the secret details), this is no robbery or heist film, and the primary characters are either financially stable or less concerned about money than lying low. Only the criminals who have crossed the border to escape US law enforcement have any need to fear, and this provides the primary tension in the film.

Emphasis on criminals fleeing persecution both opens the film and sustains its noirish suspense throughout the picture, with the mood growing more darkly ambiguous as an increasing number of the film's seven central white American male characters prove to be 'knife quick, trigger happy', and tied to crimes, mostly concerning murder.[18] The juxtaposition of fedoras and cowboy hats is particularly notable, with the cop, criminals, and blues singer sporting the former and, thereby, signifying ambiguous generic boundaries from the film's earliest moments (see Figure 4.1).

Figure 4.1   The noir western is a story told in hats in *The Walking Hills*. © Photofest

The character we first meet, walking down the aforementioned Mexicali street, is Dave Wilson (William Bishop), now hiding behind the assumed name of 'Shep'. He is trying to evade the law, having fled a scene north of the border where he accidentally killed a man during a private poker game in a hotel room. That he succeeds in reaching Mexico is rare to find in a noirish film. That we only later in the film learn about the crime he flees, through a flashback sequence, is more common, illustrating the picture's use of a common noir narrative technique to enhance tension. Dave is being pursued by private detective Frazee (John Ireland). Frazee, like Dave, sports a fedora; unlike Dave, however, he carries a gun. In keeping with what will soon become an ornate plot more typical of noir than the western, Frazee's gun will eventually be used with lethal outcome on Frazee himself, after the weapon is discovered by another criminal on the run who is part of the treasure-seeking gang, a less-developed character called Chalk (Arthur Kennedy). Among this group of adventurers, we also meet young Johnny (Jerome Courtland); this naïve cowboy, we eventually learn, has likewise come across the border after having been accused of murder. (Only after he dies from a fight injury in the desert do we learn from Frazee that he has already been exonerated.) Even our leading man, horse breeder Jim Carey (Randolph Scott), momentarily seems to be untrustworthy when he knowingly lets Johnny die. In truth, we discover, he was merely fulfilling Johnny's request to die in the desert rather than be imprisoned.

Beyond this unlikely band of men from both sides of the law, the film includes a single central female character. Chris Jackson (Ella Raines, sharing top billing with Scott) plays an independent-minded rodeo performer who learns of the search for treasure and, unwelcome, joins the party. She readily uses the threat of blackmail to demand her share, but this is a ruse. In truth, Chris's purpose is to reunite with Dave, a fellow rodeo rider for whom she left her ex-boyfriend, Jim, in the past. Somehow, she hopes to regain Jim's respect, even as she pursues Dave into the hills. In the film's first flashback, we witness how the two fell in love and, later, made plans to meet up in San Juan. Chris left only a hasty goodbye note for Jim and came to regret this when Dave never showed up in Puerto Rico. Eventually, we discover in another flashback that the accidental murder happened the day Dave was to meet Chris.

This tangled love triangle superficially links Chris with the noir femme fatale; however, the characterisation is mild and the woman redeemable. Chris is a fetish object within the male-dominated space of the picture, posed for sex appeal in tight jeans that accentuate her small waist and a scene of primping, where we watch her comb her hair in a mirror while the men just dust themselves off. As she preens and Josh (Josh White) sings, Jim comes by to admire her. When he mentions that he might have made a mistake in not taking her back (calling her a "thing" he let go and only later discovers he misses), she smiles, catlike. That Chris betrayed Jim is clear, but he has at least superficially forgiven her. Moreover, at the end of the film, he openly sends her off to Dave, exemplifying the tradition of the lone, self-sacrificing cowboy that Scott portrayed in many a western.[19] Similarly, Chris's blackmail threat is brushed off easily, with none of the men guarding his share of the treasure jealously. Jim, for one, is more concerned with a pregnant mare he brings along on the adventure; Frazee wants to capture Dave; and Dave, Chalk, and Johnny just hope to keep a step ahead of the law. After a climactic, lethal sandstorm, Chris follows Dave, who has at last decided to turn himself in. Jim wishes the two well, riding off not with the woman but with his cherished recently born foal in his arms.

In addition to narrative structure and plot, noir western hybridity is also visible in the film's casting. Randolph Scott is the most famous of the film's western stars, although character actor Edgar Buchanan (Old Willy, the old-timer who tells the others about the treasure) also appeared in multiple westerns by 1949. Arthur Kennedy, by contrast, had appeared in few films before *The Walking Hills*, but he was cast in one noir and one western, both directed by Raoul Walsh: *High Sierra* (1941) and *Cheyenne* (1947). Similarly, but with a longer list of roles, John Ireland's 1940s performances straddled the two genres. Before the *The Walking Hills*, audiences could have seen him in noir pictures *Behind Green Lights* (Otto Brower, 1946), *Railroaded!* (Anthony Mann, 1947), and *Raw Deal* (Anthony Mann, 1948), but also in the western *My Darling Clementine* (John Ford, 1946) and the proto-anti-western *Red River* (Howard Hawks, 1948). The same resume was true for Ella Raines at the time; she had starred in *Tall in the Saddle* opposite John Wayne (Edwin L. Marin, 1944), as well as in B noirs *Phantom Lady* (Robert Siodmak, 1944) – in which she plays another independent woman and faux femme fatale – and *The Web* (Michael Gordon, 1947). While perhaps typical of the studio era, in which few actors had choices in which films they would appear, this overview does help to illustrate a fluidity of performances in both the noir and the western as well as the shifting terrain of the western as it began to absorb elements of the noir style in the late 1940s.

Within this context, we can also consider the film's director and cinematographer. John Sturges is known today primarily for his directorial contributions to the western, with *The Walking Hills* his first foray into the subgenre of western noir. His next venture would be similar, with perhaps even more psychological depth. *The Capture* (1950), told in flashback, is the story of a fugitive from the law (Lew Ayres) hiding out in Mexico, seeking escape and then forgiveness with the help of a priest and the love of a 'good' woman (Teresa Wright). In the next decade, Sturges would become far more famous for the noir western *Bad Day at Black Rock* (1955) and the dark, Mexican-set *The Magnificent Seven* (1960). Cinematographer Charles Lawton, Jr served as director of photography for multiple westerns as well as several noir films, including *The Lady from Shanghai* (Orson Welles, 1947) and *Shockproof* (Douglas Sirk,

1949). Like Sturges, the 1950s brought him fame for a noirish western, *3:10 to Yuma* (Delmer Daves, 1957).

This brief overview reveals how *The Walking Hills* offers a clear early example of what would come to typify the noir western subgenre in the years ahead. However, such elements are not the only or even the most important aspects of the film from an academic perspective. What truly sets the picture apart from others of its type and era is the presence and function of its characters of colour, including a Native American sidekick and an African American performer.

The Native American

As noted above, Sturges biographer Glenn Lovell praises Jim's servant Cleve (Charles Stevens) as an image free of ethnocentrism. Close attention to the character's trajectory in the film, however, argues something more complex. Cleve has his origins in a screenplay written by prolific western author Alan Le May. Le May is best known for his novels *The Searchers* and *The Unforgiven*, the film rights to both of which were purchased quickly by Hollywood and made into films soon after. Central to these novels is a grappling with race through depictions of conflict between white men and Native Americans. The tensions – and thereby the racial politics – of the films can be seen in a brief overview of how Le May's novels were altered for the screen. The more highly lauded of the two pictures (but no less problematic) is *The Searchers* (John Ford, 1956), deemed the greatest western in film history by the American Film Institute and adopted into the National Film Registry in 1989. *The Searchers* tells the gruelling tale of a Civil War veteran who searches over the course of many years for his niece, who was taken by Comanches after her mother and several other siblings were killed by them. The veteran, Ethan Edwards (played by John Wayne in the film), is equal parts intolerance and determination, and we come to learn that he plans to kill the girl rather than rescue her because she has been, in his view, contaminated by being impregnated by a Comanche. A key problem for viewers of the film adaptation involves how we are meant to feel about Edwards's racism. Roger Ebert's review addresses this issue directly, arguing that the film's tone poses a

> difficult question, because the Wayne character is racist without apology – and so, in a less outspoken way, are the other white characters. Is the film intended to endorse their attitudes, or to dramatize and regret them? Today we see it through enlightened eyes, but in 1956 many audiences accepted its harsh view of Indians.[20]

With this tension in mind, we can explore the substantive changes the film makes to the novel in order to answer the central question of Edwards's racism. For one, the screenplay (by Frank S. Nugent, a frequent Ford collaborator) rewrites Le May's white character Martin Pawley (Jeffrey Hunter) to be biracial, part white and part Comanche. Edwards treats Pawley with utter contempt. Such racial modification could reorient viewers, arguably focusing the film even more fully on Edwards's racial hatred in order to encourage condemnation. Even more vitally, however, the film changes the novel's ending. In Le May's tale, Edwards is ultimately killed, and Pawley rescues the niece. We thus never learn whether Edwards would have murdered her as he planned. Le May seems to shy away from commentary. By contrast, in the film, Edwards becomes increasingly insane even as he returns the girl to the white townspeople unharmed. Instead of death, Nugent and Ford's reworking condemn Edwards to isolation. He is filmed alone on a porch and then walking off into a barren desert. This exile, albeit self-imposed, seems intended to hint at the isolating result of intolerance. Because we have confirmation that he is both racist *and* able to 'forgive' his niece, the film leaves an ambiguous message. As the picture's Sheriff Sam Clayton (Ward Bond) argues, Edwards 'fits a lot of descriptions'. The primary description for this contemporary viewer and critic is of a pathological white supremacist.

By contrast, Le May wrote the original story as well as the screenplay for *The Walking Hills*. The relationship of white men to Native Americans is far less gnarled and cynical than in *The Searchers*. For most of the film, Cleve is obedient and protective. Jim does in some ways treat him with respect, demanding that he get a share when he joins the treasure-hunting party, for instance, even though the others do not like it. Important is how Cleve himself comments that he would rather stay at a distance or, better yet, return home with the pregnant mare. He declares directly to Jim that the others do not like or trust him, and he is not wrong. This may explain why reviewer Lovell identifies Cleve as part of the film's 'conscience'. However, when Cleve tells Jim he will leave, Jim makes clear who is the boss: he rejects the suggestion and makes clear he will actively stop Cleve from departing. Cleve acquiesces, and because Jim ultimately proves heroic, we are hard-pressed to see this 'Indian' as the white man's equal in understanding and decision-making. We are, by contrast, encouraged to read Jim as protective of those deemed less capable of protecting themselves (not only Cleve but also the mare and young Johnny).

When we learn about Cleve's past, however, the character shifts from either moral centre or protected servant, becoming part of the more tangled, noirish content of this western. A central reason Cleve seeks to leave the party turns out to be his own knowledge of and responsibility for the circumstances of the unearthed wagons that are said to contain treasure. Rather than wealthy Spaniards of a previous century, Cleve realises from the discovery of a finger bone in the sand that these wagons actually belonged to a party of five Chinese immigrants by whom he was surreptitiously paid for safe transport across the border. The group was swallowed up by a sandstorm instead, with only Cleve knowing their fate until he secretly tells Jim the story midway through the film.

This constellation of setting and characters provide a noteworthy gesture towards the function of composite figures in film noir. As Kelly Oliver and Benigno Trigo argue in *Noir Anxiety*, 'the representation of nationality and place can [. . .] be interpreted as a type of condensation of several images or ideas onto an idea that retains only the repressed unconscious fears or desires [. . .]'.[21] Here, Cleve – a racial other if familiar western type – is unexpectedly linked to another minority, a group that is also alien nationally. Specifically, the film's Chinese immigrants, who died during an attempted border crossing sometime in the 1920s, were likely attempting to evade the US Chinese Exclusion Act of 1886. Their brief but significant mention mark an important absent presence, marking Cleve as a 'condensed composite' figure whose presence increases (unconscious) viewer anxiety over boundaries of race and nation that, state Oliver and Trigo, are central to film noir.[22]

Cleve's history with the doomed Chinese immigrants ultimately justifies his own fate, for he, too, is swallowed up by a sandstorm at the climax of *The Walking Hills*. As Dave and Chris carry Jim's newborn foal to a small, collapsing shelter, Cleve forges on alone against the storm, calling out for Jim, who has meanwhile found a horse to ride and gathered in two others. Jim neither hears nor seeks Cleve, whose voice is increasingly obscured by the wind until the sand overtakes him. He falls and is soon buried alive, another man with a past – this time complexly racially inflected – that eventually catches up with him.

The African American

If journalist M. W. Jacobs is right in his assertion that, '[a]t a time when the subject was far too controversial to address directly, filmmakers had Native Americans stand in for African Americans as the targets of racism', *The Walking Hills* goes in another direction, featuring a Black male character who is a sidenote to the central plot but is treated with uncommon respect.[23] Josh is a blues singer living south of the border who is offered an equal share of the treasure and yields neither his life nor his dignity at the film's end.

White had already appeared in two films before this venture, including playing himself in the B noir *The Crimson Canary* (John Hoffman, 1945) and an unnamed musician in the avant-garde *Dreams that Money Can Buy* (Hans Richter, 1947). Perhaps because his third appearance included his first time portraying an actual character, his on-screen credit reads 'Introducing Josh White and his Songs'. We meet Josh when Dave veers off the sidewalk after glimpsing Chris and into an empty Mexicali club. The camera pivots to Josh, leaning back in a chair at one of the open tables, singing Bud Allen and Buddy Johnson's 'You Won't Let Me Go' and accompanying himself on guitar. The

Figure 4.2   The earnest, sensual appeal of performer Josh White. © Photofest

performance immediately showcases White's talent and appeal. He sings the blues smoothly while stylishly dressed in a loose, silky shirt with an elegant tie, posed for visual appeal.[24]

This package was White's trademark: his beautiful, clear voice; his hand strumming a guitar gently but firmly; his slender, muscular body draped in fashionable attire; and his handsome, emotive face (see Figure 4.2). Biographer Elijah Wald goes further, claiming that 'virtually everyone who saw him perform speaks first of his sex appeal'.[25] This was especially true of his days performing at Greenwich Village's Café Society (1943–5), a club that uniquely welcomed a mix of Black and white patrons. Wald quotes club founder Barney Josephson, who describes how White 'played sex to the hilt'. According to Wald, upon seeing him for the first time, Eartha Kitt found White 'irresistible and enchanting and seductive'; she lavishly praised the way he 'caressed the guitar' and gave off the message '"There's no woman I cannot have and any woman can have me."' Similarly, Lena Horne recalled, 'You used to have to beat your way through swarms of women just to say hello to him.'[26]

That the role of Josh was written for White and that he was filmed in this flattering fashion was part of its appeal for the performer, who aspired to be an actor as well as a singer. His ambitions, however, stopped at taking any part he found degrading. According to White, this included refusing $87,000 in one year for rejecting stereotyped roles in Hollywood.[27] White hoped to find a part such as Dooley Wilson's in *Casablanca* (Michael Curtiz, 1942), but he knew 'those are one in a million'.[28] He shared concert artist and actor Paul Robeson's contempt for performances such as those of Stepin Fetchit and Bill 'Bojangles' Robinson, stating, 'If our "Tom actors" would only stay away from the roles they do, Negroes could get somewhere in Hollywood.'[29]

The role of Josh was acceptable to White because the character is an equal partner in the treasure hunt. Though he has only two lines and fades from the action after the first half of the film, the part is neither demeaning nor stereotypical. As White told the *Post*:

> I don't talk in dialect, my complexion never turns white with fright or foolishness, [and] my hair doesn't, even when I'm dead scared of anything, stand up on end. [. . .] [I]t doesn't matter that I'm a Negro and the others are white; we're all together with a common destiny. I felt that it was an expression of what one world should be. And I was happy to accept the part – for its stand, rather than its merit as a movie.[30]

While White's description is accurate and his decision understandable, the character of Josh merits even closer reading. Despite resistance to degradation and some stereotyping, White's role follows traditional Hollywood marginalisation of Black performers in its emphasis on spectacle over character. This limitation is pointedly illustrated in the fact that the role, written for White, does not include a fictional character name. Such undifferentiation of actor and character further manifests in Josh's function as a performer for both the other characters and the film audience.[31] Nonetheless, the positioning of White's songs and their details serve to temper these limitations. Josh's songs do not divert but instead reinforce the film's themes and, in one case, point to social inequities of race directly. This factor makes the role remarkable.

In general terms, songs take up narrative space differently than spoken dialogue, especially beyond the musical genre. As Richard Dyer explains, songs can 'dissolve the boundaries between the self and others and take people into a realm of reality other than the separate and sequential experience of time and space in ordinary reality'.[32] In social terms, songs can bring people together across differences, as Café Society did with Black and white patrons or as in White's notion of 'what one world should be'. Additionally, while '[v]oices carry markers of gender, class, ethnic, regional, geographic, and other socio-cultural differences as well as the grain of individuality', they also unite the audience with the singer, 'at the intersection between individual feeling and the socially and historically specific shared forms available to express that feeling'.[33]

Beyond the broad parameters and functions of song, lyrics also have purpose and meaning. 'The words of songs can [. . .] tell stories, describe landscapes, promote political positions, make philosophical statements.'[34] Such functions, including the social and political, appear in a close reading of the songs that White sings in *The Walking Hills*. Returning to his opening performance of 'You Won't Let Me Go', we may note how the song features the typical blues theme of lovers who fear abandonment that ultimately causes it. The singer becomes the lover who puts his relationship to the test, suggesting he needs her, but she should show she needs him by never leaving. Such focus foreshadows the flashback in which we will learn of Dave's (unintended) abandonment of Chris and also reflect the final reunion of the couple, in which Chris will not let Dave go alone to face to his criminal punishment. The value here is mixed, however. Because the song reflects well the other characters in the film and does not, to our knowledge, reflect Josh's life (for the character is given no internal life), the authenticity of the blues as reflective of the Black experience in America is less evident than it might be. Moreover, the song arguably figures Josh as a kind of Greek chorus rather than a voice of his own.

White's next performance is another traditional blues number, 'Baby, Baby Blues', this time presented while the men rest, waiting for their evening meal. The song comes immediately after we see Chris tell Dave that her purpose in joining the group was to see Jim attack Dave once he learned his true identity, but this seems a lie. Again providing a supportive chorus type role, this time for Dave, Josh sings how life isn't worth living without the woman you love. He then foreshadows the film's mostly happy ending, referencing the sun that will again shine to drive away his blues. The sandstorm's lethality does seem to blow away Dave's criminal mindset, and the sun shines on Chris as she rides to join Dave in turning himself in to the authorities.

Another performance, while the workers rest during the dig, is far removed from the history of African American music and the darkness of noir: the fifteenth-century English ballad 'The Riddle Song' (also known as 'I Gave My Love a Cherry'). White often played it, for he was both a blues and folk musician, and the number was known to many Americans as an Appalachian lullaby. Despite its difference from the two blues songs, 'The Riddle Song' also addresses the film's content. It poses what seem impossible statements (cherries without stones) in the first verse, reflects on the puzzle in question form in the second verse, and then answers them (cherry blossoms have no stones) in the final verse. The tone of the song is sombre, raising then quelling doubts with mellow surety, reflecting what we will experience in the film's narrative arc. First, we learn of the 'impossible' hundred-year-old treasure buried in the hills. Next, we witness frustration and confusion as the treasure fails to appear, and our notions of the characters shift through flashbacks and conflict. The tension peaks in a sandstorm, and four characters die along the way. Finally, all is resolved when the puzzle is answered unexpectedly: the treasure is found but revealed to be worth $10,000 rather than the millions hoped for; it is the savings of a small group of immigrants (seemingly the Chinese men Cleve led), not that of wealthy Spaniards.

The song's relevance to the film's plot is further reinforced by its reiteration as a musical motif. First, we hear Old Willy whistle the opening measures after he safely survives the storm (and, we then learn, has the treasure). It also appears twice in the soundtrack, once soon after White sings it, as Dave tells Chris he's currently on the run, and again in the film's final moments, as Jim watches the reunited couple ride off together, wistful but not unhappy.

If songs can share 'political positions' and offer 'philosophical statements', then 'The Work Song', performed *a capella* midway through the film, speaks most loudly and poignantly in *The Walking Hills*.[35] We watch the men (apart from Cleve, who stays with the horses) working together, struggling to make headway in the ever-shifting sand. The effort is hard and slow-going. Suddenly, Josh starts to sing as he digs, in short lines that demand workers grab their shovels and dig a hole in the sand. The camera cuts between lines as the vocals continue, from distanced shots of the group with each man digging in his own spot, to close-ups of Josh, shirt unbuttoned and reaching to keep his hat on as he vocalises his determination that this will not be the place he will die. Josh croons as Frazee wipes his brow while warily watching Dave. The final verses have Josh calling for the waterboy, longing for pay day, and lamenting how long it has been since he's seen his girl.

The lyrics reflect a long tradition of African American work songs, sung by slaves and indentured servants. The steady pace reflected work rhythms, and group participation bonded men united by common oppression. Such songs are the predecessors of the blues and hold an important place in American history. In *The Walking Hills*, of course, everyone – including Josh himself – is working for a fortune. As Josh says when he agrees to join the treasure hunt, 'I've turned down a few things in my life, but I'd never turn down a million bucks.' That the character sings the work song alone is also noteworthy. This is an atypical performance for the sexy, successful club singer and musician, even in this noir western context. White brings the history of African Americans and hard manual labour, from slavery to the present day of the film, sharing it with his compatriots in a manner beyond their experience and, perhaps, understanding. For its placement in the film as well as its performance, 'The Work Song' stands out as an unexpected historical statement on the Black experience in America during the beginnings of the civil rights era.

Equally vital is that Josh survives the storm to earn his portion and comes out of his experience looking brighter and tidier than any other character. White ends the film wearing his impossibly clean pale slacks, black-and-white saddle shoes, and a black-banded white fedora. Beyond the obvious stylishness, the white hat tells us, in the classic language of the western, that Josh (unlike Cleve, in his tall, Native American style black hat) is one of the 'good guys'. He is not a hero, perhaps, but he is wise enough to stay out of the noirish conflicts and violence. He was safely hidden with Old Willy during the storm under one an overturned wagon that was uncovered – with the small treasure – during the storm.

Conclusion

The noir western in its so-called Golden Age never explored anti-Black racism deeply.[36] The subgenre primarily presented mistreated Native Americans as symbols for oppressed African Americans as befitted its mostly Old West settings and Hollywood's preference for indirection to maintain large audiences and profit. That some of Hollywood's best political writers were, like Josh White himself, blacklisted by the House Committee on Un-American Activities also speaks to the limitations of western and/or noir scripts addressing race issues.[37] Sturges's own *Bad Day at Black Rock* would be an important exception to this political rule, addressing as it does anti-Japanese racism in the post-World War II era, albeit without Japanese characters or actors.[38] Such a film validates Jacobs's claim that, '[i]n the moral atmosphere created by the civil rights movement, and in the aftermath of the unimaginable racist atrocities of World War II, some of the best Hollywood directors were compelled to take on American racism in their Westerns'.[39] Whether or not Sturges should be identified, alongside John Ford, as one of 'the best', and without overstating the power or impact of *The Walking Hills*, those noir elements that darken the western's mood alongside the casting and performance of Josh White at least suggest that it deserves greater attention than it has received to date.

Notes

1. Imogen Sara Smith, *In Lonely Places: Film Noir Beyond the City* (Jefferson, NC: McFarland, 2011), p. 178.
2. Smith, *In Lonely Places*, p. 178.
3. David Meuel, *The Noir Western: Darkness on the Range, 1943–1962* (Jefferson, NC: McFarland, 2015), p. 10.
4. Smith, *In Lonely Places*, p. 179.
5. Smith, *In Lonely Places*, p. 179. We can also separate the post-war noir western from the later (1960s and 1970s) revisionist western or anti-western, which subverts rather than darkens standard western themes and tropes, exemplified by such films as *The Wild Bunch* (Sam Peckinpah, 1969), *Little Big Man* (Arthur Penn, 1970), and *McCabe & Mrs. Miller* (Robert Altman, 1971).
6. 'Unusual Angles, Fine Cast Feature Lowe's "Walking Hills"', *The Post-Standard* (Syracuse, NY) 8 April 1949, p. 23.
7. '"Walking Hills" Due at Colonial', *The Evening News* (Harrisburg, PA) 24 March 1949, p. 24.

8. Darr Smith, 'Film Review: "The Walking Hills"', *Los Angeles Daily News*, 26 February 1949, p. 23.
9. See Darr Smith, '"Walking Hills" Due at Colonial'; 'Death Valley Thrill Story First Feature at Liberty', *Mexico Ledger* (Mexico, MO) 17 September 1949, p. 5; and "Walking Hills' Depicts Drama of Desert Hunt', *Denton Record Chronicle* (Denton, TX) 23 October 1949, p. 12.
10. Glenn Lovell, *Escape Artist: The Life and Films of John Sturges* (Madison: University of Wisconsin Press, 2008), eBook, loc. 590.
11. Lovell, *Escape Artist*, loc. 590.
12. Meuel, *The Noir Western*, p. 200, and Gene Blottner, *Columbia Noir: A Complete Filmography, 1940–1962* (Jefferson, NC: McFarland, 2015).
13. Elena Dell'Agnese, 'The US-Mexico Border in American Movies: A Political Geography Perspective', *Geopolitics* 10, no. 2 (2005), p. 207.
14. José E. Limón, *American Encounters: Greater Mexico, The United States, and the Erotics of Culture* (Boston: Beacon Press, 1998), p. 199. Also quoted in Dell'Agnese, 'The US-Mexico Border in American Movies', p. 220, n.17.
15. For more on this subject, see Sheri Chinen Biesen, *Blackout: World War II and the Origins of Film Noir* (Baltimore: Johns Hopkins University Press, 2005).
16. Smith, *In Lonely Places*, p. 137.
17. Smith, *In Lonely Places*, p. 137.
18. 'Unusual Angles, Fine Cast Feature Lowe's "Walking Hills"', p. 23.
19. Meuel, for example, declares Scott's western characters 'stoic and persevering', bearing grief 'quietly and with dignity', *The Noir Western*, p. 5. For discussion of women as a threat to men's freedom in the classic western, see Steve Neale, 'Masculinity as Spectacle', *Screen* 24, no. 6 (1983), pp. 2–16.
20. Roger Ebert, 'Review: *The Searchers*', RogerEbert.com, 25 November 2001.
21. Kelly Oliver and Benigno Trigo, *Noir Anxiety* (Minneapolis: University of Minnesota Press, 2003), p. xviii.
22. Oliver and Trigo, *Noir Anxiety*, p. xviii.
23. M. W. Jacobs, 'When Hollywood Westerns Fought Racism', *HuffPost*, 12 March 2015, n.p. https://www.huffpost.com/entry/when-hollywood-westerns-fought_b_6854854.
24. A precursor to White in such a role is Herb Jeffries (born Umberto Alexander Valentino), aka the 'Sensational Singing Cowboy' of multiple Hollywood race films, beginning with *Harlem on the Prairie* (Sam Newfield, 1937), billed as 'the first all-colored musical western'. Jeffries was born to an Irish mother and a father (whom he never met) of Sicilian, French, Italian, and Moorish roots.
25. Elijah Wald, *Josh White: Society Blues* (Amherst: University of Massachusetts Press, 2000), p. 112.
26. Josephson, Kitt, and Horne quoted in Wald, *Josh White: Society Blues*, p. 112.
27. Wald, *Josh White: Society Blues*, p. 163.
28. Quoted in Wald, *Josh White: Society Blues*, p. 164.
29. Quoted in Wald, *Josh White: Society Blues*, p. 164.
30. Quoted in Wald, *Josh White: Society Blues*, p. 165.
31. In addition, several sources reference a total of seven songs White was to sing, although only four appear in the film. Such significant cuts arguably further point

to the inessential nature of White's role. See 'The Walking Hills: Folk Balladeer Has Seven Songs in His Movie Debut', *Ebony* 3, no. 12 (1948), p. 64; and Dorothy Schainman Siegel, *The Glory Road: The Story of Josh White* (White Hall, VA: Shoe Tree Press, 1982), p. 103.
32. Richard Dyer, *In the Space of a Song: The Uses of Song in Film* (London: Routledge, 2012), p. 3.
33. Dyer, *In the Space of a Song*, pp. 7, 2.
34. Dyer, *In the Space of a Song*, p. 5.
35. The song was first recorded after the film was released, in 1951, on the British London Records label as 'Like a Natural Man (Work Song)' as the B side of the single 'The Foggy, Foggy Dew'.
36. John Ford's *Sergeant Rutledge* (1960) is a potent exception, though it has not been studied primarily through a noir lens.
37. *The Walking Hills* was Josh White's last Hollywood film. Hounded by the House Committee on Un-American Activities for his liberal political perspectives, White eventually decided to testify. He feared for his career and the financial stability it brought him, his wife, and their growing family. He also felt he had nothing to hide. As so often happened, however, his words (including defences of his participation in causes such as anti-lynching and against the poll tax) were turned against him, and he found himself blacklisted, never able to return to his acting career or the height of his former musical fame.
38. In this way, the film is somewhat similar to *The Walking Hills*, where anti-Asian racism linked to both race and nationality is reflected in the ignominious deaths of Asian characters (prior to the events of the film), as a source of tension. This tension is far more central to *Bad Day at Black Rock*, in which anti-Japanese racism is a central, overt theme.
39. Jacobs, 'When Hollywood Westerns Fought Racism', n.p.

PART II

RECONCEPTUALISING NATIONAL CINEMAS

5. 'MY MAMA DONE TOL' ME': JEWISH ÉMIGRÉ NOIR, GENERIC HYBRIDITY, AND BLACK-JEWISH RELATIONS IN *BLUES IN THE NIGHT*

Vincent Brook

Blues in the Night's (1941) outlier status in the history of American film noir is underscored thematically and stylistically. This derives partly from its having been directed by Jewish émigré director Anatole Litvak, given a Jewish émigré sensibility that infused not only Litvak's but also several other Jewish émigré directors' work. The film's distinctive generic hybridity is due largely to its production early in the classical noir cycle and to the radical political orientation of its creative team. *Blues in the Night* additionally draws on US Jews' unique historical and sociocultural relationship with African Americans, a relationship with special pertinence to the present moment. Before delineating the manner in which these three elements function in the film, examining each of them in greater detail is a useful starting point.

JEWISH ÉMIGRÉ NOIR

Jewish filmmakers in general, but particularly émigrés fleeing Nazi Germany in the 1930s and 1940s, played an outsized role in the emergence and evolution of film noir. The term 'film noir' itself, coined by French critics shortly after World War II, was predicated on seven American films – *The Maltese Falcon* (John Huston, 1941), *This Gun for Hire* (Frank Tuttle, 1942), *Double Indemnity* (1944), *The Woman in the Window* (1944), *Laura* (1944), *Murder, My Sweet* (Edward Dmytryk, 1944), and *The Lost Weekend* (1945). Four of these seminal films were directed by Jewish émigrés – Billy Wilder (*Double Indemnity* and *The Lost Weekend*), Fritz Lang (*The Woman in the Window*), and Otto Preminger

(*Laura*).[1] Noted noir scholar Alain Silver provides additional, if inadvertent, support for Jewish émigré directors' pride of place in the noir canon. In naming his 'ten best' film noirs (of which four were made by Jewish refugees), he added: 'I did have one rule: a single movie per director, otherwise [Robert] Siodmak, Lang, [Max] Ophuls and Wilder might have overwhelmed the field and made it an all-émigré list.'[2]

Besides their canonical pre-eminence, Jewish émigré filmmakers (based on a cross-referencing of taxonomies) lead the league in quantity of classical American noirs as well. Lang stands alone at the top with fourteen films, Siodmak ties Jewish American Anthony Mann in second with ten, John Brahm and Willy Wilder (aka W. Lee Wilder, Billy's brother) follow close behind with eight, and Jewish émigrés Preminger and Edgar G. Ulmer are in a pack of American Jews with six.[3] Though Billy Wilder, with 'only' three consensus noirs, and Max Ophuls (spelled Ophüls for his non-US output), with two, are further down the list, two of Wilder's – *Double Indemnity* and *Sunset Blvd.* (1950) – and Ophuls's *Caught* (1948) are among the genre's indisputable classics.

More than numerical and canonical factors justify carving a unique niche for 'Jewish émigré noir'. A distinctive Jewish*ness* in the content of much of the work further enhances the designation. The most conspicuous Jewish motif relates to the character of the male noir protagonist, who stands in stark contrast to the protagonist most preferred in the gentile-directed noirs conventionally regarded as paradigmatic of film noir as a whole.[4]

Noir classics by non-Jewish émigrés such as *The Maltese Falcon*, *Murder My Sweet*, *The Big Sleep* (Howard Hawks, 1946), *The Postman Always Rings Twice* (Tay Garnett, 1946), and *Out of the Past* (Jacques Tourneur, 1947) feature macho, tough-guy leads played by the likes of Humphrey Bogart, Dick Powell, John Garfield (the lone Jew), and Robert Mitchum. Jewish émigré directors, to the contrary, while making an occasional hard-boiler such as Wilder's *Double Indemnity*, mostly favour sensitive, artistic types. This proclivity was motivated partly by many of the filmmakers' view of themselves as artists, while working in a Hollywood system that deemed art as secondary, if not an impediment, to pecuniary demands. The émigrés' countertypes, such as professors, painters, writers, composers, and musicians, thus stood in opposition both to a crassly materialistic American society and the mass-audience driven culture industry. The actors chosen to portray these characters analogously tended towards less hyper-masculine types, such as Edward G. Robinson, Laird Cregar, Louis Hayward, Tom Neal, and Richard Whorf, in films such as *The Woman in the Window* (Robinson), *Scarlet Street* (Fritz Lang, 1945, also Robinson), *House by the River* (Lang, 1950, Hayward), *Hangover Square*, (John Brahm, 1945, Cregar), *Detour* (Ulmer, 1945, Neal), and the main object of this study, *Blues in the Night* (1941, Whorf) (see Figures 5.1).

Figure 5.1a & 5.1b Gentile versus Jewish émigré noir protagonists: Mitchum in *Out of the Past* versus Robinson in *Scarlet Street*. © Photofest

Jewish émigré directors' predilection for the less macho, even occasionally effeminate, protagonist was compounded by an aversion, with deep Jewish historical roots, to machismo in general. Daniel Boyarin, in *Unheroic Conduct: The Rise of Heterosexuality and the Invention of the Jewish Man* (1997), argues that the sensitive, scholarly male Jew devoted to religious study emerged in the early rabbinic period and was encouraged thereafter, partly as a defence mechanism, partly as an overt rejection of / alternative to the more physical, aggressive masculinity espoused and practised by the larger gentile society.[5] Sander Gilman, in *The Jew's Body* (1999), describes how the European image of the male Jew as feminised was historically overdetermined: first, by the male Jew's stereotypically stunted physiognomy, flat feet, and awkward gait, which rendered him 'innately unable to undertake physical labor'; and second, by his circumcised penis, which was deemed analogous to the clitoris of the woman.[6] Additional gender-troubling associations between Jews and gays were reinforced in the late 1800s, when antisemitism was labelled a 'scientific' term for Jew-hating at the precise historical moment that homosexuality was being clinically designated a new disease.[7]

Jewish male internalisation of the feminising discourse is evident in the early Zionist movement, whose emphasis on physical exercise and manual labour must be taken as a partial reaction against the Jewish weakling stereotype. Physician and Zionist leader Max Nordau's notion of the *neue Muskeljude* (new Muscle Jew) was conceived as an antidote to Jews' alleged physical, and thus also political, puniness and ineffectuality.[8] Nordau's therapeutic prescription would be realised, of course, in the new state of Israel's kibbutznik, Mossad operative, and army soldier. The overcompensating Muscle Jew ideal would infiltrate the United States in the twentieth century also, albeit with a more working-class, less patriotic tinge. Where would American organised crime have been, for example, without mob kingpins Meyer Lansky, Bugsy Siegel, and Mickey Cohen, or American boxing without champions Benny Leonard, Max Baer, and Maxie Rosenbloom?[9] The middle- and upper-middle-class Jewish émigré noir directors, however, steeped in European high culture and of a progressive Jewish persuasion, remained 'old school' in their primary identification with the sensitive Jewish male.

GENERIC HYBRIDITY

Blues in the Night doubly earns its Jewish émigré noir stripes by virtue of its Ukrainian Jewish émigré director, Anatole Litvak, and its Jewish-looking, virtuoso pianist protagonist with a passion for jazz, Jigger Pine (played by the non-Jewish Richard Whorf). Sheri Chinen Biesen, in *Music in the Shadows: Noir Musical Films* (2014), supports the notion that Whorf's persona countered the standard, gentile-noir type in its divergence from 'stars like Bogart [and James] Cagney', who contemporary viewers associated with 'masculine noir gangster/crime films[s]'.[10] Because of its unique combination of musical and noir elements, Biesen additionally deems *Blues in the Night* a 'definitive' example of a noir subgenre she calls 'musical noir', which subsequently led to a parade of similar films. Here, however, while I agree at least partly with Biesen's hybrid designation, I differ strongly with her placing *Blues in the Night* in the same category as its putative successors, including classics such as *This Gun for Hire*, *Phantom Lady* (Siodmak, 1944), *To Have and Have Not* (Hawks, 1944), *Christmas Holiday* (Siodmak, 1944), *The Big Sleep*, *Gilda* (Charles Vidor, 1946), *Dead Reckoning* (John Cromwell, 1947), and *Road House* (Jean Negulesco, 1948).[11]

First, unlike *Blues in the Night*, Biesen's 'musical noir' descendants are noirs above all and musicals, if at all, only as an added attraction. They are essentially noirs *with* music, using musical numbers literally to 'jazz' things up or promotionally as a showcase for a singing star such as Deanna Durbin in *Christmas Holiday* (Rita Hayworth's singing in *Gilda* was dubbed by Anita Ellis).[12] Music in *Blues in the Night*, to the contrary, is the prime narrative driver and core theme of the film, with recognisable noir elements only entering the picture midway through. Second, *Blues in the Night* is not a hybrid solely of film noir and musical but additionally of comedy and Capraesque populist fable elements that admittedly appear sporadically in a few classical noirs, but only to add spice or social relevance, not as an essential generic ingredient.

In *Blues in the Night*, humorous treatment governs the entire first portion of the film, with populism following close behind when protagonist Jigger Pine, despite the musical talent to make it big, forms a ragtag five-man combo with

Figure 5.2a & 5.2b *Blues in the Night* as musical comedy and as musical noir.
© Photofest

a female vocalist (a 'unit', he calls them) that hopscotches around the country, jumping trains and landing sporadic gigs. Only well into the film does a gangster enter the frame, derailing the band's freewheeling lifestyle and the film's buoyant tone by offering the close-knit bunch a 'real' job in a Jersey roadhouse reeking of noir ambiance. Violence and mayhem ensue while comedy and populism recede, but a strong musical undercurrent prevails to the very end and populism pops up at the conclusion as well (see Figures 5.2).

BLACK-JEWISH RELATIONS

Blues in the Night's 'unusual generic amalgam' – which Biesen, even without the comedy and populist elements, calls 'bizarre' – joins Jewish-émigré-director involvement and the film's sensitive, artistic male protagonist as the second conceptual frame for this case study.[13] A third derives from what Jeffrey Melnick terms 'Black-Jewish relations', whose foundation lies in the two groups' shared historical experience of suffering and oppression. An added benefit, for Jewish men especially, stems from the potential escape from the Jewish runt stereotype that the bond with African Americans offered – one with less socially stigmatic or physically punishing repercussions than gangsterism or pugilism, and with cultural and economic benefits as well.

It was not until the massive Jewish immigration waves of the late 1800s and early 1900s to urban areas in the north-eastern United States that Jews and Blacks began to have any significant physical interaction.[14] Already during the slavery period, however, African Americans had tied their inhumane treatment and hopes of emancipation to the biblical story of the Jewish people's bondage in Egypt, no more cogently expressed than in the most famous of Negro spirituals (echoing Moses' plea to Pharaoh), 'Let My People Go!' Once there were enough Jews in America to make a difference, they returned the favour culturally and politically: culturally, in boosting Black music through Jewish predominance in the business, creative, and performance aspects of Tin Pan Alley, vaudeville, nightclubs, the theatre, and eventually the movies; politically, in helping found the National Association for the Advancement of Colored People (NAACP) in 1909 and in disproportionate support, among Whites, of other Black causes. The cultural connection, moreover, was based on more than Jewish identification with past and present African American persecution and striving. It included a perceived kinship between Jewish and Black music that went beyond vaudeville superstar Al Jolson's idiosyncratic mixing of 'Yiddish schmaltz and Blackface sentiment' in *The Jazz Singer* (Alan Crosland, 1927).[15] It entailed a more fundamental 'mystical-genetic' bond: in 'the half and quarter tones, the sigh and the sob, the sudden inflections of the voice and the unexpected twist' of the Jewish cantorial tradition – echoed in 'the wail of the blues' and resonant in 'the pain in both jazz and klezmer'.[16]

Beyond the offensiveness (despite its popularity) of Blackface, Jewish reliance on African American experience and cultural forms in general – however sympathetically employed by performers, songwriters, and entrepreneurs – was not without its pitfalls: patronisation, cultural appropriation, and economic exploitation. Charges of inauthenticity and ransacking (both stylistic and financial) were voiced from the outset of the exchange, and certainly attended those who traded on Black musical idioms, most famously Irving Berlin and George Gershwin. One Black critic of Gershwin's *Porgy and Bess* (1935), for example, called it 'an opera about Negroes rather than a Negro opera', and a White critic went further, declaring it as 'surely the most contradictory cultural symbol ever created'.[17] The general critical consensus was more sanguine. Mainstream reviews rarely matched the hyperbole (or mixed metaphors) that hailed Gershwin's *Rhapsody and Blue* (1924) as the 'Declaration of Independence of Jazz' that 'emancipated jazz from the slums' and turned Gershwin into the 'Abe Lincoln of Negro music'.[18] But the overall response comported with what Jeffrey Melnick calls a 'slippage [. . .] between subject and form, which allowed Jewish representation of Blackness to be offered and received as Black music'.[19]

In the post-Civil Rights/identity politics era, the widening gap between Jews' and African American's socio-economic status and Israel's sudden transformation from underdog to overlord in the Middle East undermined cooperation between the two groups and, for many Blacks, created a wedge between them.[20] The radical shift in mood was stridently captured in a panel discussion on Black Power in 1965. When a Jewish audience member, as a reminder of Jewish loyalty to the Civil Rights cause, invoked the memory of Andrew Goodman and Michael Schwerner (Jewish activists killed alongside African American James Chaney in Mississippi in 1964), Black playwright LeRoi Jones (later Amiri Baraka) was not impressed. Jones not only dismissed the Jewish martyrs as 'artifacts' and 'paintings on the wall', but when asked how Jews could be of service to the Black Power movement, added derisively, 'Die, baby.'[21]

In early 1940s America, however, where Jim Crow still held sway and even Blackface was countenanced, *Blues in the Night* director Litvak, his mainly Jewish (émigré and American-born) production team, and a comparatively liberal, Jewish-owned Warner Bros. studio had little backlash to fear from a film that featured Whites identifying with African Americans and privileging the populist elements inherent to Black-based jazz and the blues. The worst the filmmakers risked confronting were charges of N-word loving and Communist sympathising – accusations which, however misguided, were not far from the truth.

Production Notes

Among major creative contributors to *Blues in the Night*, no figure reflects Black-Jewish relations more thoroughly, and ironically, than legendary American Jewish songwriter Harold Arlen, who with lyricist Johnny Mercer, 'a southern white man', wrote the eponymous, Oscar-winning theme song.[22] From its vocal introduction that functions as the film's inciting incident, to its multiple diegetic and scored permutations throughout, 'Blues in the Night' serves as both narrative driver and through-line. And composer Arlen could not have been a more appropriate wielder of the musical and thematic baton.

After Gershwin, Arlen and fellow Jewish American Jerome Kern were considered the composers 'most responsible for repositioning African American music as a province of Jewish art'.[23] Whereas Kern did not play up the intercultural connection and felt less 'at ease with the more blatant, strident side of jazz', Arlen, according to Melnick, 'happily embraced the possibilities of Jewish expressions of Blackness' and, among Jewish composers of his era, had 'the best feel for the blues'.[24] African American actor-singer Ethel Waters called Arlen 'the "Negro-ist" [sic] white man she had ever known', while other Blacks, and other 'White Negroes' (as Norman Mailer described wanna-be Blacks in the 1950s), applauded Arlen for being 'really one of them'.[25] Along with a younger generation of Jewish jazz musicians who came of age in the 1920s, Arlen, in addition to worshipping and absorbing African American music, immersed himself, like other 'hep cats', 'in the culture of Blackness'. Of special pertinence to *Blues in the Night*, this bonding with Black culture entailed a freewheeling, anti-establishment ethos and 'an entire way of life'.[26] 'Negritude', in another Mailerism, is what distinguished Arlen most from Berlin, Gershwin, and Kern, and turns him into the closest thing to a role model for *Blues in the Night*'s protagonist Jigger Pine. Besides Jigger's nickname – in its J-word variation on 'wigger' (a slang portmanteau of White Negro) – his Arlenesque Negrophilia is key to deflecting some (but not all) of my subsequent criticism of *Blues in the Night*'s representations of Black culture.

Robert Rossen, the film's Jewish American screenwriter, whether he was hired because of his leftist political leanings or lobbied for the job because of them, was ideally suited to adapting German immigrant Edwin Gilbert's unproduced play, *Hot Nocterne*. Elia Kazan, a Greek immigrant and famed film director-to-be, before becoming a cast member in the film, had reworked the play but also failed to mount it.[27] Beyond their writerly connection on *Blues in the Night*, Rossen's and Kazan's career paths were extraordinarily similar. Both men, like many (disproportionately Jewish) artists and intellectuals in the 1930s and 1940s, joined the American Communist Party (ACP). Both became involved in the heavily Jewish-populated New York theatre scene of the 1930s: Kazan as a member of the legendary Group Theater; Rossen as a writer and director of socially relevant stage and screenplays.[28] Both went on to direct Oscar-winning films on socially charged topics.[29] And both, having become disillusioned with the ACP, avoided the blacklist in the 1950s by cooperating with HUAC (the House Committee on UnAmerican Activities), thereby sullying their leftist credentials but enabling their continued film-directing in Hollywood.[30]

Blues in the Night's stylistically hybrid cinematography, by multiply Oscar-nominated and one-time winner (for Victor Fleming's 1939 film *Gone with the Wind*) Ernest Haller, though a Los Angeles-born gentile, demonstrates keen awareness and mastery of film noir's German expressionist legacy. Literally foreshadowing *Blues in the Night*'s full-fledged noir portion to come, Haller, in both the early jailhouse scene and later in the freewheeling boxcar ride, employs noir's signature prison-bar lighting (striped shadows representing actual and/or psychological imprisonment). The climactic rainstorm scene, meanwhile, is an expressionist tour de force, milking lightning-streaked darkness, creaky doors, flapping casement windows, and jerky camera movement for all the ominousness and terror they can muster.

Another tantalising kosher tidbit is served up by Jewish American Don Siegel, who would go on to direct several classical noirs (*Night unto Night* and *The Big Steal*, both 1949, among others) and neo-noirs (most famously *The Killers*, 1964, and *Dirty Harry*, 1971). Though not the chief editor on *Blues in the Night* (this credit went to non-Jewish veteran Owen Marks), Siegel edited a series of key transitional montages that brilliantly tap the African American subtext as well as the expressionist and Expressionist influence. The lower/upper case division signifies the difference between imagery that is plausibly realistic yet, like prison-bar lighting, encourages a symbolic reading, and imagery that is unrealistically distorted and, like two of Siegel's montages to be described below, demands a subjective, surreal, or dreamlike reading.[31]

Richard Whorf's second-tier billing in *Blues in the Night* – below Priscilla Lane and Betty Field, bigger stars at the time but supporting actors in the film – was justified solely for marketing purposes, given that Whorf is clearly the film's main character.³² Yet, in dealing a blow to Whorf's, and indirectly to Jigger's, masculinity, the mis-crediting further supports Jewish émigré noir's 'less manly' protagonist premise. If never a big name, either as an actor or later as a director, Whorf's creative range was as broad as *Blues in the Night*'s generic amalgam, and often veered towards noir. After his stint in *Blues in the Night*, he played a semi-heavy in one of Jewish émigré director Curtis (né Kurt) Bernhard's first noir efforts, *Juke Girl* (1942), and another shady character in Siodmak's *Christmas Holiday*, where his ethnic looks, coded queerness, and journalist occupation triply stereotype him as a Jew.³³ Whorf debuted as director in the comedy *Blonde Fever* (1944), but he returned to noir in *The Hidden Eye* (1945), a sequel to Jewish émigré director Fred Zinnemann's *Eyes in the Night* (1942). From the late 1940s on, Whorf turned increasingly to directing, largely in television.

The task of weaving these various above- and below-the-line elements together fell to director Litvak, with classical-era oversight and assistance from German émigré producer Henry Blanke (Jewish American Hal Wallis co-produced).³⁴ Blanke's affinity with the noir aspect of the material stemmed from his film work in the Weimar period, including on Lang's Expressionist classic *Metropolis* (1927). Though neither German nor Austrian, like most of the Jewish émigré directors, the Kyiv-born Litvak caught up in a hurry. After a stint with the Soviet branch of the pioneering Danish film company Nordisk, he moved to Berlin in 1925, worked as an assistant editor on the definitive 'street film', G. W. Pabst's *Die freudlose Gasse* (*Joyless Street*, 1925), and directed several Weimar-era films before fleeing Germany on the eve of the Nazi takeover. Like many of his Teutonic Jewish cohorts, he fled first to France, then traded time between Paris and London from 1933 to 1936. His direction of comedies and musicals during this period would stand him in good stead on the generically eclectic *Blues in the Night*, as would the policier *Coeur de Lilas* (*Lilac*, 1932), a harbinger of noir in its crime-drama theme and early association with French poetic realism. Hired in the late 1930s by Warner Bros., Litvak was an ideal choice to direct the historic *Confessions of a Nazi Spy* (1939). This was Hollywood's first overtly anti-Nazi film, and quite controversial at a time when the United States was still officially politically neutral and the studios were leery of stoking antisemitism and beholden to Production Code rules against demeaning other nationalities.³⁵ *Confessions of a Nazi Spy* also laid the groundwork for Litvak's dramatic, progressively tinged films to follow. These included a string of noirs, both fledgling – *Out of the Fog* (1940), *Blues in the Night*, and *City for Conquest* (1942) – and, after a wartime hiatus, full-fledged – *The Long Night* (1947) and *Sorry, Wrong Number* (1948).³⁶

Storylines: Part 1, Musical Comedy / Populist Fable

Blues in the Night opens in a cheap St Louis nightclub with Jigger's band-to-be's clarinetist, Nickie (Elia Kazan), making his first of several phone calls to his mother. Along with this running gag and his small-boned, big-nosed, dark-curly-haired appearance, Nickie's studying to be the fourth lawyer son in the family seals his coding as a Jew. The similarly short, dark-haired, large-nosed Jigger Pine is introduced playing a jazzy piano that moves an obnoxious older customer to offer the second nod – third, given Jigger's nickname – to the film's Black-Jewish relations. Combining antisemitic and anti-African American tropes, the man drunkenly complains that he does not like Jigger or his music. This affront triggers, apparently not for the first time, Jigger's temper, flying fists, and an escalating brawl that lands him, Nickie, and his also arguably Jewish-coded (smallish, sickly, dark-curly-haired) drummer, Peppi (Billy Hallyup), in jail.

The opening mayhem and onset of the jail scene – high-key lighting, no marks on the combatants – clearly register as comedy. This defuses the tough-guy overtones of the fisticuffs, yet in its action element hints at the noir turn to come. From a film noir perspective historically, the light-hearted, brightly lit beginning also signals a genre that had not yet found its bearings or settled on its tonal parameters. And confusion continues as the jail scene unfolds, which, while it ends on *Blues in the Night*'s first truly noir note, is more concerned with establishing Black-Jewish relations and the film's populist core.

When one of Jigger and the boys' cellmates turns out to be an old acquaintance, Pete (Peter Whitney), his blondish hair, beefy figure, and goofy manner mark him as a comic foil and the least stereotypically Jewish of the bunch. Most importantly, his bass-playing serendipitously plays into Jigger's dream of forming the pitch-perfect musical combo, as he expounds in a passionate soliloquy whose populist strain will course through the film:

> It's gotta be *our* kinda music, *our* kinda band, the songs we've listened to, knockin' about the country! Blues, *real* blues, the kind that comes outta people, *real* people! Their hopes and their dreams, what they've got and what they want! The whole USA in one chorus! Five guys, no more, who feel, play, live, even think the same way! That ain't a band, it's a unit! It's one guy multiplied by five! It's got a style that's theirs and nobody else's!

Well, almost nobody else's, for the *real* people Jigger extols happen to be holed up in a segregated, more darkly lit cell adjacent to his, one of whose African American inmates commences to demonstrate what the *real* blues is all about. Or almost all, for the eponymous theme song the Black man begins to wail, as we learned, was the work of Johnny Mercer and White Negro Harold Arlen. And the song's alternate title and opening, oft-repeated line, 'My mama done tol' me . . .' – like Al Jolson's signature minstrelsy tune 'My Mammy' (also written by a White man, Walter Donaldson) – clearly resonates with the 'Jewish mother' routine that Nickie 'just happened' to reprise moments before.[37] Yet the film does not leave us with this seemingly comforting – at least from a liberal Jewish perspective – hymn to Black-Jewish solidarity. Rather, the *mise en scène* adds a strikingly discordant note. Besides the segregation of the African American from the White inmates, the Black singer's (William Gillespie) downtrodden demeanour and dirge-like voice, backed by a similarly sad chorus of hunched-over Black cellmates, contrasts starkly and tellingly with Jigger and his wanna-be grassroots band's reaction. Rather than showing any understanding of the wellspring of suffering the song evokes, the White men jump up, rush forward, and break into broad smiles at hearing the 'real thing'.

That the joke is on them, for which some awareness of the song's faux authenticity is required, was likely lost on most contemporary viewers (at least until the Oscar ceremony), and thanks to Ella Fitzgerald's and other Black singers' adding the song to their repertoires, likely lost on more recent listeners as well. What is less amusing is that beneath Jigger and his bandmates' upbeat reaction lies a disturbing truth, one that the film, on the whole, fails to address. Namely, Jigger and his pals, bailed out by Nickie's mom, will soon be free to gleefully indulge in performing Blackness, while their seeming African American mentors, in 1940s St Louis and elsewhere, will continue to suffer its racist curse.

To its credit, at least for the time, the jail scene does show us the separate but unequal treatment of the Black prisoners and also implies a darker backstory than we presume applies to their White counterparts. But the scene's main function is to propel the film's narrative. Thus, when Mercer's lyrics refer to a train's lonesome whistle and a mama's warning about a woman who will sweet-talk and give you the eye, the words become more than just the impetus for Jigger and his band's pilgrimage to the Mecca of the Blues, New Orleans, and their obeisance at the altar of the 'real thing'. They also become a Greek chorus's foreboding of *Blues in the Night*'s eventual segue to 'real film noir'.

But we're not there yet. Don Siegel's first transitional montage instead manages to tap the film's political unconscious – if in a bifurcated manner in keeping with the film's generic hybridity. The montage's short, dissolving, archival shots of Mississippi steamboats and Black men and women picking, baling, and toting cotton, function narratively to speed up Jigger and company's trek from St Louis to New Orleans. The musical backdrop, meanwhile, reprises the Black prisoners' noir prophesy of a two-faced woman who will leave a man singing blues in the night. The song's montage version, however, is not rendered dolefully, as before, but in a slick, big-band style that clashes with the ominous lyrics, and even more portentously with the cotton-field worker images. As a whole, the sequence brilliantly capsulises both the blues' African American roots and their appropriation, as well as emphasising how appallingly little has changed for southern Blacks, in their social conditions, since their alleged emancipation.[38]

Alas, Siegel's probing of the blues' racial dynamic remains a footnote. Instead, we return to musical comedy during Jigger and the boys' brief stay in the Big Easy. There they join a Whites-only crowd enjoying (Jimmy Lunceford's) Black big-band Dixie – hardly the 'real blues' they supposedly came to experience and absorb, though the discrepancy appears lost on them. What they do acquire is the missing link in their five-piece combo: a talented, if rambunctious, White trumpeter, Leo (Jack Carter), plus the bonus of his talented, more wholesome wife, nicknamed 'Character' (Priscilla Lane). Character shows her singing chops and that she's 'one of the guys', when the team heads back on the road, playing honky-tonks and ending up in a freight train's boxcar – all in Siegel's second, less symbolic, more purely narratively motivated montage.

The outset of the boxcar scene, in which Character belts out a lively 'Here We Go Again!' to the boys' jubilant accompaniment, leaves no hint of the generic turning point to come. Indeed, Jigger's slightly amended populist dream appears fulfilled – of 'five guys [and a gal] who feel, play, live, even think the same way, knockin' about the country'. Then, as the train slows while passing through a small town, film noir comes knockin' – or rather bursts through the boxcar door in the grimy, unshaven figure of escaped convict Del Davis (Lloyd Nolan). Del hops aboard with a helping hand from Jigger, then returns the favour by robbing the band of their meagre earnings at gunpoint. But he also shows a little heart. Struck that they do not turn him in at the next stop – 'We've been broke and hungry, too. You probably need it more than we do' – he offers them a long-term gig at the aforementioned Jersey roadhouse, whose neon 'The Jungle' sign underscores the film's unequivocal entry into the noir world.

Storylines: Part 2, Musical / Populist Noir

This abrupt tonal shift, midway through the film, clearly threw reviewers at the time, who found it difficult to reconcile not just a blending but a seeming exchange of musical comedy and populist fable for what they saw as a gangster film. *The Baltimore Sun*'s Donald Kirkley gave up trying to peg the genre altogether, deeming *Blues in the Night* 'a bizarre screen oddity', while *St. Petersburg Times* critic Frederick Othman utterly ignored the noir aspect in dismissing the film as 'the worst musical of the year'.[39]

Oddly and bizarrely enough, both Kirkley and Othman were on to something. Because unlike *Blues in the Night*'s noir turn, which trades heavily on gangster-film clichés, its musical underpinning was decidedly atypical. Standard Hollywood musicals at this juncture – whether of Twentieth Century-Fox's cuddly Shirley Temple type, RKO's glamorous Fred Astaire/Ginger Rogers variety,

MGM's wholesome *Andy Hardy* series, the fairy-tale *Wizard of Oz* sort, or Warner Bros.' backstage brand – mostly tended towards splashy production numbers with elaborate costumes and what Biesen calls a 'utopian idealism' centred on romance and the quest for stardom.[40] *Blues in the Night*, in eschewing these conventions and adding a downbeat tone to boot, was closer, in the contemporary context, to an experimental, avant-garde, or even anti-musical.[41] Nor did Warner Bros. fail to recognise the film's singularity and thus the need for a marketing strategy that prepared audiences for 'a novel drama set to music', a 'different kind of musical', and even a 'jazz opera' (a nod to Gershwin's *Porgy and Bess*), whose characters extolled jazz and the blues as 'the true folk music of their country'.[42]

Playing up the folkish aspect also resonated with Warner Bros.' reputation as the studio most inclined – since spearheading the gangster-film genre during the Great Depression – to deal with populist, social realist themes.[43] The populist fable, specifically, had become a Hollywood staple since Frank Capra's *Mr. Deeds Goes to Town* (1936), *You Can't Take It with You* (1938), and *Mr. Smith Goes to Washington* (1939). Populist fable and musical or screwball comedy were a natural fit. Populist fable and film noir, not so much. Thus, another generic challenge loomed, at least for contemporary viewers and reviewers, when, upon crossing 'The Jungle's' threshold, Jigger's high-minded ideals confront not only violent crime but film noir's ace in the hole: the two-faced woman the Black prisoners had forewarned their neighbouring White inmates about.

The femme fatale is Kay Grant (Betty Field), The Jungle's down-in-the-mouth resident singer, of sorts. The roadhouse itself had seen better days before Del, who ran the place, was locked up, and will see them again thanks to his speakeasy gambling den and Jigger's spirited band. That major trouble lies ahead, as well, is obvious from Jigger's immediate reaction to Kay, which broadcasts loud and clear – despite or because of her pouty mien and nasty manner – that the black widow's web has been spun. No matter that Kay carries a torch for Del, and that Leo, the married horn player, is even more turned on than Jigger by her orneriness. As Leo remarks to her lame-legged piano accompanist, Brad (Wallace Ford), who is also stuck on Kay but stands no chance with her: 'I think any dame that looks like her oughta flare up once in a while – gives her style, class, you know what I mean?'

Kay knows what he means and gives Leo the come-on, but only as a way to rekindle a flame with Del – a plan that fizzles when Character's pregnancy brings out Leo's better nature and he returns to the fold. So, Kay casts her net at Jigger, who welcomes it and sees his chance when the pregnancy forces Character to forego her singing and Jigger starts training Kay as her replacement. Yet, while the song she sings in Siegel's third, highly Expressionist montage – 'Somewhere, someday, we'll be close together, wait and see' – sounds hopeful, the montage ends with Kay blowing a fuse over the drudgery of the training and her mediocre talent. When Jigger tries luring her back by professing his love, she tells him to show it – by breaking free from the band and making something of *himself*.

And thus, courtesy of noir, we have the film's core conflict – the collective versus the individual, populism and solidarity versus personal ambition and raw desire – a conflict that will send Jigger on the anti-hero's journey into noir's nether regions. When Brad wisely advises Jigger to get her 'out of his system', his muttered reply tells the tale: 'I just don't think I can.' Or, as Character, echoing her own ambivalent relationship with Leo, explains Jigger's obsession to the rest of the band when he deserts them to go solo: 'Don't you know you can be in love with someone and know it's wrong and know it's poison but not be able to do anything about it?'

Flash-forward to Jigger tickling the ivories in a shiny gold tux at a swank New York ballroom as Guy Heiser's band's (actually Will Osborne's) 'big new discovery'. A bejewelled, fur-coated Kay, after being rebuffed by Del, is in the audience, basking in Jigger's financial windfall. That Jigger is wallowing rather than basking is evident from his brooding expression and mechanical playing, emphasised during a surreal musical interlude. This riotously funny tap-dance number, which Jigger robotically accompanies with his glowering bandmates hovering over his shoulder and the four male dancers and female singer (Mabel Todd) mirroring the bandmates and Character, is meant to evoke Jigger's stricken conscience and troubled emotional state. Incongruously, however, due to the hilarious and superbly performed routine, the number is actually a scene-stealing knockout and brief musical-comedy reprise.

Back in the noir world, Jigger's ten-count comes soon after, when Kay tells him she's had it, that, as with Leo, 'I played you for a chump. I never loved you – and it's over.' Although he should have seen it coming, the verbal haymaker sends Jigger over the edge, on a bender, and into the hospital – where Siegel's most Expressionist montage penetrates Jigger's mind as it teeters on the brink of insanity.

Expressionist touches, however masterfully achieved, are by themselves nothing exceptional in film noir. But can you imagine Bogie's, Powell's, Garfield's, or Mitchum's characters, or any other tough-guy protagonist, *literally* going crazy over a dame? Falling head over heels, sure. Getting 'played like a chump', comes with the territory. But then, like any self-respecting macho, you get even, not go bananas! With the sensitive, perhaps overly sensitive Jewish émigré protagonist, it is often another story. *Scarlet Street*'s Criss Cross, for example, though he vengefully stabs to death his double-dealing 'true love', Kitty (Joan Bennett), ends up a psychotic, street-wandering wretch.

But *Blues in the Night* is musical-comedy-populist noir, so Jigger is not going to fall quite that far. He returns to The Jungle after three months in an institution and highlights his turnaround by playing a Gershwin-style variation on the 'Blues in the Night' theme to a wildly enthusiastic, still all-White, but younger and hipper crowd. By going the Gershwin route, of course, Jigger has also, for the moment, betrayed his earlier Arlen-esque ideal – that is, not only to absorb real Black blues but also to adopt Negritude and a way of life that resonated with Blackness. Thus, Jigger is not fully recovered, or even fully freed from his obsession with Kay. So, when she returns to The Jungle to give Del one last try, instead of blowing her off – as his macho noir cousins would have done and Del does now – Jigger plans to escape with her after Del slaps her around and she shoots him point-blank. Jigger's bandmates try to convince him that going with Kay now would turn him into another pathetic hanger-on like the crippled Brad. In the end, it is Brad himself, or more accurately, the Production Code, that comes to the rescue. Together they ensure that no-good Kay is duly punished for her sins (and Del was already taken care of), while Jigger is allowed, morally bloodied but unbowed, to live another day.

A *deus ex machina* ending is appended, in which benighted Brad, having overheard Jigger's bandmates' belittling comments, sees a way out for himself, Jigger, Kay, and the Code's demands for moral redemption. He drives away with Kay into the stormy night and plunges the car off a cliff to a fiery death, thus enabling a chastened Jigger and the band, including Leo (whose adulterous intentions were punished, with collateral damage to Character, when we learn that their baby was stillborn), to wash their hands of The Jungle – and film noir. In a musical-comedy-populist coda, the five guys and a gal are back where they started, and where they belong: tearing it up in a boxcar headed for who knows where, but who cares – 'We're in a groove.'

Summation

In tabulating the success of *Blues in the Nights* in meeting this chapter's tripart criteria, its satisfying the demands of Jewish émigré noir – by virtue of director Anatole Litvak and Jigger Pine's more sensitive, artistic rather than macho tough-guy protagonist – was a foregone conclusion. The film's generic hybridity, as I have detailed, was realised many times over, and in more radically eclectic fashion than Biesen proposes or Warner Bros. advertised. Rather than mounting a trend in musical noir or in dramas set to music, this 'unusual generic amalgam' and 'bizarre screen oddity', while an outlier for the time, now qualifies as a precursor for the even wilder mash-ups of the postmodern age. Assessing the film's Black-Jewish relations is less self-evident, given their inherent complexity and ambivalent treatment in the film, as punctuated by the film's boxcar-receding image and 'We're in a groove' farewell.

On the one hand, one can read the vanishing train travellers as White Negro time travellers, an allegorical vanguard of the Beat Generation's hipsters to come, drunk (or stoned) on Negritude and 'on the road' again.[44] On the other hand, for all their good intentions, some of the same complications that marred the boxcar band's earlier connections to Blackness still apply. The Civil Rights movement of the 1950s and 1960s, increasingly supported by Whites (progeny of the younger 'Jungle' crowd at film's end), produced a sea change in overall US attitudes towards African Americans and other oppressed groups. LeRoi Jones-like dismissals notwithstanding, this new generation's actions contributed to the groundbreaking anti-discriminatory measures of the 1960s and the multicultural movements to follow. All Jigger and company seem to have learned from their Negrophila and immersion in noir is to steer clear of America's baser, materialistic instincts. Populism has indeed triumphed, but only in a delimited sense. As with the White boys' departure from the St Louis prison that left their Black 'blues brothers' confined, a more comprehensive, systemic sense of the country's woes eludes them. Then again, given that a more fully enlightened racial consciousness is a bit much to ask of a mainstream Hollywood film of the 1940s, maybe it is enough to celebrate their 'groove' and leave it to neo-noir to take up the cause.

Notes

1. Alain Silver and Elizabeth Ward, eds, *Film Noir: An Encyclopedic Reference to the American Style*, 3rd ed. (Woodstock, NY: Overlook Press, 1992), p. 334. Fritz Lang's Jewish identity is the most ambiguous of the Jewish émigré directors listed here and discussed later in the chapter. His mother was Jewish and his father was Protestant, but in response to rising antisemitism in Austria, his parents converted to Catholicism and raised young Fritz as a Catholic. Lang's first wife was Jewish and the woman he fled Nazi Germany with and eventually married was as well. Most of his Jewish colleagues considered him Jewish and the Nazis did also, as evidenced by their labelling his film *M* (1931), in the antisemitic pseudo-documentary *Der ewige Jude* (*The Eternal Jew*, Fritz Hippler, 1940), an example of 'degenerate Jewish art'.
2. Alain Silver, 'Introduction', in *Film Noir Reader 4: The Crucial Films and Themes*, ed. Silver and James Ursini (New York: Limelight Editions, 2004), p. 3.
3. For a more detailed breakdown of Jewish émigré, Jewish American, and non-Jewish noir directors, see Vincent Brook, *Driven to Darkness: Jewish Émigré Directors and the Rise of Film Noir* (New Brunswick, NJ: Rutgers University Press, 2009).
4. Jewish émigré noir also features a disproportionate number of strong female characters and protagonists, which I describe in detail in *Driven to Darkness*.
5. Daniel Boyarin, *Unheroic Conduct: The Rise of Heterosexuality and the Invention of the Jewish Man* (Berkeley and Los Angeles: University of California Press, 1997).
6. Sander Gilman, *The Jew's Body* (New York and London: Routledge, 1991), pp. 52, 76.
7. Karoly Benkert coined the term 'homosexuality' in 1869; Wilhelm Marr, 'antisemitism' in 1879. See Gilman, *The Jew's Body*, p. 126.
8. Gilman, *The Jew's Body*, p. 53.
9. For more on Jewish gangsters, especially, see Rich Cohen, *Tough Jews: Fathers, Sons, and Gangster Dreams in Jewish America* (New York: Simon and Schuster, 1998).

10. Sheri Chinen Biesen, *Music in the Shadows: Noir Musical Films* (Baltimore: Johns Hopkins University Press, 2014), p. 35.
11. Biesen, *Music in the Shadows*, pp. 2–3.
12. Gerald W. O'Brien, 'The Heat is On . . . Quinn Lemley's Musical Journey as Rita Hayworth', *jazzreview.com*, 25 July 2006; archived 27 August 2006.
13. Biesen, *Music in the Shadows*, p. 5.
14. Jeffrey Melnick, *A Right to Sing the Blues* (Cambridge, MA: Harvard University Press, 2001), p. 7.
15. On Jews and Blackface, particularly in relation to *The Jazz Singer*, see Michael Rogin, *Black Face, White Noise: Jewish Immigrants in the American Melting Pot* (Berkeley: University of California Press, 1998); Joel Rosenberg, 'Rogin's Noise: The Alleged Crimes of *The Jazz Singer*', *Prooftexts: A Journal of Jewish Literary History* 22, no. 1/2 (Winter/Spring 2002), pp. 221–39; Mark Slobin, 'Putting Blackface in Its Place', in *Entertaining America: Jews, Movies, and Broadcasting*, ed. J. Hoberman and Jeffrey Shandler (New York: The Jewish Museum and Princeton University Press, 2003), pp. 93–9; and Eric Lott, *Love and Theft: Blackface Minstrelsy and the American Working Class* (New York: Oxford University Press, 1993).
16. Irving Howe, with Kenneth Libo, *World of Our Fathers* (New York: Touchstone/Simon and Schuster, 1976), p. 563; Melnick, *A Right to Sing the Blues*, pp. 4, 172; Biesen, *Music in the Shadows*, p. 28; Herbert Goldman, *Jolson: The Legend Comes to Life* (New York: Oxford University Press, 1988), p. 302.
17. Quoted in Melnick, *A Right to Sing the Blues*, p. 48.
18. Melnick, *A Right to Sing the Blues*, p. 48.
19. Melnick, *A Right to Sing the Blues*, p. 48.
20. Jews were officially designated as 'white' for the first time in the 1940 census. See Janet Brodkin, *How the Jews Became White Folks . . . and What That Says about Race in America* (New Brunswick, NJ: Rutgers University Press, 1998).
21. Quoted in Brodkin, *How the Jews Became White Folks*, pp. 1, 15.
22. Quoted in Brodkin, *How the Jews Became White Folks*, p. 51.
23. Melnick, *A Right to Sing the Blues*, p. 50.
24. Melnick, *A Right to Sing the Blues*, p. 50.
25. Quoted in Melnick, *A Right to Sing the Blues*, p. 50; Norman Mailer, 'The White Negro: Superficial Reflections on the Hipster', *Dissent* 4, no. 3 (Fall 1957).
26. Melnick, *A Right to Sing the Blues*, p. 50.
27. I could find no conclusive evidence that Gilbert was Jewish, but he foregoes Jewish coding for explicit and sympathetic Jewish representation of two main characters in his novels (*Native Stone*, 1956, and *The Hourglass*, 1959).
28. With his adaptation of Tennessee Williams's play *A Streetcar Named Desire* (1951), Kazan also introduced to Hollywood film the Method acting style, adapted from the Russian Constantin Stanislavski's System by Lee Strasberg. One of Rossen's early screenplays was *They Won't Forget* (1937) about Leo Frank, the Jewish American factory manager lynched in Georgia in 1915 for the alleged murder of Mary Fagan, a young white woman. The case highlighted rising antisemitism in America and became a 'touchstone' in Black-Jewish relations, because, surprising for the South, the other suspect in the case, a Black worker at Frank's plant, avoided prosecution. See Melnick, *A Right to Sing the Blues*, p. 9.

29. Kazan's Oscar winners were *Gentleman's Agreement* (1947), the first major Hollywood film about antisemitism, and *On the Waterfront* (1954), about corrupt labour unions; Rossen took the prize with *All the King's Men* (1949), adapted from Robert Penn Warren's novel based on leftist demagogue Huey Long. Kazan also made *Pinky* (1949), the first to confront anti-Black racism, and Rossen made *Body and Soul* (1947), about corruption in professional boxing.
30. For more on Rossen, see Brian Neve, 'The Hollywood Left: Robert Rossen and Postwar Hollywood', in *Film Studies* 7, no. 1 (December 2005), and Alan Casty, *Robert Rossen: The Films and Politics of a Political Idealist* (Jefferson, NC: McFarland, 2012). For more on Kazan, see Richard Schickel, *Elia Kazan: A Biography* (New York: HarperCollins, 2006) and *Kazan Revisited*, ed. Lisa Dombrowski (Middletown, CT: Wesleyan University Press, 2011).
31. The expressionist/Expressionist dialectic is explained in John D. Barlow, *German Expressionist Film* (Boston: Twayne, 1982), and applied extensively in Brook, *Driven to Darkness*.
32. Biesen, *Music in the Shadows*, pp. 26–7.
33. Michael Walker, 'Robert Siodmak', *The Book of Film Noir*, ed. Ian Cameron (New York: Continuum, 1993), pp. 138–9.
34. For more on production parameters in the classical era, see David Bordwell, Janet Staiger, and Kristen Thompson, *The Classical Hollywood Cinema: Film Style and Mode of Production to 1960* (New York: Columbia University Press, 1985).
35. For more on Hollywood's reluctance to make anti-Nazi films, see Lawrence Baron and Joel Rosenberg, with a Coda by Vincent Brook, 'The Ben Urwand Controversy: Exploring the Hollywood-Hitler Relationship', in *From Shtel to Stardom: Jews and Hollywood*, ed. Michael Renov and Brook (West Lafayette, IN: Purdue University Press, 2017), pp. 23–46.
36. Paul Buhle and David Wagner, *Radical Hollywood: The Untold Story Behind America's Favorite Movies* (New York: New Press, 2002).
37. The alternate title can be found in parentheses on album covers or liner notes as well as on sheet music. See, for example, https://www.musicnotes.com/sheetmusic/mtd.asp?ppn=MN0026341 or https://www.oktav.com/en/d/54d99086.
38. Quoted in Biesen, *Music in the Shadows*, p. 32.
39. Frederick C. Othman, 'Movie Critic Invites Dirk in Back as He Selects 10 Worst Film Plays of 1941', *St. Petersburg Times*, 6 December 1941, p. 1; Donald Kirkley, 'Blues in the Night', *Baltimore Sun*, 22 December 1941, p. 8.
40. Biesen, *Music in the Shadows*, pp. 9, 35.
41. Biesen, *Music in the Shadows*, p. 19.
42. Warner Bros. publicity, quoted in Biesen, *Music in the Shadows*, pp. 26, 29.
43. Biesen, *Music in the Shadows*, p. 24. See also Thomas Schatz, *The Genius of the System: Hollywood Filmmaking during the Studio Era* (Minneapolis: University of Minnesota Press, 2010).
44. Jack Kerouac's *On the Road* (New York: Viking, 1957), along with Allen Ginsberg's epic poem 'Howl', in *HOWL and Other Poems* (San Francisco: City Light Books, 1956), are considered the urtexts of the Beat Generation.

6. EXPRESSIONISM, EXISTENTIALISM, AND SOCIALISM IN *SCARS OF THE PAST*

Milan Hain

INTRODUCTION

In early 1959, *Scars of the Past* (*Zde jsou lvi*) – a powerful psychological drama from veteran director Václav Krška – was sharply criticised by the committee and members of the Communist Party at the inaugural Festival of Czechoslovak Films in Banská Bystrica. Almost immediately, the film was withdrawn from distribution and banned from public screening for several years. The story of traumatised mining engineer Alexandr Štěrba, struggling with a guilty conscience after causing a fatal accident, was viewed by party officials as subversive and critical of the system. Moreover, its formal properties were in stark contrast to the doctrine of socialist realism, which (in this pre-New-Wave climate) was still the norm of the state-sponsored film industry. To dramatise Štěrba's subjectivity, the authors use a flashback structure, expressionist lighting schemes, and complex *mise en scène*, all of which have become trademarks associated with the classical film noir cycle of the 1940s and 1950s.

Even though I am not in favour of expanding the film noir canon ad infinitum, as has been the case with numerous publications of the recent past,[1] I share the opinion of the editors of the present volume that sometimes framing a film as noir might be useful to illuminate its obscured or underexplored elements. When viewed through the noir lens, so to speak, the incompatibility of *Scars of the Past* with the prevailing ideological and aesthetic norms in Czechoslovakia of the late 1950s becomes more apparent. The film tackled sensitive issues (individualism, crisis of conscience, alcoholism, infidelity) in a highly unconventional manner, which explains why it became such a welcome target for the threatened communist regime. In what follows, I focus on the film's noir-inflected narrative strategies, visual properties, tonal qualities, and character construction and relate these to the specific historical situation of its production and theatrical release.

Banská Bystrica and the Political Thrashing of Czechoslovak Cinema

The first Festival of Czechoslovak Films that took place in late February 1959 in the city of Banská Bystrica is a convenient starting point for the discussion of *Scars of the Past* and its place in Czechoslovak film history. Banská Bystrica in the eastern part of the country (today's central Slovakia) was selected as the site of the event for mainly symbolic reasons: in 1944 it became the centre of a large, though ultimately unsuccessful, anti-Nazi opposition known as the Slovak National Uprising. Fifteen years after this historic episode, the city once again witnessed a powerful resistance – this time sanctified by the state and directed against a certain tendency in Czechoslovak cinema, for the purpose of the festival was not only to present new films but also to critically evaluate the production of the past year and set goals for the coming term.

Unquestionably, the outcomes of the event were not random, nor entirely unexpected. Banská Bystrica became merely a platform for voicing what had already been collectively decided at the 11th Convention of the Czechoslovak Communist Party in June 1958.[2] The high officials of the party observed with great concern the liberalisation of Czechoslovak culture that mirrored similar processes launched in the whole Eastern bloc after Nikita Khrushchev's appointment as the first secretary of the Communist Party of the Soviet Union in 1953 and, three years later, his open criticism of Stalin's purges and the cult of personality. Political elites in Czechoslovakia were determined to make a powerful gesture by publicly denouncing ideologically faulty films and restoring the film industry's commitment to preserving and promoting socialist ideals.

The most vociferous critique in Banská Bystrica came from the Minister of Education and Culture, František Kahuda. In his report, delivered on 23 February 1959, he identified remnants of bourgeois thinking in several recent films which needed to be eradicated in order to bring the socialist cultural revolution to its successful end. Specifically, he objected to pessimistic stories that showed the regime as erring: 'It doesn't correspond with objective truth to present central contemporary characters as broken and hurt individuals who are capable of experiencing nothing more than their private problems, which leads them to skepticism and faithlessness typical of the petite bourgeoisie.'[3] In Kahuda's view, cinema should fully submit to the intentions of the party, otherwise it might risk being misused by the class enemy. In other words, films ought to serve the regime as prolonged arms of its apparatus, and their value rests solely on faithful reproduction of socialist ideological patterns: 'The director has to be thoroughly versed in Marxism-Leninism, [. . .] has to love the socialist present and be able to enthuse over our life and our people and for this life and for this people dedicatedly work.'[4]

Four films in particular fell victim to what Jan Žalman (born Antonín Novák), long-time editor-in-chief of the magazine *Film a doba*, called 'political thrashing whose aim was to restore unconditional obedience in the impatient Czechoslovak culture':[5] *Three Wishes* (original title *Tři přání*, Ján Kadár and Elmar Klos, 1958), a scathing satire, masked as a fairy tale, on current mores in socialist society; *The Star Goes to the South* (*Hvězda jede na jih*, Oldřich Lipský, 1958), a kitschy musical comedy, whose main 'sin' was that it was made as a co-production with Tito's Yugoslavia;[6] *The End of the Clairvoyant* (*Konec jasnovidce*, Vladimír Svitáček and Ján Roháč, 1957), a 25-minute comedy about a fortune teller, whose mystical job is by virtue of a state decree transformed into a purely bureaucratic affair; and, finally, *Scars of the Past*, Václav Krška's first film on a contemporary subject in more than ten years, after spending most of the 1950s making historical biopics – *The Herald of Dawn* (*Posel úsvitu*, 1950), *Mikoláš Aleš* (1951), *Youthful Years* (*Mladá léta*, 1952), *From My Life* (*Z mého života*, 1955) – and fairy tales with oriental settings – *Labakan* (1956), *A Legend about Love* (*Legenda o lásce*, 1956). Several other films were mentioned as representing an undesirable trend in recent Czechoslovak cinema. These included Ladislav Helge's directorial debut *School for Fathers* (*Škola otců*, 1957), which traces the gradual disillusionment of a reformist teacher at a small-town elementary school; *At the Terminus* (*Tam na konečné*, Ján Kadár and Elmar Klos, 1957), a bleak, yet poetic portrait of several residents living in a tenement house at the end of a tramline; and *September Nights* (*Zářijové noci*, Vojtěch Jasný, 1957), an adaptation of Pavel Kohout's play about the disturbing treatment of army servicemen by their incompetent officers.

The effects of the festival in Banská Bystrica were far-reaching: films that were singled out as ideologically problematic were immediately withdrawn from distribution; their makers were reprimanded – some of them were banned from making another movie for several years (the creative hiatus of the duo Ján Kadár and Elmar Klos, makers of *Three Wishes* and *At the Terminus*, lasted for five years), while others – including Václav Krška – were allowed to work only on less thorny subjects; and the most innovative production unit headed by František Daniel and Karel Feix (responsible for *Scars of the Past*, *Three Wishes*, and *The End of the Clairvoyant*) was dismantled, thus undermining the process of decentralisation of film production which had contributed to the creative outburst of the short period between 1956 and 1958 in the first place.[7] Overall, most of the revisionist tendencies of Czechoslovak cinema were abruptly and firmly put out, causing a general regress to the rigid norms of socialist realism. It was not until 1962 or 1963 that another relaxation of political conditions led to the formation of what would become the Czechoslovak New Wave.

Films for the People: A Few Notes on Socialist Realism

So, what exactly was meant by 'socialist realism', which was again and again cited as a model to which all filmmakers should unconditionally subscribe, both before and certainly after the 1959 festival in Banská Bystrica? As Valérie Pozner remarked, there is no single, all-encompassing definition of the term,[8] even though it is arguably less nebulous than the notoriously difficult concept of film noir, which is constantly being redefined and renegotiated both in scholarly and popular literature. Cultural historians Jiří Knapík and Martin Franc specify five features that are characteristic of artistic production in the mode of socialist realism: (1) standardisation (for instance, characters are clearly marked by their social class); (2) loyalty to the Communist Party and principles of socialist society; (3) folksiness and popular appeal (intelligibility, because art should be accessible to the masses); (4) the working-class hero as a positive role model; (5) and, finally, emphasis on current topics (such as industrialisation, aspiring to a socialist ideal, emancipation of the proletariat, etc.).[9]

Most generally, these directives were derived from the Soviet experience and the doctrine proposed by the leading communist ideologist Andrei Alexandrovich Zhdanov in 1946, even though the term itself originated in the early 1930s. In Czechoslovakia, it became the only method of cultural production sanctified by the state in 1948 after the communists assumed total control. Almost immediately, ideological motives were given precedence over artistic aspects, and the main criteria for evaluating art's worth became limited to those directly related to furthering the socialist cause. Culture became one of the domains closely controlled by the regime because it was an effective platform for delivering the socialist message to the masses. To reach as wide an audience as possible, mimetic forms of art were preferred over more experimental or formalist ways of expression. Socialist art was supposed to celebrate and glorify the party and the common folk, while individualism, elitism, and intellectualism were all discarded as undesirable throwbacks to capitalism.

Cinema, as the most dominant mass medium of the time, was not exempt from the obligation to promote positive socialist values and criticise everything that was deemed incompatible with these strictly defined ideals. In most cases, this led to a schematic treatment of a stable inventory of subjects: primacy of the collective over the individual; responsibility to the party and the people; class struggle; glorification of the working class and its positive relationship to labour; industrialisation and technological progress; identification of traitors of the regime and diversionists in intellectuals or members of the petite bourgeoisie; elimination of the remnants of the prior (and inevitably fallacious) social order; transformation of the country on the road to socialism; leadership of the USSR and the Communist Party; gratitude to and love for the liberators; or friendly coexistence of socialist nations. On the other hand, negative aspects of communism and socialism were carefully suppressed, and history was falsified for ideological purposes.[10]

The motto of the festival in Banská Bystrica read 'For Tighter Union Between Film Production and the Life of the People', and, in the final analysis, this is as good a definition of socialist realism as any because it plainly states the ambition of the state to address the masses on a large scale and unite them in the struggle to build a utopian socialist society.

Scars of the Past as Film Noir?

As I have already elucidated, the years 1956 to 1958 brought several reformist films which challenged the hegemony of socialist realism (Peter Hames rightfully calls this brief period of creativity 'the first wave').[11] In the words of historian Ivan Klimeš:

> artists showed great willingness to break loose from cultural isolation [that was enforced after the 1948 communist *coup d'état*] and absorb contemporary stylistic and philosophical movements from the West. This meant, at the formal level, a lack of concern for socialist realism and, at the thematic level, a disdain for big topics related to the building of socialism that were preferred by the party cultural politicians.[12]

To accomplish this end, however, the filmmakers used diverse methods. Take for instance the two films made by the tandem of Ján Kadár and Elmar Klos. In *Three Wishes*, they opted for an allegorical statement, fusing a contemporary story about a married couple struggling with a lack of money with a fantastical element where a magic old man reciprocates a small favour by granting the husband three wishes. On the other hand, *At the Terminus*, made a year earlier, eschewed all artifice and emulated the style of Italian neorealism by focusing on the everyday experiences of a group of characters inhabiting a typical suburban tenement house.

In *Scars of the Past*, experienced director Václav Krška and noted playwright and first-time screenwriter Oldřich Daněk chose yet another mode of expression which, as I argue further in this chapter, is closely related to film noir. That is not to say that they were consciously influenced by the American or international variations of film noir (one of the reasons being that the import of Western films was severely circumscribed in Czechoslovakia during the 1950s). But I believe that we can identify a close affinity with film noir on several levels, including narration, style, character construction, atmosphere, and ideology, which have traditionally been the domains in which 'noirness' has been located.[13] In that, my approach is probably closest to David Bordwell's historical poetics of cinema which assumes that 'the filmmaker selects among constructional options or creates new choices' based on his or her ends.[14] Bordwell also emphasises 'the institutional dimension of practice [which] forms the horizon of what is permitted and encouraged at particular moments'.[15] As I aim to show, the very same elements that are responsible for *Scars of the Past*'s affinity with film noir also made it incompatible at the time of its original release with the principles of socialist realism required by the state.

Out of the Past (Plot Construction)

The story of *Scars of the Past* is quite simple and straightforward. Alexandr Štěrba (Karel Höger) is a talented mining engineer known for his resourcefulness and imaginative approach to solving problems. One of his more unorthodox ideas, however, causes a fatal cave-in with one miner dead. After this, Štěrba becomes a *persona non grata*: he is stigmatised as a murderer and spends some time in jail for negligence. His marriage slowly disintegrates, and he begins to drink heavily. Because the system does not know what to do with such a maladjusted individual, he is transferred from one mine to another until, finally, he ends up in the godforsaken Mine Žofie, which is scheduled to close soon. When the hard-working junior engineer Radim Vochoč (Svatopluk Matyáš) suggests a bold plan to extract coal from the old mine galleries, Štěrba is reminded of his own failure from years before and sharply dismisses the idea without providing any explanation. Interpreting the reaction as an expression of vanity and ignorance from an arrogant superior, Vochoč and his colleagues decide to continue with the plan anyway. This results in another cave-in, though this time, no one is seriously hurt. Štěrba, selflessly assisting in the rescuing operations, understands that Vochoč's career is now jeopardised. To make sure his young colleague does not follow in his unfortunate footsteps, he tries to prevent fellow miner Palivec (František Kreuzmann) from sending a message about the incident to the headquarters. Racing against time (and not knowing that Palivec has changed his mind at the last minute), he has a motorcycle accident and ends up undergoing serious surgery. Everyone at the mine is relieved when copyist Vilma (Dana Medřická), secretly in love with Štěrba, reports that he will survive after all.

Based on the synopsis above, one might assume that the film presents events in linear fashion, with causes neatly leading to effects (and effects always preceded by causes) and each character's action explained by overt psychological motivation. However, this is not how Krška and Daněk organised the plot. As is the case with numerous classical film noirs, *Scars of the Past* uses an elaborate flashback structure and stimulates audience interest by withholding crucial information and offering part of the story as an enigma.

The film's opening pre-credit sequence shows the frantic motorcycle ride leading to an accident, but it refuses to provide any meaningful context: at this moment we do not know the reason for the rider's hurry or his identity because we do not get to see his face and there is no dialogue to guide us; we can only tell from visual cues that it is a man. The rapid montage of the ride and the ensuing crash is followed by an extremely long take (more than 150 seconds) of a hospital corridor: first we see a body on a stretcher being carried to an operating room, after that a woman enters the frame at a leisurely pace and stops by the door; only then do the opening credits start to roll. This exposition is deliberately frustrating because it presents a succession of dramatic events (near-fatal accident, surgical operation, woman's nervous expectation of its outcome) without indicating any of the causes, thus producing a flaunted narrative gap. As is typical for film noir, we are thrown in the middle of an already highly developed sequence of actions with no alternative but to wait until the film provides answers to our questions, thereby satisfying our curiosity.

When we return to the motorcycle accident near the end of the film – after eighty minutes of screen time – our sense of the events is completely different: we know the characters, their relationships and personal histories, and understand what is at stake for each of them. The main focus, as always in *Scars of the Past*, is on Štěrba, who is trying to prevent Palivec from delivering a message that might be potentially devastating to his young colleague's future. Moreover, the filmmakers use the technique of cross-cutting to intensify suspense (alternating shots of Štěrba on the motorcycle with Palivec getting nearer to the post office), even though by the ending we already know the basic outcome. The extended flashback structure is known from classic noirs such as *Double Indemnity* (Billy Wilder, 1944), *Murder, My Sweet* (Edward Dmytryk, 1944), and *Out of the Past* (Jacques Tourneur, 1947), but, in my opinion, the closest equivalent to *Scars of the Past* is *Mildred Pierce* (Michael Curtiz, 1945) which, in the climax, also revisits scenes from the beginning (Monte Beragon's murder in the beach house) and gives them new meaning.[16]

After the opening credits and again, briefly, near the end of the film, we can identify another familiar technique of film noir: voice-over narration. But it is not Štěrba's voice we hear at this point, nor does it belong to any other character. Its positioning outside of the story world and the authority it generates (almost inevitably, the voice belongs to a male) might remind us of newsreel-like narrators known from docu-noirs such as *The House on 92nd Street* (Henry Hathaway, 1945) and *The Naked City* (Jules Dassin, 1948). Upon closer inspection, however, the effect is different. The source of the voice seems impartial and detached at first, describing matter-of-factly Štěrba's injuries ('a skull fracture, four broken ribs, severe internal injury'), but it soon becomes clear that this narrator has access not only to objective facts but also to characters' most intimate thoughts and emotions. Moreover, the flawless synchronisation of his commentary with images on screen and the present tense he uses to frame the story ('How many people here are fighting for the life of engineer Alexandr Štěrba?' he asks while we watch surgeons performing the operation) suggest that he might be more than a mere mediator dryly recounting events from the past, as is customary in newsreels. He seems to be fully in control of the unfolding story, similar to third person omniscient narration in literature. For instance, when he says, 'three days ago', a dissolve initiates a flashback that will form the majority of the film. A reference to Štěrba's wife Jana (Jarmila Smejkalová) is accompanied by a cut to a shot of her, and a similar technique is repeated on two other occasions. Finally, when the voice says that Štěrba has abandoned all people but is not alone altogether, we see him sitting at a restaurant table and drinking liquor ('he has found a friend'), thus introducing alcoholism as an important aspect of his current state. On the one hand, the voice-over commands authority by evoking newsreel techniques or the 'voice-of-God' narration in semi-documentary noirs,[17] on the other hand it also creates a sense of unease because it soon relinquishes its strictly objective tone and its source remains unknown to the audience. In socialist art, specifically, such ambiguity as to who is actually speaking can be seen as problematic and undesirable because it associates control with an unidentified source as opposed to an officially sanctioned power (representative of the state or public official, for example).

Within the main retrospective, there is another flashback (or rather a series of flashbacks), this time presented as Štěrba's memories and accompanied by his own voice-over narration. The extended flashback covers three days, from Vochoč's bold suggestion to use the old galleries and Štěrba's sharp rejection of the plan to the latter's motorcycle accident and surgery. The inserted flashbacks cover a much longer period of plot time, detailing Štěrba's professional and personal decline after indirectly causing the fatal cave-in. Significantly, this crucial part of the story – providing explanation for Štěrba's moroseness and reclusion – comes after fifty minutes of screen time. For the majority of the film, then, the narration is highly uncommunicative, rendering Štěrba's behaviour inexplicable and thus seemingly lacking motivation. This also makes any identification for the audience difficult, if not impossible. We simply do not have any explanation that would justify his social isolation and harsh treatment of people around him, even though they often mean well.

The flashback thus finally satisfies our desire for knowledge: introduced as a confession to his former teacher and mentor Hron (Bedřich Vrbský), Štěrba recounts the way he was ostracised after the mining accident, both by individuals and the system at large. It is only at this point that we realise that his actions in the present are not whims of an antisocial person but have deep psychological roots. Moreover, they also help to explain other moments in the film – for instance, the strange reaction of Štěrba's wife when she hears for the first time about Vochoč's plan. Again, many film noirs take the form of a confessional flashback, recounted by the troubled protagonist – for instance, *Double Indemnity*, *Detour* (Edgar G. Ulmer, 1945), and *The Lady from Shanghai* (Orson Welles, 1947)[18] – but rarely does it come as late in the plot as in *Scars of the Past*, frustrating our sense of closure and testing our patience.

Even when judged against noirs from the classical period, the film uses a highly complex narrative structure – with two voice-over narrators and layered, multiple flashbacks – to defy many norms of plot and character construction typical for the socialist realist tradition, including clear exposition, linear causality, and explicit character motivation. Foregrounding the process of narration in this way was often criticised in contemporary reviews of the film. For example, several commentators complained that the retrospective was an unnecessary and distractive device and that the film presented its events in an artificial, fabricated manner.[19] While the socialist norm called for direct address and comprehensibility to appeal to the masses, Krška and Daněk opted for a more challenging narrative form which refused to provide answers right away and instead required active participation of the audience.

Cast a Dark Shadow (Visual Style)

Another ground for criticism was the film's visual style. In the prescriptive mode of socialist realism, form (by which I mean the combination of narration and style) should be invisible or transparent and always in service of the ideological intention of the work.[20] In *Scars of the Past*, however, style is a very prominent aspect, transcending realism by facilitating access to Štěrba's subjectivity or forming visual patterns and motives that might be read independently of the recounted story. Krška and respected cinematographer Jaroslav Tuzar employed a wide range of techniques, many of which belong to film noir's stylistic and iconographic inventory as described by Janey Place and Lowell Peterson in their classic essay 'Some Visual Motifs of *Film Noir*'.[21] Chiaroscuro lighting, night scenes, deep focus, odd camera angles, asymmetrical compositions, cobblestones wet with rain, cigarette smoke and fog, crowded interiors and inhospitable urban places – all can be found in *Scars of the Past* in no small measure.[22] On the other hand, the mining background – far removed from the modern metropolitan jungle that provides setting for most classical noirs – seems to situate the film more emphatically in the socialist realist tradition that was often preoccupied with places associated with physical labour. Even here, though, one can point to several Hollywood precursors, most prominently Billy Wilder's *Ace in the Hole* (1951) where a self-centred reporter ruthlessly exploits a story about a man trapped in a cave.[23]

Like the narrative structure, many of the film's stylistic strategies are used to convey Štěrba's psychological states and his position within the community. His agitation is often communicated by Dutch angles, rocking camera movement, low-key lighting, off-kilter *mise en scène* and other striking effects. On one occasion we see him pour out the contents of his glass directly into the lens of the camera, thereby communicating to the viewer his frustration and aggression reinforced by alcohol. In a scene that forms part of the main flashback, Štěrba and his wife are forced to clear out their apartment and move to another place. The concluding shot shows Štěrba's dark silhouette from a low angle as he watches a manual worker disassemble their glass chandelier. It is heavily raining outside and the raindrops, reflected through the glass windows, make large, moving patterns on the ceiling. When the chandelier is finally taken down, the electrical wire that remains in the wall is reminiscent of a noose. The downpour and the irregular clinking produced by the glass parts of the chandelier can be heard from the soundtrack. All technical means of the medium (camera placement, lighting, staging, décor, sound) are mobilised in this extraordinary scene in order to dramatise Štěrba's loss of professional status and personal stability and his growing estrangement from wife Jana. Specifically, the noose-like image of the wire (evoking death by hanging and electrocution), shot from a low angle with Štěrba's silhouette on the right and the workman's ladder on the left, suggest that psychologically and emotionally, the protagonist has sunk to the bottom, perhaps contemplating suicide as a way out of his misery.

Most scenes in the film are characterised by oppressive, low-key lighting which produces a claustrophobic atmosphere. Often, the edges of the frame are darker than the centre, thus emphasising Štěrba's (and, occasionally, other characters') social ostracism. Contemporary reviews often criticised this aspect, pointing out that darkness (both explicitly and figuratively) is not adequately balanced by light in the film's overall composition.[24] The only notable exceptions are the overexposed shots introducing the inserted flashback before the fatal cave-in that initiates Štěrba's downfall. The rest of the film is characterised by night-time exteriors and dimly lit interiors with distinct shadows.

While dominated by darkness, the style of the film is not static. Framing, *mise en scène*, and editing involve dynamic shifts and often mediate the material and spiritual decay of the society. Scenes showing isolated characters, often in deglamourising close-ups (for instance apathetic Štěrba drinking alcohol), alternate with crowded scenes of committee meetings and other work situations where faces and bodies are crammed close to one another. Seedy, comfortless interiors (apartments, offices), mostly built in the studio, are shown side by side with the inhospitable industrial scenery shot on location around Příbram in Central Bohemia. A stunning effect was achieved when Jaroslav Tuzar and Václav Krška went more than one kilometer (3,280 feet) below ground to get several shots of the mining cabin in motion and miners operating in the shaft.[25] The film thus produces instability and unpredictability not only by its complex narrative structure, but also visually, by employing scenes with varied content and movement.

Michal Večeřa has noted another strategy used by the filmmakers to complicate the audience's sense of temporal and spatial relations. Beginning with the pre-credit/opening credits sequence, they alternate rapid editing (motorcycle ride, excited conversations) with longer takes, often utilising deep focus. Movement and anxiety are thus followed by peace or resignation and vice versa.[26] A sense of unease is further produced by violating one of the fundamental rules of continuity editing: establishing shots are often omitted and new scenes begin with close-ups or medium shots emphasising characters' faces.

Writing in the early 1990s, Jan Žalman viewed *Scars of the Past* as a singular attempt to break away from stylistic conformity that characterised much of Czechoslovak cinema of the late 1950s and produce a film that would reflect Krška's unique artistic vision.[27] Just as he did with plot construction discussed earlier, the director eschewed the seemingly objective style of socialist realism and instead embraced highly expressionist techniques that were closely aligned with the protagonist's animated emotional and psychological states and that, taken in their totality, contributed to the film's dark, oppressive mood.

I Walk Alone (Character Construction, Tone, and Ideology)

The greatest challenge against socialist realism in *Scars of the Past* is arguably the construction of main characters and the way they embody certain ideological perspectives. The film was criticised by party representatives for 'significant defects of ideological nature'. A report from 20 January 1959 stated that

> the most serious problem is that marginal shortcomings, that might manifest in our society, are emphasised in such a manner that they seem to represent general disagreement with certain institutions and forms of our life. [. . .] This misguided interpretation is a result of a faulty political approach of the makers.[28]

Many state officials were concerned that the film might be used as a foundation for 'expressions of disapproval with the necessary and correct measures of our party'.[29] Reviewers in the contemporary press took a similar stand. Jan Nový, writing for the literary weekly *Tvorba*, called *Scars of the Past* an ideologically imperfect work, primarily because Štěrba's story is not only 'improbable' but also 'made-up and untrue'.[30] The main protagonist was described as a weakling, unable to confront his past and instead stylising himself as a martyr, all of which was perceived as contrary to socialist ideals.[31]

The film met with such a vociferous resistance because it tended to problematise the present instead of glorifying it. The party ideologues preferred patriotic biopics and historical epics or escapist comedies and musicals. Psychological dramas, of which *Scars of the Past* was a prominent example, were undesirable since they prioritised the individual's troubled experience over his or her flawless integration into the wider social community. It was for this reason that Krška's and Daněk's film was labelled, fittingly but rather unflatteringly given the contemporary interpretation of the term, as a case study in 'socialist existentialism'.[32]

Protagonist Alexandr Štěrba certainly fits the description of the existentialist (anti-)hero who, according to Robert Porfirio, is one of the mainstays of film noir.[33] As played by Karel Höger, Štěrba is a highly ambivalent character – arrogant yet full of doubt, cold, detached, and emotionally fragile. Ostracised by society, he becomes a lonely, alienated nonconformist, suspicious of everything and everyone. He spends his time in seclusion – often sitting alone in a pub, smoking cigarettes and chasing away his problems with liquor. As we soon find out, his marriage is in ruins and he is not part of any official structures, as he was unanimously expelled from the Communist Party after the cave-in. His individualism and nonconformism are further emphasised by his preferred means of transport, the motorcycle, which, using a term borrowed from literary criticism, becomes his objective correlative (see Figure 6.1).[34]

As already described, a large part of the film presents Štěrba as a mysterious person. He opposes the young and passionate Vochoč – in many ways his counterpart – without any apparent motive. His seemingly irrational resistance

Figure 6.1 Karel Höger as the alienated mining engineer Vochoč. [frame capture]

sets everyone against him, exacerbating the mutual hostility. But the inserted flashback, narrated by Štěrba himself, changes the audience's perspective in a crucial way. Suddenly, we realise that Štěrba is mostly a victim of the system. After making one mistake, he finds no solace and relief in his misery, only blame and apathy. Unsupportive friends and relatives, indifferent coworkers, and the impersonal party apparatus are all to blame for his subsequent downfall. As Štěrba himself says, 'The question is whether a person who has once stumbled, has a right to strive for anything at all'. In this way, according to Petr Bilík, the film made a powerful statement 'against hypocrisy, background checks, and reckless building of socialism'.[35]

Karel Höger, one of the most celebrated Czechoslovak actors of his generation, was adept at portraying anguished intellectuals, coping with guilt or inner dilemmas. For example, Ladislav Helge's *School for Fathers* showed him as Jindřich Pelikán, an elementary schoolteacher who flees from his failing marriage to take a position in a small provincial town. There, he runs into conflict with his pupils, their parents, and other members of the teaching staff who disagree with his methods. Totally disillusioned, he leaves the town after failing to accomplish any real change in the community. In *School for Fathers*, Höger opted for minimalist performance signs. As shown by Veronika Zýková, 'everything that is important is expressed through glances or simple gestures, very economically and functionally'.[36] In *Scars of the Past*, though, Höger's performance is more varied, alternating moments of serenity with extreme agitation, thereby presenting Štěrba both as resigned, reconciled with his fate, and defying his expulsion from society. In this way, Höger renders the protagonist as a complex individual, far from one-dimensional types that frequently populate socialist realist dramas and more akin to the morally ambiguous antiheroes of film noir.

Scars of the Past's spotlight on outsiders is further demonstrated in the character of copyist Vilma who defies social conventions by her provoking appearance, plain outspokenness, and courageous conduct. In two scenes, we see her climbing on Štěrba's motorcycle (in the second instance disregarding his vehement protests) and riding in high speed without a helmet. The community has a low opinion of her. After her husband left her, we learn, she had many other relationships, thus acquiring the reputation of a loose woman. Under her cynical, seemingly impenetrable exterior, however, she harbours a sensitive, vulnerable soul. It becomes obvious that she has feelings for Štěrba and, in the end, she is the only one who really stands up for him. Štěrba's wife is also portrayed as a lonely figure but she does not arouse much empathy, mainly because she is unfaithful to her husband with Vochoč and does not support him in the moments of greatest need. Contrary to Vilma, for example, she does not wait for the outcome of the operation and instead leaves with a young doctor, possibly to seduce him.

Figure 6.2 Vilma (Dana Medřická) defies many social norms and conventions, yet she comes off as a less threatening partner for Štěrba than his own wife. [frame capture]

The film at first evokes two female archetypes most readily found in film noir: the alluring, independent, yet also treacherous femme fatale, and her counterpart, the passive, nurturing and unexciting *femme attrapée*.[37] This interpretation is underscored by the characters' appearance and visual presentation: Vilma has dark hair and we often see her with a cigarette, while Jana is a blonde and is usually shown in domestic situations. Yet these archetypes are ultimately problematised and reversed as Vilma proves to be a less threatening romantic partner for Štěrba than his own wife. Significantly, the marriage is presented as unproductive (in the literal sense of the word – the Štěrbas have no children) and wholly lacking in harmony and understanding. In contrast, Vilma as the hardened and individualistic tramp demonstrates capability to stand by the man she loves (see Figure 6.2). Once again, *Scars of the Past* challenges the norms of socialist realism (and thereby audience's expectations) by contesting accepted tenets of communist society, in particular its emphasis on domesticity and family life. Just as in numerous film noirs,[38] the concepts of home, marriage, and family are called into question: instead of providing comfort and stability, they become causes of uneasiness and even hate.

The ending does suggest hope for Štěrba: in the attempt to save Vochoč's career he has found a hint of redemption and Vilma's faithfulness (demonstrated by her patiently waiting for the result of his surgery) is a promise that they might form a couple. Nevertheless, the film refuses to confirm any of such hypotheses. Krška and his collaborators do not dwell on any sense of moral or emotional uplift and instead end the picture with shots of the still unconscious Štěrba being carried away and Vilma, seen behind hospital bars, walking away from the camera. One thing is clear, though: while Štěrba's individual situation might change for the better after all, the impersonal, apathetic system, which caused his misery in the first place, remains the same.[39]

In a way, *Scars of the Past* presented its audiences with a highly humanistic message: that people should not be judged too harshly based on their momentary conduct. They are complex, often contradictory beings whose actions are determined by past events. When someone slips or goes astray, it is the society's obligation to offer a helping hand. In reality, though, this is hardly ever the case. As the original Czech title *Zde jsou lvi*[40] (taken from the Latin phrase *hic sunt leones*, here are lions) makes clear, we usually expect danger or wrongdoing from something we do not know or understand. Making such a statement at the height of socialism, when everyone was supposed to be unequivocally happy, was a bold gesture which, as we have seen, did not go unpunished.

Conclusion

Scars of the Past was released in August 1958, only a few months after the premiere of *Touch of Evil* (Orson Welles, 1958) and a full year before *Odds Against Tomorrow* (Robert Wise, 1959), two films which are often viewed as self-reflexive epitaphs to the classical film noir of the 1940s and 1950s and precursors to the neo-noir cycle that came into full bloom a decade later.[41] Contrary to Hollywood directors Orson Welles and Robert Wise, though, Václav Krška was not part of a rich film noir tradition, and in this chapter, I have not argued that he and his collaborators (mainly screenwriter Oldřich Daněk and cinematographer Jaroslav Tuzar) were consciously trying to imitate or react to models originating in the United States or elsewhere. Instead, I wished to demonstrate that their film's narrative, visual, and tonal affinity with film noir was a result of their sharp resistance to the restrictive norms of socialist realism. In this way, film noir's potential for ideological subversion becomes again apparent. In post-war Hollywood, film noir was often used to implicitly critique capitalism and class inequality and promote leftist ideas, as Dennis Broe has convincingly shown.[42] Ten years later, similar tropes were, ironically, mobilised to undermine the principles of the Czechoslovak communist regime.

Not surprisingly, then, *Scars of the Past*'s bold formal conception and ideological nonconformity led to its sharp dismissal from official circles. To add to some of the comments quoted earlier, Stanislav Zvoníček in *Film a doba* complained that the film was too dark and pessimistic and lacking in heroism, joy, and the poetry of contemporary life. Moreover, it was guilty of asking painful questions without offering at least a glimpse of a solution.[43] As late as 1972, film critic Jiří Hrbas was still embittered by the notion that the film 'devoted so much effort, energy, talent, and skill – but also other resources at society's disposal – to a depiction so full of shadows, gloom, darkness, and negation'.⁴⁴ Only in recent retrospect has it been recognised – for the very same reasons – as one of Krška's crowning achievements and a fitting candidate for the potentially interesting, though as yet necessarily tentative list of Czechoslovak film noirs.⁴⁵

Notes

My sincere thanks go to Kristýna Kovářová who helped me with bibliographic research for the chapter and, as always, my wife Ksenia. This work was supported by the grant of the Czech Ministry of Education, Youth, and Sports for specific research under Grant IGA_FF_2022_028.

1. See especially the many film noir guides and encyclopedias, for example Spencer Selby, *The Worldwide Film Noir Tradition* (Ames, IA: Sink Press, 2013), and John Grant, *A Comprehensive Encyclopedia of Film Noir: The Essential Reference Guide* (Milwaukee: Hal Leonard, 2013).
2. See Petr Szczepanik, '"Machři" a "diletanti": Základní jednotky filmové praxe v době reorganizací a politických zvratů 1945 až 1962', in *Naplánovaná kinematografie: Český filmový průmysl 1945 až 1960*, ed. Pavel Skopal (Praha: Academia, 2012), p. 56; Ivan Klimeš, 'Filmaři a komunistická moc v Československu: Vzrušený rok 1959', *Iluminace* 16, no. 4 (2004), p. 131.
3. František Kahuda, 'Za užší sepětí filmové výroby se životem lidu', *Iluminace* 16, no. 4 (2004), p. 183. Unless noted otherwise, all translations from Czech to English are mine.
4. Kahuda, 'Za užší sepětí filmové výroby se životem lidu', p. 183.
5. Jan Žalman, *Umlčený film* (Praha: KMa, 2008), p. 17.
6. In 1958, Tito resisted full integration into the Soviet-led Eastern bloc which resulted in curbing of political and cultural relations between Czechoslovakia and Yugoslavia. It is no coincidence that the central couple in *Three Wishes* was portrayed by Yugoslav actors Rade Marković and Tatjana Beljakova. For more on this subject, see Klimeš, 'Filmaři a komunistická moc v Československu', p. 134.
7. See Szczepanik, '"Machři" a "diletanti"', pp. 52–5.
8. See Valérie Pozner, '"Socialistický realismus" a jeho využití pro dějiny sovětské kinematografie', in *Film a dějiny 3: Politická kamera – film a stalinismus*, ed. Kristian Feigelson and Petr Kopal (Praha: Casablanca, Ústav pro studium totalitních režimů, 2012), pp. 17–24. The same conclusion is reached in Radka Mojžíšová, *Socialistický realismus v československém filmu 50. let 20. století* (MA thesis, Vysoká škola ekonomická v Praze, 2013).
9. Jiří Knapík, Martin Franc, et al., *Průvodce kulturním děním a životním stylem v českých zemích 1948–1967*, volume II (Praha: Academia, 2011), pp. 841–2.
10. See for instance Jan Lukeš, *Diagnózy času: Český a slovenský poválečný film (1945–2012)* (Praha: Slovart, 2013), p. 37; Petr Bilík, 'Kinematografie po druhé světové válce (1945–1970)', in *Panorama českého filmu*, ed. Luboš Ptáček (Olomouc: Rubico, 2000), pp. 95–7.
11. Peter Hames, *The Czechoslovak New Wave* (New York: Wallflower Press, 2005), p. 29.
12. Klimeš, 'Filmaři a komunistická moc v Československu', pp. 132–3.

13. For instance, Mark Bould claims that 'film noirs emerge from (discussions about) the interactions of style, narrative and theme'. See his *Film Noir: From Berlin to Sin City* (London and New York: Wallflower Press, 2005), p. 12.
14. David Bordwell, *Poetics of Cinema* (New York: Routledge, 2008), p. 28.
15. Bordwell, *Poetics of Cinema*, p. 28.
16. The difference between the two films is that while *Scars of the Past* merely refuses to share crucial information with us, *Mildred Pierce* intentionally deceives us. For more on the latter film's narrative strategies, see Bordwell, *Poetics of Cinema*, pp. 135–50. Another analogy can be provided by *Sunset Blvd.* (Billy Wilder, 1950) which in the beginning also arouses audience curiosity as to what caused the tragic death of screenwriter Joe Gillis (William Holden), who ends up floating in the pool of faded movie star Norma Desmond (Gloria Swanson). Wilder's film, however, does not replay the exact same scenes as is the case with *Scars of the Past*.
17. See J. P. Telotte, *Voices in the Dark: The Narrative Patterns of Film Noir* (Urbana and Chicago: University of Illinois Press, 1989), p. 24.
18. See Gilles Menegaldo, 'Flashbacks in Film Noir', *Sillages critiques* (June 2004), http://journals.openedition.org/sillagescritiques/1561; DOI: https://doi.org/10.4000/sillagescritiques.1561.
19. See for instance Stanislav Zvoníček, 'Zde jsou lvi . . .', *Film a doba* 4, no. 10 (1958), p. 705. See also the comment in Miroslav Kratochvíl, 'Co se děje ve filmu: Zde jsou lvi', *Divadelní noviny* 2, no. 1 (3 September 1958), p. 8.
20. This meant, for example, rejection of all forms of discontinuity editing and unmotivated point-of-view. See Pozner, '"Socialistický realismus" a jeho využití pro dějiny sovětské kinematografie', p. 18.
21. Janey Place and Lowell Peterson, 'Some Visual Motifs of *Film Noir*', *Film Noir Reader*, ed. Alain Silver and James Ursini (New York: Limelight Editions, 1996), pp. 65–75.
22. Václav Krška chose a similar visual concept for his stylistically extravagant biopic *Violin and Dream* (*Housle a sen*, 1946). See my analysis of the film in '"Pocit neomezené fantazie": *Housle a sen* a žánr životopisného filmu', in *Osudová osamělost: Obrysy filmové a literární tvorby Václava Kršky*, ed. Milan Hain and Milan Cyroň (Praha: Casablanca, 2016), pp. 102–36.
23. Other noirs with mining backgrounds include *I Live on Danger* (Sam White, 1942), *The Prowler* (Joseph Losey, 1951), and *Bad for Each Other* (Irving Rapper, 1953).
24. See for instance Zvoníček, 'Zde jsou lvi . . .', p. 705.
25. The filmmakers used a portable lamp which threw constantly shifting shadows on the walls.
26. Michal Večeřa, 'Expresivita ve filmu Zde jsou lvi', *25fps*, no. 56 (February/March 2014), http://25fps.cz/2014/zde-jsou-lvi/.
27. Žalman, *Umlčený film*, p. 16.
28. Jiří Hendrych, 'Zpráva o filmu "Tři přání"', 20 January 1959, *Iluminace* 16, no. 4 (2004), p. 152.
29. Oleg Homola (Member of Czechoslovak Parliament), 26 January 1959, transcript of oral report published in *Iluminace* 16, no. 4 (2004), p. 157.
30. Jan Nový, 'Kdo zde žije?', *Tvorba* 23, no. 34 (1958), p. 800.

31. See for example Jaroslav Boček, 'Zde jsou opravdu lvi', *Kultura*, no. 37 (1958), p. 4.
32. Zvoníček, 'Zde jsou lvi . . .', p. 705.
33. Robert Porfirio, 'No Way Out: Existential Motifs in the *Film Noir*', in *Film Noir Reader*, ed. Alain Silver and James Ursini (New York: Limelight Editions, 1996), pp. 77–93. See also Stephen Faison, *Existentialism, Film Noir, and Hard-Boiled Fiction* (Amherst, NY: Cambria Press, 2008).
34. See for instance Richard Dyer, *Stars* (London: British Film Institute, 1998), p. 112.
35. Bilík, 'Kinematografie po druhé světové válce', p. 115.
36. Veronika Zýková, 'Filmové herectví Karla Högera. Část IV. Zlaté období högerismu: 1957–1962', *25fps*, no. 36 (March 2010), http://25fps.cz/2010/filmove-herectvi-karla-hogera-cast-iv-zlate-obdobi-hogerismu-1957-1962/. The article was published as part of Karel Höger's profile that ran in *25fps* from December 2009 to June 2010, see http://25fps.cz/?s=karel+h%C3%B6ger.
37. The latter term is used by Jans B. Wager in *Dames in the Driver's Seat: Rereading Film Noir* (Austin: University of Texas Press, 2005), p. 4.
38. See for instance Sylvia Harvey, 'Woman's Place: The Absent Family of Film Noir', in *Women in Film Noir*, ed. E. Ann Kaplan (London: British Film Institute, 1998), pp. 35–46.
39. A sense of discomfort is emphasised by the absence of music during the end credits.
40. The English title *Scars of the Past* is given by the Czech National Film Archive. See 'Scars of the Past', *Filmový přehled*, https://www.filmovyprehled.cz/en/film/396320/scars-of-the-past. I have not been able to locate its exact origin, but it was under this title that the film was shown on several occasions at festivals or cinematheque screenings. Currently, the film is only available online or on DVD with original (Czech) audio track without English subtitles.
41. See for instance Foster Hirsch, *The Dark Side of the Screen: Film Noir* (Boston: Da Capo Press, 2001), p. 199; I have written about both films in Milan Hain, 'Film noir znovuzrozený: Počátky neonoiru v Americe', *Cinepur* 27, no. 118 (2018), pp. 48–52.
42. Dennis Broe, *Film Noir, American Workers, and Postwar Hollywood* (Gainesville: University Press of Florida, 2009).
43. Zvoníček, 'Zde jsou lvi . . .', p. 705.
44. Jiří Hrbas, 'Václav Krška: Lyrik českého filmu', *Film a doba* 18, no. 8 (1972), p. 407.
45. For practical reasons I am leaving the whole debate about the existence and specific character of Czech/Czechoslovak film noir aside. Let me just briefly mention that as one of the programmers of the annual Czech Noir Film Festival – now in its eleventh season – I have oftentimes pondered the question. Since the foundation of the festival in 2013 we have screened more than forty titles of Czech or Czechoslovak origin which are thematically or stylistically related to film noir. These have included *The Magic House* (*Kouzelný dům*, Otakar Vávra, 1939), *Guard 13* (*13. revír*, Martin Frič, 1946), *Conscience* (*Svědomí*, Jiří Krejčík, 1948), *. . . and the Fifth Horsemen Is Fear* (*. . . a pátý jezdec je Strach*, Zbyněk Brynych, 1965), *The Murderer Hides His Face* (*Vrah skrývá tvář*, Petr Schulhoff, 1966), *A Game Without Rules* (*Hra bez pravidel*, Jindřich Polák, 1967), *Alois Nebel* (Tomáš Luňák, 2011), and *Ve stínu* (*In the Shadow*, David Ondříček, 2012). *Scars of the Past* was screened at the third festival in 2015. For more information, visit https://www.noirfilmfestival.cz/en/.

7. THE DEADLY SEDUCTION OF A RAKE: BRITISH COSTUME MELODRAMA, NOIR, AND THE 'OTHERED' WOMAN IN *THE GYPSY AND THE GENTLEMAN*

Christopher Weedman

Produced and distributed by the Rank Organisation in Britain, *The Gypsy and the Gentleman* is generally considered one of American director Joseph Losey's least accomplished films. During its staggered release across London and the British provinces in January and February 1958, this costume melodrama was deemed a critical misfire and garnered mostly mixed to negative reviews.[1] Dick Richards of *Variety* found merit in Greek star Melina Mercouri's high-energy performance as 'a hopped-up Lady Macbeth, spreading sex, sin and sorrow with an abandon that will leave all but the most avid fan completely exhausted'.[2] Nevertheless, he insisted that British writer Janet Green's 'tired script' about a half-Romani, half-British woman's plot to seduce, marry, and swindle an early nineteenth-century British baronet was encumbered with 'every possible cliché in the romantic "meller" book'.[3]

Picturegoer magazine was similarly dismissive and declared, 'The first half of the film – in which director Joseph Losey catches superbly the bawdy, amoral, Hogarthian quality of the [Regency] period – is so much better than the plot-bedevilled second. And the brilliant colour photography [by Jack Hildyard] deserved a finer, more important, showcase.'[4] This ambivalent response was echoed by the pseudonymous J.A.D.C. of *The Monthly Film Bulletin*, who found it a 'florid barnstormer' and 'a curious choice' of projects for Losey. Due to the director's background helming the original English-language stage production of Bertolt Brecht's *Galileo* (Los Angeles and New York, 1947) and the socially conscious film noir *The Lawless* (1950), J.A.D.C. could not reconcile the incongruity between the artistic pedigree of the avant-garde and left-wing Losey and his supposedly lowbrow, popular source material: Nina Warner Hooke's 1956 Gothic romance novel *Darkness I Leave You*.[5]

Equally, if not more, disparaging of *The Gypsy and the Gentleman* was Losey himself. A victim of the Hollywood blacklist, Losey made the film amid his efforts to rebuild his career in London, where he took up residence, in 1953, to avoid testifying in front of the House Un-American Activities Committee (HUAC) about his Communist associations.[6] Years later, in an interview with Tom Milne, he described the film as 'a bitter story I don't want to go into' and, when approached again for comment by Gordon Gow, bluntly called it 'largely a piece of junk' and opined, 'I'd just as soon nobody saw it again.'[7] Losey's contempt stemmed from *The Gypsy and the Gentleman*'s turbulent production history. He admitted to Michel Ciment, 'I read it and I didn't like it that much, but I thought well, I can't go on turning down scripts.'[8] Losey had hoped to transform Green's adapted screenplay into something, in his view, artistically ambitious to fulfil the first film of a three-picture deal with Rank, which he signed in May 1957.[9] As demonstrated by his prior work in American, Italian, and British noir, the experimental Losey possessed a talent for reinvigorating genre formulas with psychologically complex narratives; intricate and ornate visual stylisation; and topical themes (sometimes thinly veiled as subtext) such as the blacklist (*The Intimate Stranger*, 1956), capital punishment (*Time without Pity*, 1957), class antagonism (*The Lawless*; *The Prowler*, 1951; and *Stranger on the Prowl/Imbarco a mezzanotte*, 1952), criminal rehabilitation (*The Sleeping Tiger*, 1954), mob violence (*The Lawless* and *M*, 1951), and racial prejudice (*The Lawless* and the nightclub scene in *The Big Night*, 1951).

In retrospect, Losey and Rank, among the most formulaic and conservative of Britain's film corporations in the 1950s, were strange bedfellows and a partnership fated to go awry. Assessing this period of Rank filmmaking, Charles Drazin characterises it as a working environment where 'originality or creativity could not possibly thrive'.[10] Considering these conditions, it comes as little surprise that Rank's managing director John Davis clashed with Losey shortly after the film started shooting on 11 June 1957.[11] Among other disagreements, Davis was upset with Losey and uncredited production designer Richard Macdonald's decision to create an earthier visual design that conveyed the Regency period as 'cruel and dirty and not just lovely and elegant'.[12] Ultimately, Losey and Davis had an irrevocable falling-out when Davis commissioned a musical score by Austro-Hungarian composer Hans May without the director's input. In protest of a score that he believed 'slowed the picture' and 'changed the mood and the pace', Losey abandoned the project in post-production and, as a result, found himself dropped from his Rank contract.[13] Subsequently, Losey repudiated the film and unsuccessfully tried to block its retrospective screening at the La Royale Cinéma in Paris in October 1981, almost three years before his death on 22 June 1984 at the age of seventy-five.[14]

In the decades since its release, *The Gypsy and the Gentleman* has received minor attention in the biographies and scholarly studies of Losey by James Leahy, Gene D. Phillips, Foster Hirsch, Edith de Rham, James Palmer and Michael Riley, and David Caute. There has been a critical propensity to give the film short shrift – often recounting Losey's poor working experience and/or adhering to J.A.D.C.'s initial assessment of the film as 'a curious' diversion in the director's oeuvre – before moving ahead to his more highly regarded British and Continental European genre and art-house films such as *The Criminal* (1960), *Eve* (1962), *The Servant* (1963), *Accident* (1967), *The Go-Between* (1971), and *Mr. Klein* (*Monsieur Klein*, 1976).[15] Indicative of these tendencies is Hirsch, who insists:

> [*The Gypsy and the Gentleman*] is played for story value in a way that Losey's other films of the period are not, and the director simply hasn't the temperament for stage-managing a pulpy Regency romance. He has neither the humor to mock gently the improbable narrative conventions nor the patience to treat the coincidences and climaxes with proper respect.[16]

Among the few exceptions is Colin Gardner, who discusses the film in relationship to Losey's complication of genre tropes from British costume melodramas, particularly those produced by Gainsborough Pictures – a former semi-autonomous production unit of Rank – in Britain during the 1940s.[17] While Gardner convincingly argues that *The Gypsy and the Gentleman* 'muddies' the generic themes and conventions of Gainsborough-style costume melodrama, he does not connect this to Losey's recurring tendency to fuse noir elements within other genres and styles.[18]

This chapter aims to complicate Gardner's reading, as well as build upon my own prior reading of Losey's use of noir and genre hybridity in *The Servant*, to demonstrate how *The Gypsy and the Gentleman* exhibits a noir-informed sensibility, particularly in its first half and dark conclusion.[19] The noir elements within this costume melodrama help foreground the film's veiled critique of post-war British fears regarding sexual promiscuity and miscegenation in late 1950s Britain. These fears are embodied in the seductive characterisation of the Regency villainess Belle (Melina Mercouri), whose duplicitous disposition, uninhibited sexuality, and liminal identity as a half-Romani, half-British woman destabilises hegemonic notions of post-war British sexuality and racial/ethnic identity. Moreover, in a chaste late-1950s period of Rank filmmaking that generally depicted women as 'biddable creatures who enjoy the supposed benefits of the patriarchal order', the sexually and socially transgressive 'Other' Belle serves as a harbinger of the type of daring female performances that would become more commonplace in British cinema after the arrival of the New Wave films at the end of the 1950s.[20] By melding themes, styles, and character types from noir within the costume melodrama in *The Gypsy and the Gentleman*, Losey creates an intriguing genre hybrid that is less a strange career detour and instead an extension of his arresting work in noir during the 1950s and early 1960s.

British Costume Melodrama and Noir's Dark Interrelationship

The Gypsy and the Gentleman's relationship with noir was first posited by Raymond Durgnat, who, in his 1971 book *A Mirror for England: British Movies from Austerity to Affluence*, described Losey's Regency-set costume melodrama as 'a *film noir* in Technicolor'.[21] Subsequently, the film has gotten little, if any, critical scrutiny as a noir, including no mention in Michael F. Keaney's 2008 annotated filmography *British Film Noir Guide*.[22] In retrospect, it is not surprising that Durgnat advocated for the noir consideration of a film that expanded the cycle's traditional categorical definitions: national cinema (American); genre (crime melodrama/thriller); temporal setting (present day); and visual style (black-and-white cinematography). As explained in Durgnat's earlier article 'Paint It Black: The Family Tree of the *Film Noir*', he considered noir to be 'a bleak, cynical tone' as opposed to a genre or style in the strictest sense. Durgnat contended that this tone 'invaded' a range of national cinemas and genres before, during, and after World War II, including Britain with 'the best pre-war Hitchcocks' *Rich and Strange* (1931) and *Sabotage* (1936); the 'man-on-the-run films' *Odd Man Out* (Carol Reed, 1947), *They Made Me a Fugitive* (Alberto Cavalcanti, 1947), and *Secret People* (Thorold Dickinson, 1952); and 'an effective series of costume bullying dramas' such as *Gaslight* (Dickinson, 1940), *The Man in Grey* (Leslie Arliss, 1943), and *Fanny by Gaslight* (Anthony Asquith, 1944).[23] He found *The Gypsy and the Gentleman* more unconventional than most classical noirs due to how the film 'negates the genre's negation, to the effect that fate or the system will cross us whatever we do'.[24] Yet, despite recognising how noir permeated multiple British costume melodramas during the 1940s, Durgnat's assessment of *The Gypsy and the Gentleman* as a noir remains too brief to fully support this assertion. In order to build upon Durgnat's observation and better understand the complex interplay of costume melodrama and noir elements within Losey's film, it is vital to recognise the strong similitude between these two strains of popular British cinema, which share thematic, stylistic, and ideological commonalities.

British cinema's costume melodrama and noir cycles of the 1940s and 1950s are both widely interpreted as cinematic manifestations of the social tensions and upheavals that Britain endured during World War II (1939–45) and the 'age of austerity' (1945–51), the latter marked by post-war readjustment, high unemployment, prolonged rationing, black marketeering, and slow reconstruction from the

Blitz.²⁵ The era's genre films confronted these social concerns with varying degrees of narrative distance. According to Tony Williams, the films did not

> reflect social problems directly. They rather focus[ed] indirectly on contemporary issues. Various British contemporary genres such as costume melodrama, *film noir*, social melodrama, and crime thriller echoed the uneasy situation of a society in which things were felt to be changing. Unease and uncertainty occurred over what exactly would happen and whether it would be positive.²⁶

Noirs tended to address these contemporary conditions in a more conspicuous fashion than costume melodramas due to the former's penchant for present-day settings and a recurring thematic interest in wartime and post-war crime and urban desolation.²⁷ Conversely, costume melodramas often dealt with these issues obliquely, through an allegorical story set in the historical past with additional narrative distance necessitated by the foregrounding of 'bodice-ripping' romance. Despite their differences, both costume melodramas and noirs regularly raised the ire of establishment British critics of the period, who considered them an affront to 'good taste' and diametrically opposed to the social realist films they usually championed.²⁸

During this period, British costume melodramas were epitomised by the dark sensual style of Gainsborough Pictures, whose 1943 hit *The Man in Grey* served as a prototype. As Sue Harper explains, Gainsborough costume melodramas were frequently woman-centred narratives with 'a rich visual texture' and an 'upper class gentry' milieu, usually set during the Regency (1811–20) or Victorian (1837–1901) periods. She observes how the films generally concerned upper-class-aspiring women, 'often with gypsy blood, who seek sexual pleasure and who are ritually dispatched'.²⁹ Gainsborough costume melodramas provided 1940s British female audiences with a rare cinematic space to vicariously derive pleasure from watching women subvert dominant class, gender, and sexual structures, but the untimely deaths of these 'wicked ladies' – much like the demises of femme fatales in noir – enabled class and patriarchal norms to be restored by the conclusion.³⁰ This recurring motif is arguably best exemplified by *The Man in Grey*'s sadomasochistic image of the social climbing Hesther Shaw (Margaret Lockwood) being whipped to death with a riding crop by her lover, Lord Rohan (James Mason), for the murder of his wife.³¹

While sharing a similar transgressive impulse to obtain greater social and sexual agency, British cinema's wicked ladies and femme fatales, as observed in the scholarship of Robert Murphy and Melanie Bell, were seldom depicted as full-blooded psychopaths in the vein of archetypal American noir seductress Phyllis Dietrichson (Barbara Stanwyck) in *Double Indemnity* (Billy Wilder, 1944). Murphy finds Margaret Lockwood's Hesther in *The Man in Grey* and

Barbara Worth in *The Wicked Lady* (Arliss, 1945) to be 'essentially boisterous, good-natured villainesses, bold but unthreatening . . .', while Bell reads these depictions more generously, instead 'embody[ing] a type of fatal femininity which was inflected through a domestic lens, seemingly at odds with commonplace understandings of the "Hollywood" *femme fatale*, but rooted in a specifically British context and arguably as, or perhaps even more, threatening because of its very domesticity'.[32] At first glance, these types of sensationalist narratives would appear to be in complete opposition to the religious beliefs of J. Arthur Rank, the staunch Methodist flour magnet and owner of Gainsborough's parent company, the Rank Organisation. As Geoffrey Macnab explains, Lord Rank typically did not condone films that he deemed 'morally dubious', but he permitted Gainsborough to make costume melodramas without significant interference due to his belief that they were essentially 'moral fables: the wicked ladies always got their come-uppance and patriarchal Christian good always prevailed'.[33]

The British costume melodrama cycle of the 1940s and early 1950s was so closely identified with Gainsborough that the films have often been loosely referred to as 'Gainsborough' or 'Gainsborough-style' melodramas, but this terminology is problematic. It is important to note that Gainsborough produced films in a variety of other genres and styles during this period, notably contemporary (or, near-contemporary) domestic melodramas such as *Love Story* (Arliss, 1944), *They Were Sisters* (Arthur Crabtree, 1945), and *When the Bough Breaks* (Lawrence Huntington, 1947); and noirs such as *Waterloo Road* (Sidney Gilliat, 1945), *Dear Murderer* (Crabtree, 1947), and *The Upturned Glass* (Huntington, 1947). Furthermore, as seen in the criticism and scholarship of Durgnat, Keaney, Williams, William K. Everson, R. Barton Palmer, and Andrew Spicer, several costume melodramas – including some made by other companies in the wake of Gainsborough's financial success – have been argued to belong (or, be generically adjacent) to British cinema's noir cycle: notably Cineguild's *Blanche Fury* (Marc Allégret, 1948); Ealing's *Pink String and Sealing Wax* (Robert Hamer, 1945) and *Saraband for Dead Lovers* (Basil Dearden, 1948); Gainsborough's *The Man in Grey*, *Fanny by Gaslight*, *The Wicked Lady*, *Caravan* (Crabtree, 1946), and *Jassy* (Crabtree, 1947); Paramount British's *So Evil My Love* (Lewis Allen, 1948); Premier's *Idol of Paris* (Arliss, 1948); and Two Cities' *Hungry Hill* and *The Mark of Cain* (both Brian Desmond Hurst, 1947).[34] The films were diverse in subject matter, but several contained noirish plots concerning blackmail, murder, thievery, and/or doomed romances set against a morally or socially corrupt historical backdrop. In many instances, the directors and cinematographers of British costume melodramas and noirs moved back and forth between both cycles and frequently imbued these analogous dark-themed narratives with chiaroscuro cinematography and other expressionistic elements derived from German Expressionism, French Poetic

Realism, and classical American noir.[35] Because of the high degree of generic and stylistic hybridity seen in noirish costume melodramas like *Blanche Fury* and *Saraband for Dead Lovers*, the broad and amorphous category of British noir, as Williams aptly notes, 'may cause sleepless nights to critics preoccupied with rigidly statistical and taxonomic definitions but not to those aware of the fluid nature of generic forms'.[36]

The Gypsy and the Gentleman is a generically liminal film, which benefits from the complex hybridic approach to genre analysis advocated by Williams. A fusion of the conventions, styles, and ideological applications of both costume melodrama and noir, Losey's film was made by Rank during a fallow period when the costume melodrama was no longer achieving the same level of economic success in Britain. Not only did Rank shut down its Gainsborough production unit in 1949, but, throughout most of the 1950s, the company turned much of its attention to making light comedies aimed at domestic middle-class audiences, such as *Genevieve* (Henry Cornelius, 1953) and *Doctor in the House* (Ralph Thomas, 1954).[37] *The Gypsy and the Gentleman*, along with the earlier release *Dangerous Exile* (Hurst, 1957), was part of a short-lived attempt by Rank in the late 1950s to revive the costume melodrama in the style popularised by Gainsborough. Both shot in Eastmancolor on large budgets, the two productions were among a slate of twenty films – made in various genres at a reported cost of $14 million – that Rank designed to penetrate the lucrative US box office.[38] *Dangerous Exile* and *The Gypsy and the Gentleman* were discussed in the British press as boasting wicked lady characters (respectively played by Anne Heywood and Mercouri) evocative of those played by Lockwood in *The Man in Grey* and *The Wicked Lady*.[39]

The female antagonist Belle in *The Gypsy and the Gentleman* is depicted as a fiercely manipulative seductress with an unyielding desire to garner the wealth and social status of an aristocratic British lady – a title unfairly denied her due to her taboo parentage as the illegitimate daughter of a sexual affair between a British nobleman and a Romani woman. She holds a quasi-hypnotic control over the film's male protagonist, the downwardly mobile baronet Sir Paul Deverill (Keith Michell), who, as Hirsch observes, can be read as 'a preliminary version of the effete, well-born Tony in *The Servant* . . . an essentially weak character – easily seduced, and easily controlled'.[40] Moreover, anticipating the French femme fatale Eva Olivier's (Jeanne Moreau) domination of the Welsh novelist Tyvian Jones (Stanley Baker) in Losey's noir-informed psychological melodrama *Eve*, Deverill becomes emotionally and sexually dependent on Belle. Belle conspires with her male Romani lover, Jess (Patrick McGoohan), to blackmail Deverill into marrying her in order to take control of his country manor, Deverill Court.[41] 'I've lived my mother's way too long. If I'm to live my father's, I'll be the lady of the house', Belle insists to her future husband. This female subjugation of the male is suggested in the film's UK poster artwork.

Wearing both a devious grin and a low-cut, dark green bodice dress with a pink cape, Belle is positioned prominently in the left foreground of the image with her rival male suitors, Deverill and Jess, situated behind her. However, despite often exhibiting a callousness more akin to American noir femme fatales than Lockwood's wicked lady portrayals, Belle's agency is partially mitigated by having her own dependence on the virile Jess, who is pictured hovering over the other two members of this deadly love triangle in the right background of the poster.

The Gypsy and the Gentleman's reconfiguration of the wicked lady into a more explicitly transgressive noir femme fatale is complemented by a crime plot (involving an inheritance scheme, extortion, kidnapping, and unjustified psychiatric commitment) and gritty production design that minimises the level of opulence often associated with the costume melodrama. The film also adapts iconography associated with noir to a Regency setting, notably seedy locales such as back-room gambling venues, rowdy boxing matches, and unscrupulous bedlams. This unseemliness is heightened by Losey and cinematographer Jack Hildyard's employment of 'washed-out colour', designed to invoke the style of British artist Thomas Rowlandson's Georgian-era caricatures.[42] This muted Eastmancolor palate largely eschews the vibrant cinematography found in more conventional Rank productions in favour of a more soiled and shabby look.[43] In this respect, Losey and Hildyard's aesthetic can also be viewed as a colour variation of *film gris* ('gray film'), a visual style that Thom Andersen argues is recurrent in noirs from blacklisted American filmmakers with prominent left-wing themes. Not only have Losey's American noirs *The Lawless* and *The Prowler* been cited by Andersen as exemplars of *film gris* due to their 'drab and depressing' lighting, but elsewhere I have argued that this look is also characteristic of Losey and cinematographer Douglas Slocombe's British film *The Servant*.[44] *The Gypsy and the Gentleman*'s use of 'washed-out colour' achieves the same objective of *film gris* by highlighting a decaying British aristocracy, whose greed, selfishness, and moral depravity is slowly eating through the country's false façade of social respectability.

In addition to Losey's extensive work in noir, this narrative and visual style was familiar to other members of the film's creative team. Hildyard, costume designer Julie Harris, production designer Richard Macdonald, art director Ralph W. Brinton, editor Reginald Beck, and producer Maurice Cowan collectively worked on such key British noirs as *Thunder Rock* (Roy Boulting, 1942), *Odd Man Out*, *They Made Me a Fugitive*, *Good-Time Girl* (David MacDonald, 1948), *Turn the Key Softly* (Jack Lee, 1953), *Cast a Dark Shadow* (Lewis Gilbert, 1955), and Losey's own *The Intimate Stranger*. Perhaps, most crucially, screenwriter Green was responsible for penning the 'couple-on-the-run' noir *The Clouded Yellow* (Thomas, 1950) and the 1952 stage play *Murder Mistaken*, which served as the basis of *Cast a Dark Shadow*. Losey gave Green a backhanded compliment by labelling her 'a very successful writer of *a certain kind* of novel'.[45] However, to her credit, Green was a significant post-war British filmmaker in her own right and instrumental in collaborating with director Basil Dearden to employ a noir crime narrative framework to explore such social issues as racism and racial passing in *Sapphire* (1959) and homosexual desire in *Victim* (1961).[46]

A Liminal Noir Analysis of *The Gypsy and the Gentleman*

With this generic interrelationship in mind, this section will analyse *The Gypsy and the Gentleman*'s noir inflection of the wicked lady, particularly as a reflection of growing cultural anxiety about female sexual promiscuity and miscegenation. Not only did the September 1957 release of the Wolfenden Report with its legal recommendations on how to curb prostitution highlight British apprehension about female sexuality outside of the traditional parameters of marriage and motherhood, but also the August–September 1958 race riots in Nottingham and Notting Hill brought white British fears of increased immigration to the national forefront.[47] Admittedly, *The Gypsy and the Gentleman*'s production timeline (June to September 1957) indicates that the film could not have been a direct comment on these specific events.[48] Nonetheless, the relative concurrence of these events with the film's depiction of then-taboo female sexuality and racial/ethnic prejudice suggests that the era's social tensions were becoming increasingly palpable. If *The Gypsy and the Gentleman* can be read by Durgnat, Hirsch, and Neil Sinyard as a thematic precursor to the class issues in Losey's *The Servant*, this noirish costume melodrama should also be rightfully interpreted as an antecedent to Green's BAFTA-nominated script for the noir *Sapphire*, which subsequently dealt with themes of transgressive female sexuality and racial/ethnic prejudice in a more pronounced manner.[49]

The Gypsy and the Gentleman opens with a close-up of a burning torch mounted on the doorway of a gentleman's club in Regency-era London. Inside this seemingly respectable all-male establishment, the film's anti-hero, Deverill, is found tucked away in the dark cellar, where he is surrounded by a raucous group of upper-class gentlemen. They are placing bets on whether Deverill will break the club record by holding onto a soaped pig for twenty-two seconds straight. A proud bachelor and lascivious rake, Deverill is seemingly cocksure of his male prowess, but his masculinity is quickly undermined. After the squealing animal is lathered with soap, one of the other gentlemen announces to Deverill, 'Mademoiselle the piglet awaits your attention.' These words implicitly draw upon the derogatory slang terms 'pig' and 'sow', which have long been used as pejorative epithets for 'a promiscuous or unattractive woman' and 'slovenly woman', respectively.[50] Moreover, considering that Deverill is unable to keep a hold of the animal, the scene foreshadows the fact that he is weak and doomed to be conquered by the 'promiscuous' and 'slovenly' Belle as well. This prognostication is further emphasised when Losey and Beck cut from a ground-level medium shot of the defeated Deverill lying on the floor of the cellar (a position indicating that he will ultimately hit rock bottom both economically and emotionally) to a long shot of Belle walking over a morning hillside with Jess. The linking of these images, as Leahy observes, 'suggests the presence of some kind of fate or destiny at work, drawing Deverill and Belle inevitably together'.[51] Unknowingly, the future lovers are on a collision course, which will lead to both their marriage and eventual deaths.

The characterisation of Deverill as a man on a doomed trajectory is in keeping with his identity as a Hogarthian rake. First popularised as a stock character in Restoration comedy, the rake is an idle and debauched libertine of inherited wealth, who later in the eighteenth century became synonymous with the character Tom Rakewell from British artist William Hogarth's eight-part series of paintings 'A Rake's Progress' (1732–4). According to Harold Weber, the rake broke 'from earlier characters and traditions, not simply because of his compulsive behavior, but also because of his overt concern with the sexual act itself'.[52] *The Gypsy and the Gentleman* connects Deverill with the Hogarthian rake through his surname, which is an apparent amalgamation of Devil and Rakewell. Losey and Macdonald regularly drew inspiration from art history, the director mentioning to Milne and Ciment that he consulted Rowlandson's caricatures while making *The Gypsy and the Gentleman*.[53] Nevertheless, the Hogarthian rake had regained cultural prominence after World War II through the film characters Sir Vivian Kenway (Rex Harrison) in the British comedy-drama *The Rake's Progress* (Gilliat, 1945) and Monte Beragon (Zachary Scott) in the American noir/domestic melodrama *Mildred Pierce* (Michael Curtiz, 1945), which were two of the most popular films in Britain during the late 1940s.[54] In a marked departure from Rakewell's horrific death from tertiary syphilis that he contracted from engaging in an orgy with sex workers, Kenway was partially redeemed from his disreputable life through his self-sacrificing wartime service in Gilliat's loosely inspired contemporary adaptation. Conversely, Beragon more closely resembled Rakewell by dying from the consequences of indulging in proscribed sexual acts – in his case, an extramarital affair with his teenage stepdaughter Veda (Ann Blyth).

Due to the generally conservative nature of both Rank and the pre-Trevelyan British Board of Film Censors (BBFC) in the late 1950s, it is unlikely that Losey and Green would have ever been permitted to depict Deverill engaged in anything resembling an orgy or quasi-incest like Rakewell and Beragon, respectively.[55] At the same time, *The Gypsy and the Gentleman* aligns Deverill with the then taboo act of interethnic sex and miscegenation through his tempestuous relationship with Belle and his unusual protectiveness of his young maid, Hattie (Catherine Feller), who, as Leahy and Gardner both observe, is implied to be his illegitimate daughter from an earlier sexual encounter with a different

Romani woman.[56] Losey's films displayed a recurring thematic interest in miscegenous desire. The noir *The Big Night* includes a key scene where Georgie La Main (John Drew Barrymore) confesses his attraction to an African American nightclub singer Terry Angelus (Mauri Leighton). 'You're so beautiful, even if you are a . . .', the teenager says before catching himself from inadvertently using a racial slur – an indication that he is unable to reconcile his dual feelings of sexual desire and racial prejudice. Moreover, in *The Servant*, there is suggestion that Barrett (Dirk Bogarde) and Tony (James Fox) are both engaged, or at least interested, in interracial sex. Their desire is implied by the repeated shots of a painting of a multiracial woman that, over the course of the film, is moved from Barrett's bedroom to the dining room as Barrett starts to gain control of his master's town house.[57] In both *The Gypsy and the Gentleman* and *The Servant*, these moments of actual and implied transgressive sexuality indicate the blurring and erosion of traditional British demarcations of class, race/ethnicity, and sexuality, which, in each film, underscores the aristocracy and upper class's growing inability to keep up its false veneer of respectability.

Deverill's inherited wealth and baronetcy have afforded him the privilege of indulging in vice and idle living. However, due to his self-indulgent behaviour, he finds himself on the brink of bankruptcy. Deverill is at risk of losing his ancestral home, Deverill Court, where he resides with his unmarried, twenty-year-old sister, Sarah (June Laverick). His downwardly mobile status prohibits him from being able to pay for Sarah to attend a social season in London, where she could be introduced to eligible men of her own class and breeding. Nonetheless, he insists that Sarah follow Regency-era aristocratic marriage norms by wedding for economic and social betterment. Sarah, however, is adamant that she will instead marry her true love: a middle-class medical student, John Patterson (Lyndon Brook). The future doctor has promised to propose to her after he is able to support her financially. Deverill tells Patterson, 'Kings marry queens, boy. Lords marry ladies. Find yourself another sawbones and wed his sister.' He cannot afford for either he or his sister to break away from marriage traditions. Given his fear of bankruptcy, Deverill reluctantly proposes to Vanessa (Clare Austin), the modest daughter of wealthy gentry landowner Ruddock (Newton Blick) to pay off his debts.

The potential unions of Deverill and Vanessa, and Patterson and Sarah represent the changing marital values (i.e. marrying for profit vs. marrying for love) that took place as Britain moved into the Victorian period. Yet, before the Deverill and Ruddock families can be legally joined, Deverill's plans are upended with the arrival of Belle, who, in her own desire to use marriage as a means to improve her economic and social standing, causes Deverill to give into his libidinous impulses and instead marry for sex. A vivacious woman, she holds a liminal position in society as the illegitimate offspring of a British nobleman and a Romani travelling woman. Belle was rejected by both parents, each of whom feared ostracisation from their communities due to her multi-ethnic identity.[58] After being left in a ditch by her mother, she was raised, in her own words, by 'the wind, the trees, the sun, the brook, the night'. While rural rather than urban, Belle's youth can be seen as analogous to noir women who leave abusive homes, orphanages, or borstals to live a difficult life on the street. Also like many a femme fatale, Belle turned to crime to try and overcome her financial hardship. While denied access from birth to the aristocracy due to her multi-ethnic identity, Belle's ability to enjoy the unmitigated social privileges of white Britishness are impeded by her half-Romani heritage, since, as sociologist Emily Webb explains, Romani Travellers are situated 'at the bottom of a hierarchy of whiteness' in Britain. According to Webb, they 'emphatically fail to meet the ideals expected from performances of white racial identity and, thus, remain stigmatized "white others" existing on the margins of society'.[59] Because Belle lives at the edges of mainstream British culture, she feels a conflicting combination of intense pride for her half-British parentage as well as ethnic self-loathing at being constantly called a 'gypsy'. This compels her to prove that she is indeed her 'father's daughter' and deserving of the same level of respect as a white, non-Romani British noblewoman.

Belle finds her gateway to social mobility when she encounters Deverill at an outdoor travelling fair, which possesses an unsavoury ambience comparable to the disreputable sports venues found in British noirs such as *Night and the City* (Jules Dassin, 1950), *The Gambler and the Lady* (Patrick Jenkins and Sam Newfield, 1952), and *The Square Ring* (Dearden, 1953). The fair is populated by a cross-section of people from various class statuses (peasant, bourgeois, and noble), who are shown drinking, gambling, and watching bare-fisted boxing in a rural setting far from the disapproving eyes of polite society.[60] When Belle is caught pickpocketing Deverill's miser purse during the match, she must fend off an angry mob, which hurls ethnic slurs and threats as they attempt to apprehend her: 'a gypo', 'make sport of her', 'put her in the stocks', and 'tie her to the cart'. Deverill is instantly attracted to the feisty Belle, whose bold uninhibited sexuality is indicated by Losey and Harris's decision to drape her in a low-cut, red bodice dress that sets her apart from the other women at the travelling fair. Based on Belle's sexual allure, Deverill comes to her rescue and falsely insists that the theft was a misunderstanding. However, as indicated by a British peasant woman retorting, 'what matter, she's a gypo', it is clear that the mob was just as, if not more, fuelled by their own prejudice than the crime itself. After finally quelling the mob, the smiling Deverill reveals his rakish sensibilities by caddishly striking Belle's buttocks with a riding crop (a sadomasochistically tinged gesture that recalls the previously mentioned climax from *The Man in Grey*) and throwing her his miser purse. 'For your trouble', he tells her. As she makes her way through the crowd, Belle proudly twirls the miser purse with a devilish grin. Not only does she realise that Deverill's gallantry was sexually motivated, but, as suggested by her handling of the miser purse, she knows that he is easy prey.

Belle and her Romani lover Jess – who similarly views Deverill as 'a pigeon to be plucked' – set out to swindle the baronet of his supposed (but non-existent) fortune.[61] Later that evening, the couple arrange for Belle to stand alongside the road as Deverill and Sarah's carriage drives past in the rain. After offering Belle a ride, Deverill and Sarah take her back to Deverill Court to provide her with shelter for the night. Sexual tension is exhibited between Deverill and Belle as they exchange glances before retiring. Losey and Hildyard frame the two characters in a high-angle shot with Deverill standing at the top of the staircase and Belle positioned at the bottom. The framing highlights the class, gender, and ethnic inequities between Deverill and Belle and, more subversively, indicates Belle's aspirations to transcend her impoverished nomadic life and become, in her words, 'lady of the house'. Anticipating the changing power dynamics between master/servant and upper class/working class that Losey and screenwriter Harold Pinter subsequently explored in *The Servant*, these roles start to slowly reverse after Belle is invited into Deverill's bedroom later that same night. This implied sexual encounter marks the beginning of the seduction plot against the unsuspecting baronet and, as a result, moves him from a position of dominance in the illicit relationship to one of increasing subservience (see Figure 7.1).

Figure 7.1 The rakish Deverill (Keith Michell) succumbs to the seductive Belle (Melina Mercouri). © Photofest

According to Deborah Epstein Nord, the image of the 'Gypsy seductress' was a long-time British literary stock character and presented as 'the welcome object of male desire', but, as Johanna Laitila explains, the character type garnered new wartime and post-war-era resonance through Gainsborough costume melodramas.[62] Interethnic sexual relations between British and Romani characters figure prominently in the plots of Gainsborough's noirish costume melodramas *Caravan* and *Jassy*. Mirroring Belle in *The Gypsy and the Gentleman*, the Romani women in these films are aligned with exoticism, promiscuity, and sexual agency. Nonetheless, with the exception of *Jassy*'s last-minute reconciliation between the half-Romani, half-British woman Jassy Woodroffe (Lockwood) and the downwardly mobile British aristocrat Barney Hatton (Dermot Walsh), Gainsborough costume melodramas usually stopped short of fully endorsing their interethnic romances. Instead, there was a tendency to kill off their Romani women – notably Rosal (Jean Kent) in *Caravan* – and return to the traditional values of endogamy by the conclusion of the narrative.[63] The same doomed fate will also be true of Belle in *The Gypsy and the Gentleman*, but her death will be depicted in a darker manner that lacks the same level of pathos shown to Rosal, who takes a bullet for her British husband, Richard Darrell (Stewart Granger).

Interestingly, interethnic and interracial marriages were neither illegal nor socially uncommon in Britain prior to World War II.[64] However, the increase in anti-immigration and xenophobic sentiment after the war – exacerbated by the rising tide of immigrants from the West Indies and other territories during the early years of decolonisation – resulted in increasingly hostile response to these unions. 'The policing of sexual boundaries was seen as central to the maintenance of the nation, and "miscegenation" became a major theme of race discourse in the late 1940s', historian Wendy Webster explains.[65] This escalating antagonism towards racial and ethnic outsiders is reflected in the way Belle is presented in comparison to other Romani women from earlier costume melodramas. Whereas the Romani women in *Caravan* and *Jassy* are depicted in a generally compassionate light – in part due to the fact that they are respectively played by prominent white, non-Romani British stars Kent and Lockwood – Belle in *The Gypsy and the Gentleman* is portrayed, in the blunt words of Caute, as 'an undeviating bitch' with minimal empathy.[66] Green was seemingly attuned to this disturbing change in cultural attitudes towards interethnic and interracial relationships and, shortly after the release of *The Gypsy and the Gentleman*, wrote the script for *Sapphire*. This 1959 Rank release examined post-war Britain's racial tensions through the lens of a noir murder mystery about the stabbing of a pregnant multiracial woman, Sapphire Robbins (played by the white pin-up model Yvonne Buckingham), who is killed for passing as white and engaging in miscegenation. Regrettably, Belle is portrayed in what Jill Nelmes describes as 'a one-dimensional' manner without the general 'sensitivity' to racial and ethnic representations that Green and

Dearden later displayed in *Sapphire*.[67] Yet, at the same time, the scenes of prejudice and xenophobia in *The Gypsy and the Gentleman* – notably the previously mentioned travelling fair sequence, and the repeated scenes of Deverill's household servants treating Belle hostilely and calling her a 'gypsy' – can be read as a subversively coded rumination on post-war British attitudes towards race and ethnicity, which the noirs *Pool of London* (Dearden, 1951) and *Sapphire*, and the social dramas *Flame in the Streets* (Roy Ward Baker, 1961), *A Taste of Honey* (Tony Richardson, 1961), *The Wind of Change* (Vernon Sewell, 1961), and *Jemima + Johnny* (Lionel Ngakane, 1965) addressed in more direct ways.

Furthermore, the representation of Belle as an exoticised 'Other' aligns with classical British cinema's long history of importing Continental European stars to portray characters that, in the words of Macnab, 'jar the social, political and sexual equilibrium'.[68] Following the brief heyday of Lockwood's wicked lady characters in the early-to-mid 1940s, British cinema generally reverted back to its pre-war tradition of casting international stars to play female characters deemed too risqué or beyond the pale of British 'good taste'. Despite some notable exceptions including native-born British stars Googie Withers, Diana Dors, and, albeit very briefly, Joan Collins, British filmmakers in the late 1940s and 1950s tended to secure the services of such international actresses as France's Brigitte Bardot, Mylène Demongeot, Juliette Gréco, Simone Signoret, and Odile Versois; Italy's Claudia Cardinale, Marla Landi, and Milly Vitale; Norway's Greta Gynt; and Sweden's Mai Zetterling when casting these types of women's roles. According to Macnab, this predilection was, in part, an industry effort to produce films with greater global marketability, but, as Harper and Bell have demonstrated, it was also symptomatic of a larger cultural reticence to portray British women in a manner that laid outside the traditional patriarchal conceptions of womanhood.[69] The prevalence of Continental European actresses in British films led to a widespread, yet erroneous, perception that the country's home-grown female stars lacked the sex appeal of their international counterparts. This attitude can be seen in Dick Richards's profile of Mercouri during the making of *The Gypsy and the Gentleman*, particularly in his comment that the Greek star exuded 'an earthy loveliness which seems to be the trump that most Continental actresses hold when playing their acting hand'.[70]

Losey cast Mercouri as Belle on the strength of her prior work in the Greek melodrama *Stella* (Στέλλα, Michael Cacoyannis, 1955).[71] A Golden Globe-winning modern adaptation of French author Prosper Mérimée's 1845 novella *Carmen*, the film featured Mercouri in a 'violent, sensuous, electrifying' performance as a Rebetiko singer with a fierce independence and a penchant for short-term sexual relationships that, according to Richards, 'tagged [her as] a man-eater'.[72] The actress's budding star persona as a predatory type is maintained in *The Gypsy and the Gentleman*. However, this persona is given a noir inflection through her collaboration with both Losey and her future husband, blacklisted American noir director Jules Dassin, who lingered on the set and, according to a less-than-pleased Losey, provided 'pillow-talk' regarding his artistic choices.[73] Not only does the scheming Belle juggle multiple male lovers both before and during her marriage to Deverill, but her sexuality is also presented in a carnal manner – particularly in an animalistically erotic moment where she and Jess kiss while eating chicken meat off the bone – in stark contrast to the modest and virginal representations of British womanhood embodied by Sarah and Vanessa, who are never permitted to openly express sexual desire. While Belle's carnal sexuality can be read as a derogatory stereotype that the film aligns with her half-Romani parentage, it can also be read ambiguously as a subtle suggestion that sexual desire lies repressed in a wide array of British women waiting to be unleashed.

Belle's collusion with Jess to swindle Deverill is not entirely financially motivated. Equally important to her is securing class status and privilege by marrying the baronet and becoming Lady Deverill. In order to blackmail Deverill into calling off his engagement to Vanessa, the sexually dominant Belle beats the rake at his own seductive games by alternating between making herself sexually available and unavailable to him. This manipulative form of foreplay is displayed when Belle vanishes without notice or explanation. After spending the day frantically combing the countryside for her, Deverill returns home to find Belle waiting for him in his darkened bedroom chamber, illuminated by a candelabra and a raging fire. Losey and Hildyard reveal Belle's presence by showing her bare ankles slowly protruding from behind a lounge chair, situated behind an unsuspecting Deverill in the right foreground. The camera's lingering attention to this fetish image simultaneously evokes the memory of the femme fatale Phyllis's ankles during her introduction to Walter Neff (Fred MacMurray) in *Double Indemnity* (a particular favourite of Losey's that he admitted to seeing 'many, many times' and referred to as 'one of the best films of the sort ever made'), and anticipates the bare-legged Vera's (Sarah Miles) swivel chair seduction of Tony in *The Servant*.[74] 'Make me a lady, Deverill, make me my father's daughter', Belle insists as she draws his body closer to her. Not only does this seduction scene underscore Belle's desire to transcend her class and multi-ethnic identity to be accepted as a full British noblewoman, but it also serves as a critical turning point in her clandestine relationship with Deverill, who, from this moment onward, allows her to take complete control of both his life and the manor. Despite his need to marry Vanessa to pay off his debts, Deverill grows emotionally and sexually dependent on Belle, who informs him that she will leave him if he does not marry her. The shift in power between the two lovers is visually indicated during a subsequent heated argument over Deverill's failure to stand up to a boxer, Game Pup (Nigel Green), who accuses Belle of dishonesty. As they return to Deverill Court, Belle ascends the staircase with the hapless Deverill standing at the bottom of the landing in a low-angle shot. The image reverses the framing of the earlier staircase sequence, with Belle now in the dominant position.

Upon the couple's secret marriage, Belle achieves her goal of becoming 'lady of the house'. However, as suggested from the outset of this dark fatalistic narrative, the victory is hollow due to Deverill's diminished financial status. Learning from a vehemently disapproving Sarah that her husband is simply 'a pack of bills and a mortgaged house', Belle storms through Deverill Court destroying Deverill's ancestral belongings, all the while hypocritically ranting that he is a 'liar' and a 'cheat'. At first determined to leave him, Belle is convinced to stay by Jess – by now employed by Deverill as a stableman – who assures her that they would be fools to give up the estate's comforts. The decision to stay proves fortuitous, since, shortly afterwards, an alternative path to fortune arises when news arrives of the impending death of Lady Caroline Ayrton (Helen Haye), Deverill's wealthy aunt. A staunch derider of Deverill's rakish lifestyle, Lady Caroline has left her entire estate to Sarah with the condition that she marry before her twenty-first birthday; if not, everything will instead go to Deverill. Belle, Jess, and Lady Caroline's unscrupulous lawyer, Brooke (Mervyn Johns), conspire to defraud Sarah of her inheritance by telling her that the will says that she cannot collect unless she waits to marry Patterson *after* her twenty-first birthday. At first, Deverill abjectly refuses to take part in the scheme, but Belle cons him into participating by promising that she will bear him a son and heir. This betrayal of Sarah for profit further drives Deverill to alcohol and, like Rakewell from Hogarth's 'A Rake's Progress', leaves him a pale shell of the cocksure man he used to be.

The inheritance scheme quickly threatens to go awry. During a moment of restlessness from having to wait to collect the money, Belle rides away on her horse and chances upon the unwelcome sight of Jess exchanging sensual glances with a young Romani girl as he tries to sell one of Deverill's horses to a band of Romanis, who have set up an encampment on Deverill's land. Despite having multiple lovers of her own, a seething Belle rides in and swats at the girl with a riding crop. 'Off of my land, all of you!' Belle exclaims, adding, 'Be off, trollop! . . . I'll not have gypos on my land. Clear out. Be off, gypos!' Offended by Belle's ethnic slurs and attitude of class and ethnic superiority, an elderly Romani woman responds by callously reminding Belle of both her multi-ethnic identity and abandonment as an infant. 'You may own this land, but you're no lady. You're nothing! You belong in a ditch!' the woman declares.[75] These words cut to the core of Belle's ethnic self-loathing, while, at the same time, underscoring the fact that she will never be able to accomplish her goal of completely transcending her multi-ethnic origins. Even if the inheritance scheme is a success, the money as well as the land and marital title will not be enough for her be accepted in the eyes of either the British or the Romanis as a full British noblewoman. Belle's ethnicity is destined to remain forever liminal.

Multiple critics and scholars have cited their dissatisfaction with the inheritance scheme in *The Gypsy and the Gentleman*, which finds the narrative's focus being largely shifted away from Belle's seduction of Deverill in the second half.[76] These reservations are not meritless, particularly given the various and, at times, convoluted series of plot threads that are introduced: a night-time attack on Deverill Court by the band of Romanis seeking vengeance against Belle for her actions at the encampment; the kidnapping and imprisonment of Sarah by Belle and Jess after she discovers the will; Patterson searching Deverill Court for his vanished fiancée; Sarah's escape from a Chinese-style folly in which she was imprisoned by Belle and Jess to the home of a family friend, the renowned stage star Mrs Haggard (Flora Robson); Belle, Jess, and Brooke arranging to kidnap Sarah once again and have her committed to a bedlam run by a corrupt physician, Dr Forrester (Laurence Naismith), who has a track record of unlawfully committing patients for profit; and Mrs Haggard impersonating the recently deceased Lady Caroline to try to blackmail Dr Forrester into releasing Sarah from his institution. In this rapid series of plot developments, *The Gypsy and the Gentleman* shifts its emphasis away from the noirish seduction of Deverill into the type of sensationalist theatrics traditionally associated with the costume melodrama genre. Yet, at the same time, these scenes open up the narrative and, in the process, convey the notion that corruption, greed, and opportunism – qualities typically associated with Belle and Jess in the first half – is symptomatic of the wider degeneracy of the British social and political system during the Regency and (by allegorical extension) post-war periods. The fraudulent money-making schemes of the lawyer Brooke (emblematic of the law) and Dr Forrester (emblematic of medicine) suggest a morally bankrupt British middle and upper class, which, like the aristocracy, trades its integrity for money and power.

Having been driven to borderline madness by Belle, Deverill is shocked to discover that Sarah has been committed to a bedlam. This surprise is further compounded when he learns from Brooke that he unwittingly helped facilitate her committal when Belle got him to sign the papers while he was in a drunken stupor. Ashamed of his complicity, the baronet pulls himself together and rides to the bedlam to demand her release. He arrives just in time to witness Sarah being rescued by Mrs Haggard and Patterson, who, attempting to escape in a carriage, find themselves pursued by Jess and Belle. In a Regency-era equivalent of a climatic noir automobile chase, a carriage race ensues between the three parties. When Jess spots Deverill on a bridge, however, he decides to run the baronet over. Realising Jess's murderous intentions, Belle pulls at the harness to keep him from killing Deverill – an unconvincing moment of concern for Deverill that seems out of character and, perhaps, instead a convenient way for Rank to partially redeem her character and keep from having to entirely portray her as a femme fatale. This split-second decision causes a chain reaction that results in Deverill, Belle, and Jess tumbling off the bridge into the rapid waters of the river below. Despite all of the pain that Belle has inflicted on him and his family, Deverill rescues her. However, when she starts to call out for Jess who has swum ashore and left her for dead, Deverill succumbs to his jealous passions and commits murder-suicide by pulling them both under the water. As *The Gypsy and the Gentleman* comes to its dark conclusion, Losey ends the film with an underwater shot of Belle and Deverill's red and black cloaks wrapping around one another, an image that underscores the couple's noirish linkage to sex and death.

While not necessarily worthy of reclamation as one of Losey's finest films, *The Gypsy and the Gentleman* is certainly not the 'piece of junk' that the director claimed.[77] In addition to serving as a prime example of how classical British cinema's long-running cycle of costume melodramas was often imbued with noir elements, the film is indicative of a late 1950s British cinema in transition. With the notable exception of the Victorian-era Gothic horror films of Hammer Film Productions, British cinema was starting to break away from the type of historical escapism that was indicative of the costume melodrama and, instead, embracing the grittier 'kitchen sink' dramas that were released in the wake of John Osborne's trailblazing 1956 play *Look Back in Anger* (later filmed in 1959 by director Tony Richardson), notably the British New Wave cinema hits *Room at the Top* (Jack Clayton, 1959), *Saturday Night and Sunday Morning* (Karel Reisz, 1960), and *A Kind of Loving* (John Schlesinger, 1962). Embracing the new narrative freedoms afforded by the BBFC's X certificate – an 'adults only' rating for films aimed at audiences aged sixteen and older that the conservative Rank Organisation would distance itself from until 1961 – these contemporary-set films were able to confront issues of class, gender, race/ethnicity, and sexuality in a frank and, at times, unsettling manner that earlier British films could only suggest in veiled ways.[78] Nonetheless, as suggested in the uninhibited performance of Mercouri, *The Gypsy and the Gentleman* provides some indication that a new bolder form of national cinema is imminently coming over the horizon.

Notes

1. 'Greek Star for Rank Film Tour', *Kinematograph Weekly*, 16 January 1958, p. 7.
2. Dick Richards [as Rich.], 'The Gypsy and the Gentleman', *Variety*, 5 February 1958, p. 20.
3. Richards, 'The Gypsy and the Gentleman', p. 20. As evident from the title of the film, *The Gypsy and the Gentleman* uses the term 'gypsy' in reference to the Romani people. According to Colin Clark and Margaret Greenfields, this word is 'an abbreviation of the word "Egyptian", a name given to the Romani people in the Middle Ages as it was thought they came from Egypt'. Given the derogatory connotations associated with 'gypsy', I have selected to use the contemporary preferred term 'Romani' whenever possible. The term 'gypsy' and its derivatives will only be used in reference to the film's title and quoted dialogue. Clark and Greenfields, *Here*

to Stay: The Gypsies and Travellers of Britain (Hatfield: University of Hertfordshire Press, 2006), p. 361.
4. '"Picturegoer" Parade: "The Gypsy and the Gentleman"', Picturegoer, 15 February 1958, p. 15.
5. J.A.D.C. [pseud.], 'Gypsy and the Gentleman, The', The Monthly Film Bulletin 25, no. 288 (January 1958), p. 32. Alternatively, one mostly positive review came from Alexander Walker, who praised The Gypsy and the Gentleman's 'boldness', 'gusto', and 'energy': 'All three are qualities today's cinema needs occasionally. Here they are in full measure.' Walker [as Alex Walker], 'Wickedest Lady', The Birmingham Post & Gazette, 3 February 1958, p. 3. Among the film's few more contemporary defenders is Julian Petley, who cites it as 'an extraordinary melodrama in the Gainsborough mould'. Petley, 'The Lost Continent', in All Our Yesterdays: 90 Years of British Cinema, ed. Charles Barr (London: BFI Publishing, 1986), p. 112.
6. David Caute, Joseph Losey: A Revenge on Life (New York: Oxford University Press, 1994), p. 113.
7. Tom Milne, ed., Losey on Losey (Garden City, NY: Doubleday, 1968), p. 45; and Gordon Gow, 'Weapons: Joseph Losey in an Interview with Gordon Gow', Films and Filming, October 1971, p. 39.
8. Michel Ciment, Conversations with Losey (London: Methuen, 1985), pp. 150–1.
9. Caute, Joseph Losey, p. 128.
10. Charles Drazin, The Finest Years: British Cinema of the 1940s (London: I. B. Tauris, 2007), p. 52.
11. 'British Pulse', Variety, 2 October 1957, p. 18.
12. Edith de Rham, Joseph Losey (London: André Deutsch, 1991), p. 107; and Ciment, Conversations with Losey, p. 151.
13. Ciment, Conversations with Losey, pp. 153–4.
14. Caute, Joseph Losey, pp. 452–3. For more on the film's production history, see Caute, Joseph Losey, pp. 128–30; De Rham, Joseph Losey, pp. 106–8; Gow, 'Weapons', p. 39; and Melina Mercouri, I Was Born Greek (Garden City, NY: Doubleday, 1971), pp. 126–7. An overview of Losey's attempts to bridge popular genre and art-house cinema styles is provided in Christopher Weedman, 'Joseph Losey', in Fifty Hollywood Directors, ed. Yvonne Tasker and Suzanne Leonard (London: Routledge, 2015), pp. 143–51.
15. J.A.D.C., 'Gypsy and the Gentleman, The', p. 32. For historical and critical coverage of the film, see James Leahy, The Cinema of Joseph Losey (London: A. Zwemmer, 1967), pp. 74–9; Gene D. Phillips, 'Joseph Losey', in The Movie Makers: Artists in an Industry (Chicago: Nelson-Hall, 1973), p. 171; Foster Hirsch, Joseph Losey (Boston: Twayne Publishers, 1980), pp. 72–6; De Rham, Joseph Losey, pp. 106–8; James Palmer and Michael Riley, The Films of Joseph Losey (Cambridge: Cambridge University Press, 1993), p. 2; and Caute, Joseph Losey, pp. 128–30, 488–9.
16. Hirsch, Joseph Losey, pp. 72–3.
17. Originally established in 1924 by British producer Michael Balcon, Gainsborough Pictures merged with Gaumount-British Picture Corporation in 1928. Gainsborough subsequently became a semi-autonomous production unit of the Rank Organisation when Rank purchased Gaumount-British in 1941. For more on the

history of Gainsborough, see Pam Cook, ed., *Gainsborough Pictures* (London: Cassell, 1997); Sue Harper, *Picturing the Past: The Rise and Fall of the British Costume Film* (London: BFI Publishing, 1994), pp. 119–35; and Robert Murphy, 'A Brief Studio History', in *BFI Dossier Number 18: Gainsborough Melodrama*, ed. Sue Aspinall and Murphy (London: BFI Publishing, 1983), pp. 3–13.

18. Colin Gardner, *Joseph Losey* (Manchester: Manchester University Press, 2004), pp. 52–3.
19. Christopher Weedman, 'A Dark Exilic Vision of 1960s Britain: Gothic Horror and Film Noir Pervading Losey and Pinter's *The Servant*', *Journal of Cinema and Media Studies* 58, no. 3 (Spring 2019), pp. 93–117.
20. Sue Harper and Vincent Porter, *British Cinema of the 1950s: The Decline of Deference* (Oxford: Oxford University Press, 2003), p. 56.
21. Raymond Durgnat, *A Mirror for England: British Movies from Austerity to Affluence* (New York: Praeger Publishers, 1971), p. 254. While Durgnat is likely utilising the term 'Technicolor' in a colloquial sense to denote that *The Gypsy and the Gentleman* was filmed in colour, it was technically made using the rival Eastmancolor process. An examination of Eastmancolor within British cinema is provided in Sarah Street et al., *Colour Films in Britain: The Eastmancolor Revolution* (London: British Film Institute/Bloomsbury Publishing, 2021).
22. Michael F. Keaney, *British Film Noir Guide* (Jefferson, NC: McFarland, 2008).
23. Raymond Durgnat, 'Paint It Black: The Family Tree of the *Film Noir*', in *Film Noir Reader*, ed. Alain Silver and James Ursini (New York: Limelight Editions, 1996), pp. 37–9, previously published in *Cinema*, nos. 6–7 (August 1970), pp. 48–56.
24. Durgnat, *A Mirror for England*, p. 254.
25. For a sociohistorical examination of the British age of austerity, see David Kynaston, *Austerity Britain, 1945–51* (London: Bloomsbury Publishing, 2007); and Michael Sissons and Philip French, eds., *Age of Austerity* (London: Hodder and Stoughton, 1963).
26. Tony Williams, *Structures of Desire: British Cinema, 1939-1955* (Albany: State University of New York Press, 2000), p. 97.
27. For discussion of British film noirs and other crime films within the context of this post-war malaise, see Raymond Durgnat, 'Some Lines of Inquiry into Post-war British Crimes', in *The British Cinema Book*, ed. Robert Murphy (London: BFI Publishing, 1997), pp. 90–103; William K. Everson, 'British Film Noir: Part I', *Films in Review* 38, no. 5 (May 1987), pp. 288–9; Jim Leach, 'British Noir', in *International Noir*, ed. Homer B. Pettey and R. Barton Palmer (Edinburgh: Edinburgh University Press, 2014), pp. 19–25; Laurence Miller, 'Evidence for a British Film Noir Cycle', in *Re-Viewing British Cinema, 1990–1992: Essays and Interviews*, ed. Wheeler Winston Dixon (Albany: State University of New York Press, 1994), p. 157; Brian McFarlane, 'Losing the Peace: Some British Films of Postwar Adjustment', in *Screening the Past: Film and the Representation of History*, ed. Tony Barta (Westport, CT: Praeger, 1998), pp. 93–107; Robert Murphy, 'British Film Noir', in *European Film Noir*, ed. Andrew Spicer (Manchester: Manchester University Press, 2007), pp. 89–95; Robert Murphy, *Realism and Tinsel: Cinema and Society in Britain, 1939–1948* (London: Routledge, 1989), pp. 146–90; Robert Murphy, 'Riff-Raff: British Cinema and the

Underworld', in *All Our Yesterdays: 90 Years of British Cinema*, ed. Charles Barr (London: BFI Publishing, 1986), pp. 291–304; Tim Pulleine, 'Spin a Dark Web', in *British Crime Cinema*, ed. Steve Chibnall and Robert Murphy (London: Routledge, 1999), pp. 27–36; Andrew Spicer, *Film Noir* (Harlow: Longman-Pearson Education, 2002), pp. 182–3, 186–91; and Tony Williams, 'British *Film Noir*', in *Film Noir Reader 2*, ed. Alain Silver and James Ursini (New York: Limelight Editions, 1999), pp. 255–61.
28. Aspinall and Murphy, 'Introduction', p. 1; Geoff Brown, 'Which Way to the Way Ahead?: Britain's Years of Reconstruction', *Sight and Sound* 47 (Autumn 1978), p. 244; Pam Cook, 'Neither Here nor There: National Identity in Gainsborough Costume Drama', in *Dissolving Views: Key Writings on British Cinema*, ed. Andrew Higson (London: Cassell, 1996), pp. 52–4; Harper, *Picturing the Past*, p. 123; Murphy, *Realism and Tinsel*, pp. 168–9; and Williams, British *Film Noir*, p. 245.
29. Harper, *Picturing the Past*, p. 119.
30. Despite the seeming restoration of patriarchal norms at the end of most classical film noirs, Janey Place indicates that the fissure created by the femme fatale's destabilisation of the male-dominated order cannot be entirely resealed. Place states, 'It is not their inevitable demise we remember but rather their strong, dangerous and, above all, exciting sexuality. In film noir we observe both the social action of myth which damns the sexual woman and all who become enmeshed by her, and a particularly potent stylistic presentation of the sexual strength of woman which man fears. This operation of myth is so highly stylised and conventionalised that the final "lesson" of the myth often fades into the background and we retain the image of the erotic, strong, unrepressed (if destructive) woman.' Place, 'Women in Film Noir', in *Women in Film Noir*, ed. E. Ann Kaplan, revised and expanded edition (London: BFI Publishing, 1998), p. 48.
31. For an analysis of *The Man in Grey* in relationship to wartime British female spectatorship, see Janet Thumim, 'The Female Audience: Mobile Women and Married Ladies', in *Nationalising Femininity: Culture, Sexuality and British Cinema in the Second World War*, ed. Christine Gledhill and Gillian Swanson (Manchester: Manchester University Press, 1996), pp. 249–52. Other key works of scholarship with relevant discussions of Gainsborough and Gainsborough-style costume melodramas include Pam Cook, *Fashioning the Nation: Costume and Identity in British Cinema* (London: British Film Institute, 1996); Pam Cook, 'Neither Here nor There: National Identity in Gainsborough Costume Drama', pp. 51–65; Johanna Laitila, *Melodrama, Self, and Nation in Post-War British Popular Film* (London: Routledge, 2018); Marcia Landy, *British Genres: Cinema and Society, 1930–1960* (Princeton: Princeton University Press, 1991), pp. 209–21; and Tony Williams, *Structures of Desire*.
32. Murphy, *Realism and Tinsel*, p. 107; and Melanie Bell, 'Fatal Femininity in Post-War British Film', in *The Femme Fatale: Images, Histories, Contexts*, ed. Helen Hanson and Catherine O'Rawe (Houndmills: Palgrave Macmillan, 2010). For more from Murphy on this subject, see Steve Chibnall and Robert Murphy, 'Parole Overdue: Releasing the British Crime Film into the Critical Community', in *British Crime Cinema*, ed. Chibnall and Murphy (London: Routledge, 1999), p. 5; and

Murphy, 'British Film Noir', p. 85. In his discussion of femme fatale characters in the British film noirs *Forbidden* (George King, 1949), *The Long Haul* (Ken Hughes, 1957), *Blind Corner* (Lance Comfort, 1964), Jim Leach, like Bell, diverges from Murphy about his assertion that British cinema had few femme fatales: 'In the British films, the distinctions between "decent" and "transgressive" women are often much less clear than in American noir.' Leach, 'British Noir', p. 27.

33. Geoffrey Macnab, *J. Arthur Rank and the British Film Industry* (London: Routledge, 1993), p. 117.
34. Many, but not all, of the Gainsborough and Gainsborough-style costume melodramas in this list are also given entries by Keaney, *British Film Noir Guide*. For more noir consideration of this list of films, consult Durgnat, 'Paint It Black', p. 39; Williams, 'British *Film Noir*', pp. 244–8, 252, 255–9; William K. Everson, 'British Film Noir: Part II', *Films in Review* 38, nos. 6–7 (June/July 1987), pp. 342–5; R. Barton Palmer, 'Film Noir Begins: Some Thoughts', *South Atlantic Review* 86, no. 4 (2021), pp. 1–30; and Spicer, *Film Noir*, pp. 181–4.
35. Additional discussion of this melding of cinematic styles can be found in Everson, 'British Film Noir: Part I', p. 289; Spicer, *Film Noir*, pp. 183–4; and Williams, 'British *Film Noir*', pp. 244–6.
36. Williams, 'British *Film Noir*', p. 246.
37. Macnab, *J. Arthur Rank and the British Film Industry*, pp. 223–4.
38. Rank was planning more historical films, but these projects were abandoned – presumably due to both the expense and the failure of *Dangerous Exile*, *A Tale of Two Cities* (Ralph Thomas, 1958), and *The Gypsy and the Gentleman* to make a significant dent in the American market. The other unfilmed projects included film adaptations of Thomas Hardy's 1886 novel *The Mayor of Casterbridge*, Mary Webb's 1924 novel *Precious Bane*, John Masters's 1951 novel *Nightrunners of Bengal*, and an early pre-David Lean attempt to dramatise the life of T. E. Lawrence ('Lawrence of Arabia') with Dirk Bogarde. 'Rank Will Produce 20 at $14 Million', *The Independent Film Journal*, 26 October 1957, p. 19; and Charles Swann [as C.S.], 'Pinewood Dips into the Past', *Picturegoer*, 28 December 1957, p. 30. For more on Rank's late-1950s initiative to market its films to American audiences, see 'Rank Personalities to Boost Lineup for American Market', *The Independent Film Journal*, 1 March 1958, p. 12; Macnab, *J. Arthur Rank and the British Film Industry*, pp. 226–9; and Sarah Street, *Transatlantic Crossings: British Feature Films in the USA* (New York: Continuum, 2002), pp. 140–54.
39. Representative press coverage includes Walker, 'Wickedest Lady', p. 3; S.S.L. [pseud.], 'Our Cover Girl Wants to be a "Wicked Lady"', *Picturegoer*, 15 June 1957, p. 13; 'Dangerous Exile', *The Monthly Film Bulletin* 25, no. 288 (January 1958), p. 5; and 'Entertainments Guide: Next Week's Programmes', *Reading Mercury*, 1 February 1958, p. 8.
40. Hirsch, *Joseph Losey*, p. 73. Interestingly, *The Gypsy and the Gentleman* was hailed by Durgnat as 'a fancy dress draft' for *The Servant*, but this interpretation was later downplayed by both Caute and Gardner who both found this reading problematic. According to a rather caustic Caute, 'to compare the grotesque Belle to the subtle Barrett, as interlopers, is to give comparative analysis a bad name'. Despite these

reservations, this chapter demonstrates that there are multiple shared thematic and stylistic elements within the two films that remain worthy of comparison. Durgnat, *A Mirror for England*, p. 254; Caute, *Joseph Losey*, p. 129; and Gardner, *Joseph Losey*, p. 57.

41. In an apparent attempt to heighten the film's semblance of realism, Losey shot the exteriors at Shardeloes Manor, an eighteenth-century country house near Amersham, Buckinghamshire. 'A Gypsy at Shardeloes', *Bucks Examiner*, 23 August 1957, p. 3.
42. Milne, *Losey on Losey*, pp. 62–3.
43. Another exception is cinematographer Geoffrey Unsworth's work on *Dangerous Exile*, which 'employs high contrasts for the interior scenes, forming expressive shadows that add to mounting tension in the film, evoking a Gothic horror aesthetic'. Street et al., *Colour Films in Britain*, p. 143.
44. Thom Andersen, 'Red Hollywood', in *Literature and the Visual Arts in Contemporary Society*, ed. Suzanne Ferguson and Barbara Groseclose (Columbus: Ohio State University Press, 1985), pp. 183–4; and Weedman, 'A Dark Exilic Vision of 1960s Britain', p. 104.
45. Ciment, *Conversations with Losey*, p. 151, emphasis added.
46. A critical re-evaluation of Green can be found in Jill Nelmes, *The Screenwriter in British Cinema* (London: British Film Institute/Palgrave Macmillan, 2014), pp. 108–33.
47. For more on the Wolfenden Report and the Nottingham and Notting Hill race riots of 1958, see, respectively, Gillian Swanson, *Drunk with the Glitter: Space, Consumption and Sexual Instability in Modern Urban Culture* (London: Routledge, 2007), pp. 73–99; and Joe Mulhall, *British Fascism After the Holocaust: From the Birth of Denial to the Notting Hill Riots 1939–1958* (London: Routledge, 2021), pp. 150–6.
48. Caute, *Joseph Losey*, p. 128.
49. Durgnat, *A Mirror for England*, p. 252; Hirsch, *Joseph Losey*, p. 73; and Neil Sinyard, 'Intimate Stranger: The Early British Films of Joseph Losey', in *British Cinema of the 1950s: A Celebration*, ed. Ian Mackillop and Sinyard (Manchester: Manchester University Press, 2003), p. 120.
50. *Oxford English Dictionary*, 'pig, n.1', https://www-oed-com.ezproxy.mtsu.edu/view/Entry/143654; and *Oxford English Dictionary*, 'sow, n.2', https://www-oed-com.ezproxy.mtsu.edu/view/Entry/185355.
51. Leahy, *The Cinema of Joseph Losey*, p. 75.
52. Harold Weber, *The Restoration Rake-Hero: Transformations in Sexual Understanding in Seventeenth-Century England* (Madison: The University of Wisconsin Press, 1986), p. 4.
53. Milne, *Losey on Losey*, p. 62; and Ciment, *Conversations with Losey*, pp. 153–4.
54. The popularity of both *The Rake's Progress* and *Mildred Pierce* is demonstrated by Sarah Street's analysis of post-war audience surveys in Street, *British Cinema in Documents* (London: Routledge, 2016), pp. 125–8, 130–1.
55. John Trevelyan's 1958–71 tenure as board secretary of the BBFC is generally viewed as a period where the board's censorship practices started to become more liberalised to reflect the changing cultural climate in Britain during the late 1950s and 1960s. For more information on Trevelyan's tenure, see Anne Etienne, Benjamin Halligan,

and Christopher Weedman, eds, *Adult Themes: British Cinema and the X Certificate in the Long 1960s* (London: Bloomsbury Academic, 2023); Edward Lamberti, ed., *Behind the Scenes at the BBFC: Film Classification from the Silver Screen to the Digital Age* (London: Palgrave Macmillan, 2012); and John Trevelyan, *What the Censor Saw* (London: Michael Joseph, 1973).

56. Leahy, *The Cinema of Joseph Losey*, p. 76; and Gardner, *Joseph Losey*, p. 54.
57. For my analysis of these scenes, see Weedman, 'A Dark Exilic Vision of 1960s Britain', pp. 113–14.
58. During the late nineteenth century, people of half-Romani parentage began to be referred to derogatorily as 'didicoi', an offensive British Romani term meaning a person 'not solely of Romani descent'. *Oxford English Dictionary*, 'didicoi, n.', https://www-oed-com.ezproxy.mtsu.edu/view/Entry/52365. Additional discussion can be found in David Cressy, *Gypsies: An English History* (Oxford: Oxford University Press, 2018), p. 177; and Judith Okely, *The Traveller-Gypsies* (Cambridge: Cambridge University Press, 1983), pp. 15–18.
59. Emily Webb, 'An Invisible Minority: Romany Gypsies and the Question of Whiteness', *Romani Studies: Journal of the Gypsy Lore Society* 29, no. 1 (2019), p. 1.
60. The scandalous nature of these travelling fairs is subsequently underscored by Vanessa, who, after Deverill tells her that her father Ruddock was in attendance, laughs and naïvely replies, 'Paul, father doesn't gamble.'
61. 'A pigeon to be plucked' is an animal metaphor that dates back to the fourteenth century that means '[a] gullible person . . . an easy mark for con artists'. Robert A. Palmatier, *Speaking of Animals: A Dictionary of Animal Metaphors* (Westport, CT: Greenwood Press, 1995), p. 288.
62. Deborah Epstein Nord, *Gypsies & the British Imagination, 1807–1930* (New York: Columbia University Press, 2006), pp. 40–1; and Laitila, *Melodrama, Self, and Nation in Post-War British Popular Film*, p. 32.
63. Another example of this type of narrative tendency is in the death of the DID-suffering (dissociative identity disorder) Maddalena Labardi (Phyllis Calvert) – a socially reserved, upper-class housewife, whose alternative personality, Rosanna, is a sexually bold and transgressive Romani woman – in Gainsborough's *Madonna of the Seven Moons* (Crabtree, 1945), which does not fit cohesively within either the British noir or costume melodrama cycles due to its limited noir tropes and near-contemporary setting.
64. Chamion Caballero and Peter J. Aspinall, *Mixed Race Britain in The Twentieth Century* (London: Palgrave Macmillan, 2018), p. 116.
65. Wendy Webster, *Imagining Home: Gender, 'Race' and National Identity, 1945–64* (London: University College London Press, 1998), p. 33.
66. Caute, *Joseph Losey*, p. 128.
67. Nelmes, *The Screenwriter in British Cinema*, pp. 110–12.
68. Geoffrey Macnab, *Searching for Stars: Stardom and Screen Acting in British Cinema* (London: Cassell, 2000), p. 143.
69. Sue Harper, *Women in British Cinema: Mad, Bad and Dangerous to Know* (London: Continuum 2000), pp. 98–9; and Melanie Bell, *Femininity in the Frame: Women and 1950s British Popular Cinema* (London: I. B. Tauris, 2010), pp. 124, 132.

70. Dick Richards, 'The Greeks Have a Word for It', *The Sketch*, 9 October 1957, p. 346. Among those who took issue with the notion that 1950s British female stars lacked sex appeal was actor Stanley Baker, who, in a 1958 British television interview, insisted, 'Only give the girls a chance in this country and they have the sex appeal. Look at Anne Heywood, for instance. Don't tell me that she doesn't have sex appeal.' MacDonald Hobley, 'Interview with Stanley Baker', special features, disc 1, *Hell Drivers*, Blu-ray, directed by Cy Enfield (London: Network Distributing, 2017).
71. Ciment, *Conversations with Losey*, p. 151.
72. Richards, 'The Greeks Have a Word for It', p. 346.
73. Ciment, *Conversations with Losey*, p. 250.
74. Ciment, *Conversations with Losey*, p. 106.
75. The actresses who played the two Romani women in this scene are uncredited.
76. For representative criticism, see Gardner, *Joseph Losey*, p. 57; Hirsch, *Joseph Losey*, p. 72; and '"Picturegoer" Parade', p. 15.
77. Gow, 'Weapons', p. 39.
78. Melanie Williams, 'No Love for Johnnie', in *The Cinema of Britain and Ireland*, ed. Brian McFarlane (London: Wallflower Press, 2005), p. 127.

8. ARGENTINE GOTHIC-NOIR FUSION IN *THE BLACK VAMPIRE*

Osvaldo Di Paolo Harrison and Nadina Olmedo

In Argentina, the history of horror films can be traced to the 1930s when the country was beginning its cinematographic Golden Era. According to Tamara Falicov, Argentina entered a production phase of massive tango, detective, gangster, melodrama, and comedy films, allowing this South American country to become one of the most important movie industries within the Hispanic film market.[1] Some of the first Gothic horror films to appear included *El hombre bestia* (*The Beast Man*, Camilo Zaccaría Soprani, 1934) and *Una luz en la ventana* (*A Light in the Window*, Manuel Romero, 1942).[2] However, while the production of such films was not prolific during the first half of the twentieth century, one was particularly popular: *El vampiro negro* (*The Black Vampire*, Román Viñoly Barreto, 1953), a Gothic picture usually considered an Argentine version of Fritz Lang's *M* (1931). Notably, *The Black Vampire* presents a hybridity between Gothic horror – monsters, gloomy underground spaces, mad men, and anxiety over cultural limits and boundaries – and detective noir – criminal investigation, victims, violence, and murder. This Gothic-noir fusion occurs through inclusion of suspense, mystery, ominousness, horror, terror, and the macabre, confusing the notions of good and evil and exploring the darkest sides of the individual and of society. As Fred Botting vividly describes: 'Gothic shadows flicker among representations of cultural, familial and individual fragmentation, in uncanny disruptions of the boundaries between inner being, social values and concrete reality and in modern forms of barbarism and monstrosity' (see Figure 8.1).[3]

Figure 8.1 A publicity poster for *El Vampiro Negro* that includes Gothic and noir imagery. © Matías Gil Robert

During the Argentine cinematographic Golden Era, Gothic-noir film production in Argentina converted the literal monster into the savage killer, following the juxtaposition within nineteenth-century thought of civilisation and barbarism. This binary construct emerged during the Argentine's nation-building process with its desire to mould its citizens according to European cultural conventions. President Domingo Faustino Sarmiento (1811–88), an educator and writer, designed an intensive plan to modernise the country and fostered the importance of public education in rural areas to sophisticate the population and defeat the violence of *caudillos* – regional leaders – in the countryside. Sarmiento authored *Civilization and Barbarism* (1845), a foundational text that has shaped modern Argentine politics and ideology to the present day.

In *The Black Vampire*, this dichotomy is left ambiguous because the killer is a monster that lurks behind a 'civil man' – an English teacher. He, in turn, is investigated by a detective whose morals are also unreliable. Gothic-noir emphasises such complex characters, confusing the boundaries of good and evil; absolutes are not easy to detect as the presence and threat of an uncivilised being among civilised citizens becomes increasingly difficult to discover. In the following analysis, we focus on these oppositions and the ways they are deconstructed through the film's use of Gothic-noir aesthetic and techniques, with emphasis on liminality as it reflects a particularly Argentine world view.

The evolution of Gothic-noir films in Argentina derives from the transnational popularity and distribution of German Expressionist films in Latin America, such as *Das Cabinet des Dr. Caligari* (*The Cabinet of Dr. Caligari*, Robert Wiene, 1920), *Metropolis* (Fritz Lang, 1927) and *M*, as well as Expressionistic US Gothic-horror films such as *Dracula* (Tod Browning, 1931), which appeared in Argentina immediately following their releases in Europe and the United States. In *Gothic Imagination: Latin American Fiction and Film*, Carmen Serrano explains that

> German Expressionist films were innovative compared with those produced by France or Hollywood up until then, and these commercially successful German Expressionist films not only resonated with filmmakers in the 1920s but also influenced Hollywood horror films of the 1930s and film noir produced in the 1940s and 1950s.[4]

From the nineteenth century, Argentina has been fascinated by European cultural movements. Almost every film director's goal was to study abroad and import new cinematic trends, blending them with a Latin American flair – *gaucho* and *compadrito*[5] characters, tango and bolero singers, and Buenos Aires as a setting. The resulting aesthetic appears in remakes of European and American productions, such as *El extraño caso del hombre y la bestia* (*The Strange Case of the Man and the Beast*, Mario Soffici, 1951), based on the classic *Dr. Jekyll and Mr. Hyde* (Rouben Mamoulian, 1931) and Román Viñoly Barreto's adaptation of *M*, *The Black Vampire*.

At the same time, political disturbances – including multiple dictatorships and economical upheavals – provoked fear and repression among citizens.[6] Argentine films made use of such tensions through Gothic-noir distancing. As Gandolfo and Hojman explain, terror based on the supernatural has the function of providing an escape from fearful events that are too real and close, such as 'wars, plagues, crises, famines'.[7] Nonetheless, as Carina Rodríguez states, Argentine society has not been able to exorcise its own demons: 'colonization, historical struggles between centralism / federalism and civilization / barbarism, changes in national identity after the waves of immigrants, hyperinflation, fear not to make ends meet and dictatorships'.[8] Therefore, audiences, living frightening and repressive realities, both escape from and identify with the horror that emanates from creatures, monsters, and criminals.

As far as the progression of detective-noir movies in Argentina, the 1940s and 1950s saw a film noir boom with the production of more than one hundred detective films. The works of directors such as Daniel Tinayre, Carlos Hugo Christensen, Hugo del Carril, Hugo Fregonese, Don Naypy, and Román Viñoly

Barreto are representative of this expansion.⁹ Their films also reflected Argentine city life. Buenos Aires of the era was a cesspool of murder and corruption, where serial killers, paedophiles, and scammers roam freely with impunity and without any criminal receiving punishment. So too is the Buenos Aires of *The Black Vampire*.

Viñoly Barreto's first incursion into film noir resulted in *La bestia debe morir* (*The Beast Must Die*) in 1952. Following this production, he experimented with a Gothic-noir fusion in *The Black Vampire*. In addition to directing, Barreto also co-authored the film's script with Narciso Ibáñes Menta, known as the father of Argentine Gothic terror in film and theatre. *The Black Vampire* narrates the investigation of a series of murders of young girls in 1950s Buenos Aires. Dr Bernar (Roberto Escalada) is the detective in charge of solving the crimes, a solitary and unhappy individual married to a paralysed upper-class woman (Gloria Castilla). He becomes entangled with Rita (Olga Zubarry), a cabaret singer and witness to one of the crimes. Tension rises when Rita's friend and fellow performer Cora (Nelly Panizza) asks her admirer, Teodoro Ulber (Nathán Pinzón), to take Rita's daughter to the amusement park. Cora does not know that Teodoro is a serial killer and a predator of little girls. As the investigation continues, a blind street person who sells toys and his homeless friend realise, after listening to the news, that Ulber purchased a doll for one of his victims from them. In the end, the serial killer surrenders himself to the police after an intense pursuit.

An obvious reworking of Lang's *M*, the plot of *The Black Vampire* follows the outline of hard-boiled detective fiction. Its title and aesthetics, however, align with the Gothic and film noir. Oblique angle shots, chiaroscuro lighting effects, and long, dark shadows, distort the image of the murderer, turning him into a monster – in this case identified as a 'vampire'. For instance, when Rita is changing outfits in her dressing room, a close-up shows her scream after witnessing the dumping of the body of a little girl into the sewer system. Her terror is enhanced by camera and light distortions and because she only sees him from the back, dressed in a black trench coat with the collar up. This visual composition accentuates the silhouette of a 'creature of the night', while the close-up focuses on her wide eyes and mouth, typifying horror convention and thus convincing the viewer that Rita is experiencing a darkly supernatural event.

In addition, the use of the subjective camera increases the dramatic expression of individual inner experience. As Lee Horsley mentions in *The Noir Thriller*, the representation of the protagonist's point of view is crucial for the viewer to perceive his state of mind, his desires, obsessions and anxieties.¹⁰ For instance, when Cora asks Ulber to babysit Rita's daughter he hesitates because he knows that he cannot control himself and desperately responds 'no, not the girl'. The subjective camera shows the point of view of the killer and his facial expressions reveal his nightmarish thirst for blood, accentuating him as an ambiguous figure of noir.

This perception of the murderer as a Gothic devil is reinforced when the detective addresses Ulber as a 'black vampire'. Bernar states that:

> Medieval fantasy created a specter, a horrendous being that at night approached the living to suck their blood little by little until it killed them and called them vampires. There are certain kinds of abnormalities among humans who release their anguish when they see blood. All they need is blood. Immediately lucidity ensues, the dreadful lucidity that tells them how to get rid of their victims without leaving a trace. We have to lock up or eliminate that satanically intelligent freak. He is the most terrible threat to society because as long as he is on the loose, there will be no safety for any creature.[11]

Throughout the film, there is a pendulum that portrays Ulber as swinging from vampire to criminal, reinforcing the Gothic-noir fusion. The oscillation also allows the audience to perceive Ulber as a monster, in spite of being an ordinary member of society. As Winfried Fluck explains, the threat in film noir 'is now the ordinary citizen who has committed the crime or is suspected of having committed a crime or comes dangerously close to the world of crime'.[12] The character represents the 'white' European male and the construction of a civilised nation. Fitting into the semblance of the 'ideal' citizen, he is the face of civilisation against barbarism, which allows him to commit his crimes with total impunity, diminishing his potential of being seen as a suspect.

Since the nineteenth century, Argentina has tried to import European cultural models, viewed as well educated and sophisticated in direct opposition to the diverse population composed by indigenous 'mestizos' and 'mulatos',[13] who were regarded as barbarians. This social division is a constant struggle throughout the centuries; however, during the twentieth century, film noir contributed to the subversion of the idea of white male supremacy. In other words, the combination of Argentine racism and noir links the monster to non-white (darkness and dark skin). The discomfort for the viewer is thus ultimately the way the figure crosses *multiple* boundaries linked to the civilised/barbarous binary: good citizen/criminal, human/monster, and white/racial other.

Simultaneously, *The Black Vampire* also implies a strong moralising message directed to Argentine citizens. As Claudio España argues in *Cine Argentino: Industria y clasismo 1933–1956*, 'Argentines went to the movies to learn to be Argentine.'[14] In the film, the judge in charge of the murder trial reads the sentence of the jury stating that

> your case has been considered by the court. During the entire investigation and the judicial process, nothing has been done to your detriment. You

> have received the protection that the law grants to all, to those who are subjected to the supreme decision of justice [...] Having recognized that what has been said throughout this process is the most exact truth, this court sentences you to be suspended from the neck by a rope until death.

This verdict clearly conveys the ultimate respect for the rule of law and the valuable role of the jury, portrayed as a fair body of respectable peers. Breaking the social order is unacceptable and the criminal must be severely punished. It is worth noting that the serial killer is condemned to death, even though this punishment has never been part of the Argentine criminal code. The insertion of this severe sanction is taken from the United States. Argentines have always respected their social order and the sense of justice. The shocking effect in the audience is a warning of the strong consequences that could derive from breaking the law. In other words, it is unacceptable for barbarism to take over the civilised self.

For Ulber, this sense of a divided self is a constant struggle, and it is shown in the movie as a pendulum that opens a play of ambivalence between vampire (Gothic) and criminal (noir). When represented as a Gothic monster, he cannot repress his erotic appetite and thirst for killing. His own presence hides a sexual desire that cannot be declared because it is either prohibited, immoral, or clandestine. These creatures are selfish in essence and have no anguish or remorse for their vulnerable victims. At the beginning of the film, the prosecutor, detective Dr Bernar, informs the jury that

> Freud points out that there are erotic instincts that neutralize aggressive desires from the death instinct. The examples that I have presented refer to this instinctive sublimation. It has been said here, it has been reiterated, that the murderer is anguished, a repressed individual, who releases his anguish with the crimes committed against those most vulnerable, but we also know that when the crime is finished, he acts with strange lucidity.

According to the prosecutor, the lack of 'normal' erotic urges brings forward the lethal behaviour of the serial killer. Like a 'true vampire', Ulber does not conform within the socially accepted sexual norms. In 'Beyond the Pleasure Principle', Sigmund Freud explains that multiple killings are linked to the concept of repetition compulsion.[15] This pathology derives from the resistance of the repressed unconscious, which makes an individual relive unpleasant past experiences.[16] The vampire cannot stop attacking his victims. It has the constant need to feed and is impossible to satisfy. In the film, there is a scene where the police perform undercover stings to capture the murderer. Nevertheless, due to his need to kill and the shortened term of the satisfaction of the previous victim, he follows a girl watched by the cops, risking getting caught out of desperation.

Even more starkly, in the final sequence Ulber kidnaps the daughter of his friend Rita, who trusted him to babysit her, showing that the intensity of his need for blood makes him betray his friendship and he realises this vice cycle gets harder and harder to break, causing him a sense of anguish.

At the same time, Ulber is a victim of his inner monstrosity when the pendulum sways to film noir. In this case, the focus is on the criminal. Once Ulber is caught, he reveals his vexatious memories from the past:

> It is not my fault. I never wanted to hurt anyone. I was always lonely. Everyone made fun of me. All of them harassed me. Other kids were afraid of me. I would hear the music. I have always heard it since I was a kid. Why did they mock me?

In one scene, the psychiatrist administers the Rorschach Test to Ulber, revealing the traumatic experiences of the killer by showing him inkblot images and asking him what he sees. Ulber responds, 'I do not know.' The camera narrates the effect of confusion by overlapping a composition of chiaroscuro and smoke that hides Ulber's face. In *Film Noir: A Very Short Introduction*, James Naremore explains that 'psychoanalysis was in vogue, and because characters suffered from neurosis or quasi-Freudian obsessions, flashbacks were common in various sorts of movies'.[17] In the film, the subjective camera shapes the pathology of the killer with close-ups of surreal faces of women who humiliated him and victimised girls, along with their loud and grotesque laughter in voice-overs.

This trend is noticeable in Argentine Gothic-noir, where the arrival of psychoanalysis and the focus on pathological characters derives from its popularity among citizens. Going to the therapist is a voguish practice. Unlike other cultures, Argentines do not have the same stigma about seeking mental health. For instance, Buenos Aires is the city with the highest number of psychologists per capita in the world. According to José Juan del Col, the rise of psychoanalysis in Argentina responds to factors such as overcoming or sublimating the bitterness and frustration caused by the socio-economic reality, the search for identity in a young country that has not yet shaken the trauma of European emigration, the tendency towards introspection and individualism in the face of the decline produced by public institutions, and the impassivity in large urban concentrations.[18]

In *The Black Vampire*, psychoanalysis permeates throughout the vampire's complex psyche. As a Gothic subject and following Fred Botting's concept, Ulber is alienated and divided from himself, a product of 'reason and desire' and a 'subject of obsession, narcissism and self-gratification as much as reasonable, responsible code of behavior'.[19] In one scene, after a failed attempt to kill a young girl – showing his compulsion for blood – Ulber goes to a bar and asks for a drink. The camera moves from a medium shot to a close-up to show him immersed in sadness. Gloomy lighting accentuates his monstrous features and the tremendous guilt that the vampire bears. Next, an extreme close-up fix on his delirious eyes, reflecting the surrealist and expressionist aesthetics of film noir. This scene reaches its climax when another close-up shows him crushing a glass of cognac with his hands. He then proceeds to mutilate himself with a piece of broken glass, as if he would like to achieve the maximum pleasure: his own death.

In 'Beyond the Pleasure Principle', Freud states that pleasure is connected to death instincts and is correlated to external stimuli, seen as danger, but mainly in connection with internal catalysts that make life difficult.[20] In *Knowing Freud and His Work*, Francesc Gomà explains that the ultimate pleasure will be that of maximum relaxation, the ending of all longing – in other words, nirvana. The consequence is paradoxical, but inescapable: maximum pleasure is achieved with total relaxation, death.[21] According to Freud's interpretations in 'Mourning and Melancholia', the analysis of melancholy teaches us that the ego can only kill itself if, by virtue of the retreat of the object investiture, it can treat itself as an object, if it is allowed to direct against itself that hostility that falls on an object and subrogates the original reaction of the ego towards objects of the external world.[22] In this sense, Ulber is trying to destroy his own shadow. His ego intends to shatter itself in the attempt to destroy the displeasure that he finds in being a savage vampire.

At times, Ulber's alienated and divided Gothic psyche represses his violence and aggression by replacing it with submission and insecurity. Following the scene in which Ulber mutilates himself, he visits Cora, the cabaret dancer. She scolds him as if he were a child. She reprimands him, saying, 'What are you doing here this late? I have to go to work. Sit down. You are stupid. You cannot be left alone because you end up doing crazy things.' Moreover, when she notices the evidence of his self-mutilation, he shows her his hands, palms up, in the manner of a child revealing a guilty misdeed to his parents. In another scene, two students of Ulber approach him, and he displays nervousness and discomfort at being alone with young ladies. His hands start shaking and he accidentally drops his teacup, exhibiting his immaturity and lack of social skills. Such moments illustrate how Ulber's harmless appearance, education, and social class situate him out of the line of the investigation. Instead, the detective focuses on the usual suspects, frequently seen in the realm of the marginal world.

As Naremore states, film noir 'occupies a liminal space' because 'it often centres on a zone between the law and the underworld; and its action keeps moving back and forth between respectable and disreputable areas of town, bringing together people of different status'.[23] *The Black Vampire* reflects this space in the contrasts between Ulber's life and locales and that of the criminal investigation. For example, after the first victim is found in the sewer system, the police interrogate a man who was apprehended while collecting trash to make a living. Bernar, following the stereotype that crime is mostly perpetrated by the lower classes, assumes that he could be a potential killer. The camera reinforces the monstrous appearance of the trash collector through the pre-eminence of darkness, pronounced shadows, vertiginous camera angles, and unbalanced compositions, all of which combine to present the suspect with a blurry face, deformed silhouette, elongated extremities, and a pronounced and constant limp.

Ironically, this discriminatory association of crime and low socio-economic status dissipates at the end of the film. When detectives finally pursue Ulber, he tries to hide in the sewer system, where a group of homeless people live. These indigents, knowing that he is the black vampire, surround and capture him. In this case, the marginals contribute to obtaining poetic justice. To this group, Ulber is not an example of civility and, by virtue of the grisly murders, has fallen into the lowest social category. In opposition, by the film's conclusion Bernar is perceived as the centre of the world and nucleus of the investigative organism.

Bernar is a psychiatrist and a responsible detective who upholds traditional values and lives by societal norms. He bears the responsibility to ensure the protection of the citizens. He is a devoted husband whose wife is confined to a wheelchair, and he provides care for her. However, he does not stop at living ethically. Bernar goes further, pushing his world views on others. For instance, when he interviews Rita, he tells her that her job in the cabaret as a dancer is not appropriate for a woman who is raising a child. He even threatens her with reporting her to social services. In another scene, Bernar interrogates a sailor who is involved in illegal businesses as a potential suspect for the second murder. The sailor states that he is not the killer and that he was in the apartment complex having an affair with a married woman at the time. The detective interviews the adulteress and confirms the illicit romance alibi. Once again, Bernar threatens this female character and labels her shameless, revealing his sexist double standard because he does not judge the sailor.

These two examples illustrate a sexist double standard in Bernar, which is extended when he sexually harasses Rita, trying to force intimacy. This behaviour aligns with the popular concept of 'machismo', typical of Hispanic patriarchal societies. In 'Cinematic Categorization of Gender Identities from the Gaze of Sociological Imagination', Shilpa Khatri Babbar explains that 'through the popular cinematic discourses the aim to reclaim traditional hegemonic masculinity from 'emasculated' peers creates a 'retributive masculinity'.[24] In other words, popular film genres such as Gothic-noir, especially as nuanced for Hispanic audiences, present a narrative and a visual aesthetic that reinforces traditional masculinity, legitimating a double standard. In addition, the typical hard-boiled story emphasises male violence, sexual harassment, and the objectification of female characters. That we see this sexism reflected in Bernar's behaviour as well as that of Ulber illustrates the problematic gender politics of Argentine genre film.

Women in these films become reflections of such politics. *The Black Vampire* portrays male characters as powerful while showing women as weak. Reading through Khatri Babbar, such cinematic constructions illustrate the concept of 'contingent femininity', which 'is brought to the audience in the contingent frame, where [woman] is representative of dependability and reliability. Her gendered essence is shown to be relational, either as a wife, mother, daughter, or daughter-in-law.'[25] This is the case of detective Bernar's wife, whose name is never revealed. She is presented as a typical submissive housewife of the 1950s, having the duty of submission to please and obey her husband. Furthermore, she is disabled, rendering her more pitiable object than active subject.

Not all women in the film are so passive, however. Another female image that the film introduces to the audience exemplifies the category of 'intractable femininity', which includes the nonconformist woman who 'can be further subdivided into the aggressive and the autonomous types. The assertive feminine selves bring to the audience the girl power, emphasizing on sex as fun and throwing importance of female friendships as mechanism of coping with masculinity.'[26] Cora, the cabaret singer, being independent and confrontational, fits this model. She embraces her sexuality and has no shame about dancing in a nightclub for the gaze of men despite these types of activities being considered immoral.

The group of detectives who work with Bernar judge Cora and Rita harshly, assuming without evidence that they are sex workers and treating them with disrespect. To endure this hostile treatment, Cora and Rita maintain a strong friendship. They support each other as they navigate a disreputable job and male-dominated social environment. This bond reflects the sentimental type of relationship that Karen Hollinger finds reflected in the woman's film that dominated Hollywood cinema of the 1940s. Such a friendship can be 'nurturing and psychologically enriching', but 'it rarely leads to the promotion of significant cultural change. Its function is primarily to serve as a temporary respite [. . .]'.[27] Such relationships are rarely seen in horror or noir cinema, in which women tend to be isolated figures, achieving potence through manipulation of men or in acts of violence typical of the femme fatale. In the words of Sylvia Harvey, 'The two most common types of women in film noir are the exciting, childless whores, or the boring, potentially childbearing sweethearts.'[28] Again, *The Black Vampire* illustrates its ambiguity. Cora may have the fiery spirit of the femme fatale, but she has none of the treachery. And Rita may be more passive, but she is a caring mother, devoted to her daughter. Nonetheless, both are minor characters, trapped in the machismo of the world around them.

The complexity of female characterisation in the film and especially the presentation of female friendship links the Gothic-noir of *The Black Vampire* with melodrama. This sentimental style/genre is central to dictates for proper citizenship in Latin American cinema. In 'The Manual of Urbanity and Good Manners by Manuel Antonio Carreño: Rules for the Construction of the Ideal Citizen', María Fernanda Lander explains that

> in both the old and the new continent, the sentimental text served to train readers in a specific type of social behavior. In Latin America, an attempt was made to offer the independent subject of the new republics a code of 'civilized' behavior that was understood as following the rites and customs of the ruling class. [. . .] The sentimental discourse was the one that best aligned with the need to teach citizens capable of confronting the challenges that progress entailed.[29]

The sentimental mood of cinematic melodrama has the intention of moulding conservative Argentine citizens and is clearly conveyed in the film. Beyond Rita and Cora, the adulteress character exemplifies social demands for conventional moral 'decency'. The detectives have no remorse for exposing her to her family, for example. She desperately cries and begs them not to put her personal information in the murder case files; however, Bernar shows no pity and denies her request. In 'Norms and Deviation of Sentimental Genres' Nicolas Balutet points out that hyperbole is a resource of this type of narrative, which we see in the woman's desperate pleading.[30] The embedding of such emotive, melodramatic elements illustrates how Argentine popular culture explores social anxieties. Beyond the resolution that condemns the child murderer, behavioural norms are reinforced through the judgement of unacceptable people and behaviours, particularly women.

Melodrama also produces catharsis for viewers, central to Gothic tropes. In one of the final scenes, Rita goes to Ulber's house to pick up her daughter. As he refuses to give her the child, she quickly reaches overdramatic heights of sadness and frustration. She dramatically begs the vampire to return her daughter to her and repeatedly screams, 'You are crazy!' The emphatic evocation of strong suffering provokes empathy and compassion in the viewer. Such a scene produces cathartic emotions and facilitates 'the expulsion of the object of fear', argues Nicolas Balutet. 'Transgression, provoking fears of social disintegration, thus enable[s] the reconstitution of limits and boundaries.'[31] The conflict between Ulber and Rita illustrates well the blending of the Gothic (the predator vampire), hard-boiled noir (criminal and victim), and the melodramatic (hyperbolic sentimentalism).

In conclusion, *The Black Vampire* can be most usefully explored as a film that revisits the tension of civilisation and barbarism of the 1950s Argentina, nuanced by the Gothic mode and the content and visual effects of film noir. In addition, psychoanalysis permeates the aesthetics of the film in its presentation of Freudian neurosis. Moreover, the film exhibits a traditional hegemonic masculinity as the cinematic gaze weakens female representation to reaffirm social norms. This process creates a melodramatic effect that promotes 'proper' behaviour in accordance with the customs of the Latin American ruling class. Ultimately, this Gothic-noir picture offers a macabre story of a predator vampire that fuses horror and mystery to explore the darkest places of Argentine society of the 1950s.

Notes

1. Tamara Falicov, *The Cinematic Tango: Contemporary Argentine Film* (London: Wallflower Press, 2007), p. 16.
2. Fernando Pagnoni Berns, 'Cine de terror argentino: Historia, temas y estética de un género en el período clásico', in *Horrofílmico: Aproximaciones al cine de terror en Latinoamérica y el Caribe*, ed. Rosana Díaz-Zambrana and Patricia Tomé (San Juan, Puerto Rico: Editorial Isla Negra, 2011), pp. 432, 436.
3. Fred Botting, *Gothic* (Routledge, 2007), p. 156.
4. Carmen Serrano, *Gothic Imagination in Latin American Fiction and Film* (Albuquerque: New Mexico University Press, 2019), p. 61.
5. *Compadritos* are lower-class males from marginal suburban areas who behave violently.
6. The proliferation of Gothic-noir films occurs alongside multiple dictatorships such as that of José Uriburu (1930–2), the Revolution of 1943 (1943–6), and the Liberating Revolution (1955–8).
7. Elvio Gandolfo and Eduardo Hojman, *El terror argentino* (Buenos Aires: Alfaguara, 2002), p. 14.
8. Carina Rodríguez, *El cine de terror en Argentina: producción, distribución, exhibición y mercado* (Bernal: Universidad Nacional de Quilmes, 2014), p. 52.
9. Osvaldo Di Paolo and Nadina Olmedo, *Negrótico* (Madrid: Pliegos, 2015), p. 205.
10. Lee Horsley, *The Noir Thriller* (New York: Palgrave Macmillan, 2001), p. 9.
11. Dialogue from *The Black Vampire* is our translation.
12. Winfried Fluck, 'Crime, Guilt, and Subjectivity in "Film Noir"', *American Studies* 46 (2001), p. 384, https://www.jstor.org/stable/pdf/41157665.pdf.
13. The Spanish Royal Academy defines 'mestizo' as a person born of a mother and a father of different races, specifically white and Indigenous and 'mulato' as a person born of a mother and a father of different races, specifically black and white.
14. Claudio España, *Cine argentino: Industria y clacismo. 1933/1956* (Buenos Aires: Fondo Nacional de las Artes, 2000), p. 130.
15. Sigmund Freud, 'Más allá del principio del placer', in *Psicología de las masas y análisis del yo y otras obras (1920–1922) XVIII* (Buenos Aires: Amorrortu, 2013), p. 20.
16. Freud, 'Más allá del principio del placer', p. 32.

17. James Naremore, *Film Noir: A Very Short Introduction* (Oxford: Oxford University Press, 2019), p. 76.
18. José Juan del Col, *Psicoanálisis de Freud y religión* (Buenos Aires: Centro Salesiano de Estudios San Juan Bosco, 1996), p. 22.
19. Botting, *Gothic*, p. 12.
20. Freud, 'Más allá del principio del placer', p. 61.
21. Francesc Gomà, *Conocer Freud y su obra* (Barcelona: Dopesa, 1979), p. 8.
22. Sigmund Freud, 'Duelo y melancolía' in *Obras completas. Contribución a la historia del movimiento psicoanalítico. Trabajos sobre meta-psicología y otras obras (1914–1916) XIV* (Buenos Aires: Amorrortu, 2013), p. 252.
23. Naremore, *Film Noir: A Very Short Introduction*, p. 58.
24. Shilpa Khatri Babbar, 'Cinematic Categorization of Gender Identities from the Gaze of Sociological Imagination', *IORS Journal of Humanities and Social Sciences* 23 (2018), p. 23, http://www.iosrjournals.org/iosr-jhss/papers/Vol.%2023%20Issue7/Version-5/D2307052025.pdf.
25. Khatri Babbar, 'Cinematic Categorization of Gender Identities from the Gaze of Sociological Imagination', p. 21.
26. Khatri Babbar, 'Cinematic Categorization of Gender Identities from the Gaze of Sociological Imagination', p. 22.
27. Karen Hollinger, *In the Company of Women: Contemporary Female Friendship Films* (Minneapolis: University of Minnesota Press, 1998), p. 7.
28. Sylvia Harvey, 'Woman's Place: The Absent Family of Film Noir', in *Women in Film Noir*, ed. E. Ann Kaplan (London: British Film Institute, 1998), p. 38
29. María Fernanda Lander, 'El Manual de urbanidad y buenas maneras de Manuel Antonio Carreño: reglas para la construcción del ciudadano ideal', *Arizona Journal of Hispanic Cultural Studies* 6 (2002), p. 84, https://muse.jhu.edu/article/378590/pdf. The translation is ours.
30. Nicolas Balutet, 'Normas y desviación de los géneros sentimentales en *Como agua para chocolate* de Laura Esquivel', *Polifonía* 9 (2019), p. 3, https://www.apsu.edu/polifonia/volume_9/2019-1-balutet.pdf.
31. Botting, *Gothic*, p. 8.

PART III

AESTHETICS AND ANTECEDENTS

9. A 'FEELING OF SUSPENSION': TRADITION AND MODERNITY IN *LA POINTE COURTE*

Alicia Byrnes

'In Paris it seemed normal to have you as a partner. Here, I can feel the strangeness of our connection.' So Elle (Silvia Monfort) tells Lui (Philippe Noiret) on one of their many jaunts through La Pointe Courte in Agnès Varda's debut film, *La Pointe Courte* (1955). Elle and Lui's predicament constitutes just one part of Varda's film; the other half treats the routines and hardships of La Pointe Courte's citizens. Varda arranges the film's two parts so that they alternate, forming a dualistic structure that many consider *La Pointe Courte*'s distinguishing feature.[1] This chapter seeks out further dualisms in order to foreground the unifying space of La Pointe Courte. I contend that the lens of noir encourages us to understand Varda's film as about its titular location on the precipice of significant social and cultural change.

Elle's assertion reveals *La Pointe Courte*'s profound relation to space in several ways. For one, her comparison of Paris, where the couple live, to La Pointe Courte, where they holiday, conveys the dissimilarity of these places despite their connection by train (or boat, as is the case for the village's less modern inhabitants). The figurative distance between the locations is underscored by Elle's changed relationship to her marriage: in Paris, she could get on with Lui; in La Pointe Courte, things feel different. The film's depiction of its setting suggests that the 'strangeness' Elle experiences here is not just a symptom of her dislocation but has something specific to do with La Pointe Courte. Indeed, the film's titular location displays a stuck-in-time quality that would seem capable of transforming one's view of their relationship. Moreover, the purpose of Elle and Lui's conversation – whether to stay together or separate – speaks to the circumstance of La Pointe Courte at this time. The couple's predicament turns on a question of stasis versus change that encompasses the process of modernisation underway in post-war France.

Film noir, specifically as it is framed by Jennifer Fay and Justus Nieland as a response to the global force of modernity, brings this understudied but crucial aspect of *La Pointe Courte* into view.[2] In this chapter I situate Varda's film as a meditation on the modernisation of her native France. 1954 marks both the year that *La Pointe Courte* was produced, thus beginning Varda's long and vibrant film career, and the year that France began to modernise. I heed this confluence of events to propose the film as a document of Varda's recognition that national change is afoot. To do so, I consider a number of dialectics present across multiple levels of the film – including tradition-modernity, stasis-movement, inside-outside, realism-artifice, marriage-separation – that altogether convey Varda's concern about the transition from old to new. Indeed, what makes *La Pointe Courte* especially noirish, I contend, is the anxious timbre of Varda's meditation. She portrays the film's dual stories and the unifying backdrop of La Pointe Courte (a location with which she has a personal affinity) with a level of apprehension about modern life – its industrial components, its sense of time, its disregard for tradition. The lens of noir clarifies Varda's apprehension and provides new context for this unusual film.

La Pointe Courte is something of an anomaly within film history. Varda herself asserted that the film began the French New Wave, insofar as it laid the foundations for 'another approach, another vision' for the cinema.[3] Relevant scholarship corroborates Varda's claim, pointing towards the film's low budget (it was made for approximately seven million old francs or $14,000), its development outside of the French studio system, its use of location shooting, its modernist aesthetic, Varda's age (she was only twenty-five during filming), and the fact that it was her first film as proof that *La Pointe Courte* anticipated the New Wave.[4] Such affinities granted, Varda's film still seems to sit uncomfortably in relation to that movement. For one, *La Pointe Courte* was largely brushed over by the *Cahiers du Cinéma* critics who would become central to the New Wave. At the Paris premiere of her film, Varda remembers 'feeling small, ignorant, and the only woman among the guys from *Cahiers*'.[5] François Truffaut subsequently penned a review of the film that Kelley Conway calls 'oddly malicious', wherein he criticised Varda's framing, her dialogue and her direction, and noted her likeness to Lui.[6] *La Pointe Courte* never received distribution and was subsequently 'obliterated in the tidal wave' of the French New Wave proper, including such films as *Hiroshima mon amour* (Alain Resnais, 1959), *Les quatre cents coups* (*The 400 Blows*, Truffaut, 1959), and *À bout de souffle* (*Breathless*, Jean-Luc Godard, 1960).[7] The *Cahiers* critics' appreciation for the former film is especially curious given its numerous similarities to

La Pointe Courte (namely, a focus on the dialectic between public and private, writerly dialogue, and the incorporation of documentary-style footage), not least of which pertains to the involvement of Resnais, who edited Varda's film.[8] In toto, *La Pointe Courte* stands as a film that anticipated the New Wave by some years, but was never properly embraced by the movement.

The awkwardness of this embrace stems in part from Varda's disposition as a filmmaker. Varda, by her own admission, knew little about the cinema when she made *La Pointe Courte*.[9] Prior to this point she had studied fine art and literature and worked as a photographer for the Théâtre National Populaire, only turning to the cinema because she 'simply felt the need to make this film'.[10] Moreover, at the time of *La Pointe Courte*'s conception, Varda had not encountered any film theory nor even *seen* many films (when pressed, she recalled having seen Orson Welles's *Citizen Kane* (1941), Marcel Carné's *Quai des Brumes* (1938), and *Les Enfants du paradis* (1945) – all of which, notably, evince a noir pedigree). Hardly a cinephile, Varda drew inspiration for her film from cinema-adjacent mediums (for instance, literature, photography, drawing). Her peculiar profile as a filmmaker makes *La Pointe Courte* a perplexing film, one that resists easy categorisation. Prevailing discourse is apposite: André Bazin, the lone *Cahiers* critic to champion the film, calls *La Pointe Courte* 'miraculous';[11] and Richard Neupert, in his monograph on the New Wave, describes Varda's film as 'unusual' and 'haunting'.[12] At the risk of qualifying a film that derives power from its uniqueness, part of my purpose with this chapter is to lend new understanding to *La Pointe Courte* through the lens of noir.

La Pointe Courte could be associated with film noir in a number of ways. For one, the film reveals noir roots through its source material. Varda drew the inspiration for the film's unusual structure from William Faulkner's *The Wild Palms* (1939), a novel which likewise alternated two unconnected stories in a series of chapters. Not only was Faulkner an avid fan of detective fiction with reportedly twenty-five works of the genre sitting on his desk when he died, but *The Wild Palms* has also been likened to a detective story due to its fragmented form.[13] Faulkner was also involved in a network of cross-medial influence crucial to the invention of film noir.[14] He worked a brief stint in Hollywood as a screenwriter, most notably penning the screenplay for *The Big Sleep* (Howard Hawks, 1946). In fact, during his time in Hollywood Faulkner also came across a film treatment written by Sergei Eisenstein that incorporated montage elements.[15] That Faulkner subsequently incorporated such elements into his literary practice, foremost the structure of *The Wild Palms*, suggests Varda might have been indirectly influenced by the cinema. Furthermore, Faulkner was among a pantheon of American modernist writers, including John Dos Passos, Ernest Hemingway, and John Steinbeck, who enjoyed popularity among French intellectuals during the 1930s. The taste for such novels surely served as a primer for the similar mood of film noir, and James Naremore goes so far as to note that early 'critical discourse on [film noir] usually consists of little more than a restatement of familiar modernist themes' inaugurated by these writers.[16] Varda's adaptation of Faulkner's novel thus links *La Pointe Courte* to a system of transnational, cross-medium exchange responsible for film noir's formation.

La Pointe Courte also displays some stylistic qualities typical of film noir. Most plainly, the film uses harsh Mediterranean sunlight to naturally contrast light and shadow, creating a chiaroscuro look that Varda describes as 'rigid'.[17] A key noir cinematographic trope, the canted camera angle features heavily in the sections of the film concerning the couple to contribute to that story's overall modernist aesthetic. *La Pointe Courte*'s dualistic structure points towards film noir's interest in binary oppositions, specifically as they serve to unsettle 'unifying [myths]' like the American Dream.[18] Moreover, Varda's film features an ambiguous ending, the meaning of which has become a fixation for film scholars. As this brief list attests, *La Pointe Courte* displays a number of genealogical and stylistic connections to film noir. While I am mindful of these connections, I contend that the film can be most productively linked to film noir through its use of setting.

That Varda chose La Pointe Courte as the setting for her treatise on modernity is no accident. Varda came to the project with a personal tie to the location, one that was only strengthened during the process of filming. Varda spent time living in La Pointe Courte as a child and initially returned as an adult 'to record images and sounds as a favor for a terminally ill friend who could no longer visit his home'.[19] Her stay proved fateful; after reviewing the footage she decided to shoot a film in the village. In preparation, Varda spent 'weeks and weeks' in La Pointe Courte, 'talking to people, walking around, observing the inhabitants of the place'.[20] Her fieldwork ultimately formed the basis for parts of the film; Varda plotted the things that she observed into scenes and used the villagers as actors. Events dramatised for the film include a quarrel between a couple and their teenage daughter about her marriage; gossip among local women as they undertake housekeeping duties; and the hardships of the local fishermen.[21] Varda was so moved by the latter story that she even said *La Pointe Courte* was 'created for and with the fishermen'.[22] As this dedication suggests, Varda is extremely fond of La Pointe Courte, its people, and customs. It is therefore telling that she chose to tell this particular story of modernity here. Given that Varda holds the village so dear, it follows that she sees the changes to its culture wrought by modernisation as unwelcome.

Varda's project gains clarity through film noir, specifically a theory of the style that foregrounds local crises. Jennifer Fay and Justus Nieland's framework is instructive: they understand film noir as 'a fully internationalized phenomenon, and as an expression of disquiet with the conditions of a modern, globalized age'.[23] Per their rubric, film noir has, since the 1930s, figured as a response to modernity 'in its traumatic, catastrophic, or irrational registers'.[24] They write:

> Our story of noir's internationalism is ... linked to the broader condition of global disquiet with the mobile and dislocated social and cultural relations of modernity itself: of rootless and wandering desire; of chance, accident, and class instability; of local traditions and spaces either imperiled or energized by global flows of culture and capital; and of homelife across the world that has become unsettled, uncanny, or newly foreign.[25]

Noir films thus rehearse anxieties about the state of national life – 'its rootedness in tradition, or its movement into the future, or its traumatic upheavals, displacements and confusions' – in the face of the levelling force of modernity.[26] Such anxieties are typically registered through the motif of 'local crime', which articulates 'the crises of local spaces' through generic features such as sex, violence, and corruption.[27] Importantly for the case of *La Pointe Courte*, Fay and Nieland's emphasis on the local allows for the existence of film noir outside of the national and temporal boundaries posed by the classical Hollywood period. Because the local is both universal and eternal, noir films are liable to appear in diverse contexts relative to internal patterns of change.

With Fay and Nieland's framework in mind, *La Pointe Courte*'s fraught articulation of place becomes legible as a response to the contemporaneous process of modernisation. Filmed in 1954, Varda's film captures the village during the early stages of French modernisation, a process that Kristin Ross describes as especially abrupt. Although post-war France was poised for a new way of living, the nation's state-led modernisation process was so swift as to be experienced as 'highly destructive' to traditional culture.[28] Ross details the expediency of the process beginning around 1954: 'In the space of just ten years a rural woman might live with the acquisition of electricity, running water, a stove, a refrigerator, a washing-machine, a sense of interior space as distinct from exterior space, a car, a television, and the various liberations and oppressions associated with each.'[29] The brash introduction of modern products and systems into a society that 'still cherished prewar outlooks' engendered feelings of ambivalence amongst its citizens.[30] Excitement about the new was counterbalanced by a sense of loss or nostalgia for the nation's old way of life.[31]

It seems likely that Varda shared in such feelings of ambivalence. The filmmaker's affection for the village of La Pointe Courte, as well as her subsequent involvement in the Situationist International, bespeak her attachment to traditional French culture and corresponding wariness of modern life.[32] In what follows, I propose *La Pointe Courte* as a document of Varda's ambivalence. I demonstrate that a tension between old and new is central to the film, foremost through its featured cinematographic technique of the wandering camera, its juxtaposing structure, and the narratives contained by its dual parts. While in all instances the balance of the tension is skewed to favour France's traditional way of life, modern signs and systems are detailed in an intrusive way that suggests social and cultural change is as unwanted as it is inevitable. The terms of Varda's meditation on modernisation certainly chime with Fay and Nieland's understanding of film noir – the rub of the film's binary oppositions suggests a culture in the throes of transformation, grappling for stability as old and new ways of life converge. Fay and Nieland's framework in turn allows us to better appreciate the anxious register of Varda's film.

La Pointe Courte's opening tracking shot presents the titular village in a manner that evokes the film's undergirding tension between the old and new. After an initial shot that delivers the film's title credits over a close-up of a plank of wood, the camera pans left and tracks down an empty street of La Pointe Courte. The setting itself displays a static quality; the narrow street is silent, bar the sound of distant seagulls, and its gravel footing is dissected by dense, angular shadows traced by the terracotta houses that flank it. Varda's mobile camera seems intent on unsettling the stillness of the space. For one, the camera's view is unsteady and set at an awkward height that produces the sense that it is hovering. It tracks down the empty street and subsequently observes a health inspector waiting outside one home in the village (thus inaugurating one of the film's key narrative threads) and then wanders into a home where a mother serves up food to her brood of small children. The camera moves fluidly through these scenes, satisfying its interests (a peak through a window into the first home; a look at the knitted children's clothes draped over the doorway of the second home; a passage through the second home to a room located at its rear where a child lies under a blanket) as it continues its forward movement.

The camera technique featured in this scene – the wandering camera – is one used throughout *La Pointe Courte* to produce a sense of tension. The technique does so in this opening scene in a few ways. For one, the camera's unsteadiness and its mobility both accentuate and corrupt the apparent stillness of La Pointe Courte. Moreover, the camera's journey through the village is characterised by detachment; it is curious about the villagers and their dwellings but does not allow these things to disrupt its progress. Such detachment sets up an inside-outside dichotomy for the setting's presentation, one that encourages us to witness the space as if it were historically distant, like a museum. Finally, the wandering camera establishes a break between the film's diegesis and form. Its pace and roaming perspective inhibit our immersion in the story world, instead distinguishing the diegesis and the lens by which we view it as discrete entities.

This latter feature of the technique is especially evident in another scene, where the wandering camera introduces Elle and Lui as a couple. In this later scene the camera seems restless, tracking the couple's gaze rather than foregrounding their movements and altogether exercising a will of its own. The camera pans to objects that it finds interesting (such as when it drifts from the couple's conversation to attend to a nearby pile of wood) or arrives in spaces ahead of the couple so that their entry into the frame is delayed. Such camerawork is redolent of film noir in its alienating effects, instigating a rupture between form and content that echoes the stasis-movement and inside-outside dialectics of *La Pointe Courte*'s opening scene. These oppositions altogether generate a sense of tension that figures to convey La Pointe Courte's place between the poles of tradition and modernity.

La Pointe Courte's juxtaposing structure offers a more overt articulation of the conflict between old and new. Varda replicates the organisation of Faulkner's novel, *The Wild Palms*, with two distinct stories connected by setting arranged in alternation. Varda said that she admired the 'feeling of suspension'[33] generated by Faulkner's structure; the way that, in the course of reading, 'two unrelated things become superimposed in your mind'.[34] This notion equally applies to Varda's film. The sections concerning the villagers and those involving the Parisian couple are composed to express a contrast between tradition and modernity. By pitting the film's parts against each other, we come to see them in a system of exchange. Varda effectively makes a dialectic of the film's structure, one that encompasses the untidy process of modernisation.

Varda pays homage to France's old way of life through the formal language of the sections featuring the villagers. As has been widely noted, these sections are shot in a neorealist style, using real locations, natural light, non-actors and dialogue scripted from local events and interactions witnessed by Varda. Moreover, Varda dedicates much of the frame of these sequences to the documentation of local practices. She seldom uses close-ups and scales the shots at a certain distance, often using mid- or high-angle shots, so that the tasks that the villagers complete while they converse (for instance, packing fish, mending fishing lines) can be studied. Rebecca DeRoo takes this idea a step further: she situates Varda's method of framing as an effort to archive the traditional practices of La Pointe Courte. DeRoo, in her valuable study of the role of intermediality in Varda's work, likens such shots to *petit métiers*, or minor trades, a genre of photography driven by 'preservationist ideas – the notion of documenting local practices disappearing in the face of modernization, and capturing vernacular practices – people and labor – that might not otherwise be part of the visual archive'.[35] Given her background in photography, Varda's awareness of the genre seems likely.[36] In lieu of a cinematic touchstone, this reference here serves to verify the filmmaker's exigent desire to document traditional French culture.

Varda gives equal attention to local housekeeping practices in these sections. She demonstrates the centrality of women to the daily running of La Pointe Courte through their depiction packing shellfish, rearing children, and air-drying laundry. Varda seems most enchanted by this latter activity, with numerous shots dedicated to capturing the movement of white linens suspended in the breeze. One particularly memorable sequence sees two local women retrieving sheets draped along clothes lines at the edge of the canal. The wandering camera passes through a line of sheets to reach the women, momentarily arching to observe a man who sits at the right edge of the frame pedalling a manual sewing machine. The camera presents a series of close-ups depicting one woman taking the sheets down from the line, her hand moving in and out of frame to remove each peg. In a most evocative shot, her hand reaches up from the bottom of the frame and grasps at a sheet that the wind has carried up out of reach. Varda's poetic treatment of this banal activity suggests her reverence for La Pointe Courte's traditional way of life. Alas, the breeze that carries the sheets marks the women's task with a tinge of melancholy; the breeze is the mistral, a strong, cold, northwesterly wind that blows from Southern France into the Mediterranean at times of seasonal change.

France's future is exemplified by Elle and Lui. The sections of *La Pointe Courte* concerning the couple are appropriately dense with visual associations to modernity. Where the villagers' story is presented in a neorealist style that largely aims to offer a transparent recreation of reality, the couple's story is highly constructed in a way that has been understood as distinctly modern. Conway observes that in these sections of the film, 'style, far from serving to support or clarify the plot, often draws attention to itself, seemingly for its own sake'.[37] The couple's story is articulated using the previously discussed canted camera angles, careful blocking (including a seminal shot that anticipates one from *Persona* (Ingmar Bergman, 1966), wherein Elle and Lui's faces are momentarily framed in close-up at a perfectly adjacent angle), and editing designed to test the rules of cinematic perception (such as the disruption of the 180-degree rule). Such emphatic stylistic choices serve not only as a counterpoint to the subtle visual language of the villagers' sequences, but also suggest Varda's regard for modern culture as aloof and perplexing.

Signs of industrial modernity proliferate the *mise en scène* of the sections concerning the couple. Tellingly, the scene of their debut sees Lui on his way to meet Elle from the train. Lui, a native of La Pointe Courte, arrived in the village on his own and expected Elle to join him a couple of days later. Alas, she arrives after five days. A pair of onlooking locals commentate Lui's journey to the local train station:

> Villager 1: He already met the Paris train yesterday.
> Villager 2: Who's he expecting?
> Villager 1: His wife.
> Villager 2: Doesn't he know when?
> Villager 1: He says he doesn't.

The villagers' dialogue and the attendant introduction to the couple reveal Varda's suspicions about modernity. The couple are aligned with modern time, a regulated system that dictates the once-daily arrival of the train in La Pointe Courte and that has some hand in their disconnection. The train schedule facilitates Elle's evasion of the couple's plans – she relies on the timetable to announce her prospective arrival, rather than correspond directly with Lui – and foretells their miscommunication prior to her arrival. Our first proper look at Lui reflects the confusion begotten by the train systems: he is presented in a long shot traversing a mess of intersecting train lines on his way to meet Elle. The shot is framed to convey the train system's immenseness, with the train tracks assuming the width of the frame and the overhead electrical wires segmenting the clear sky.

The subsequent sections depicting the couple feature elements of industrial modernity that disrupt their contact to more or less overt degrees. Tall cranes, telephone lines, and black smoke from oil refineries are clearly visible in the background of a number of mid-shots. Twice, the couple's jaunt around La Pointe Courte is circumvented by passing trains. Especially notable is the rickety old train that interrupts their journey back to their homestay in this introductory sequence. We hear the train before we see it; the sound of its squeaking gears bleeds into the scene prior, wherein Elle first hints at her intentions to separate. The next shot sees the train approaching at the centre of the frame with the couple stationed at its left side. 'Let's talk about it at once!', Lui demands as they pause to let the train pass. Clearly impervious to this pivotal chain of dialogue, the train moves at a glacial pace and emits a screeching sound that amplifies as it nears the camera. Here again, the train gets in the way of Elle and Lui's clear communication. Even after it passes out of shot, its screeching is still audible, muffling Elle's grave admission: 'I came to tell you we should separate.'

The presentation of the landscape in the sections featuring the couple further conveys their association with modern France, and therefore their displacement in La Pointe Courte. In distinction from the locals' scenes, which are centrally set and dense with people and objects, the couple are largely depicted in isolation and often in vast, empty exterior spaces. They map an alternate terrain of La Pointe Courte, one which is landlocked, desolate, and littered with debris. Varda uses long shots and distant high-angled shots to show the couple passing through a field of unruly brush, a marsh, and a swampy stretch of beach strewn with washed up barrels and broken wicker baskets. Moreover, if the landscape that the couple pass through is bordered by water, Varda frames the shot so that signs of open water are eliminated. The couple's vantage on La Pointe Courte is thus as something of an abstracted wasteland.

The arrangement of *La Pointe Courte*'s dual stories insists that we perceive them in association, despite their many differences. The sense of care and attention apparent in the villagers' story is offset by its pairing with the sections involving the couple. As a result, the former story takes on something of the sinister quality of the latter and, inversely, the couple's story is softened by the scenes of the villagers. Varda effectively builds a tension – a 'feeling of suspension' – into the film's structure that distils the process of modernisation. Her coding of that process here – as jarring; as subject to friction – is made acute by the lens of noir, thus augmenting the film's resonance.

Varda's concern about this transition reverberates within the narratives of the film's respective parts. The narrative thrust, such as it is, of the villagers' story involves the surveillance of local fishing practices by the health department. The government is specifically concerned that the villagers are fishing in waters without a permit and catching shellfish from a nearby bay which is supposedly polluted. This thread illustrates, in quite literal terms, the struggle between the new and old ways of life. The health inspectors figure as a form of bureaucracy that impinges on the traditions and livelihood of the villagers. Varda emphasises the inspectors' affiliation with modern France through their presentation. The government officials who appear at the home of one fisherman in the film's opening scene are dressed in suits and dress shoes. The fisherman's daughter comments that they look 'like a couple of gangsters'. The semantics of this description do not seem coincidental. The French health officials are likened to a noirish emblem of American cinema, one of modernity's chief exports. Soldering this link between the health officials and a new order, another set of government workers arrive in La Pointe Courte via a flashy new motorboat that one local woman calls 'a real thunderbolt'. The health officials effectively represent a modern France that is wealthy, businesslike, and decidedly un-French.

Additionally, the cause for the health department's interest in the fishing practices of La Pointe Courte would seem to be an offshoot of modernisation: the waters are noxious due to industrial run-off. Varda's film draws inspiration from the recent history of the lagoon in which the fisherman harvest shellfish, *étang de Thau*, where 'the thriving shellfish practices in the 1950s were being threatened by pollution (from the growth of nearby cities, industry, and tourism), and were being heavily regulated due to fears of bacterial contamination'.[38] This historical detail gives real weight to the fishermen's narrative and in so doing underscores the threat to traditional French culture imposed by modern systems.

The process of modernisation is portrayed in equally problematic terms in an earlier scene also involving the regulation of water. In a rare moment of coincidence between *La Pointe Courte*'s two parts, the couple hosting Elle and Lui in La Pointe Courte show them to their newly refurbished room. The couple are pleased with its modernness: Elle comments, 'Very nice!'; and Lui, 'It's brand new! Clean!' Their host proudly announces that the room's attached basin has running water. Alas, when he releases the tap no water appears. 'I mean, [there's] water when there's water', he explains. 'It was connected this year at Issanca. Then they cut it off. I hope we'll have water next year.' Varda's suspicions about modernity are signalled by the awkward refurbishment of this guest room. The room is outfitted with modern luxuries, which Varda underscores through a slow pan of its interior and Elle and Lui's delighted reactions. The visage of modernity is punctured, however, by the erratic functioning of the water. This particular house received running water only for it to be cut off, perhaps reconnected next year. The stymied arrival of modern systems to La Pointe Courte exemplified here upends illusions of modernisation as a smoothing functioning, even process.[39]

Appropriately, the sections of *La Pointe Courte* concerning Elle and Lui narrativise the transition from tradition to modernity through dialogue rather than action. The couple are, after all, visiting La Pointe Courte for a reprieve. (Although, as one local woman observes, their retreat appears to be far from leisurely: 'Some vacation! . . . They talk too much to be happy.') As the couple meander through the more landlocked spaces of La Pointe Courte they discuss their relationship (including the revelation that he has cheated), and contemplate whether to stay together. As previously noted, their discussion centrally reflects the film's tension between old and new as it involves a decision for sameness – staying together – or change – separating.

The couple's lines of dialogue evince this tension through recurring phrases pertaining to pastness or stillness and change. In a sequence occurring about halfway through the film, which is perhaps the couple's most significant and tense exchange, they repeatedly refer to their relationship in terms of pastness: 'Our love's like an old beau'; 'You can't tell me our love hasn't aged.' Such associations between their relationship and pastness are counterbalanced by lines regarding newness as forward movement: 'When I met you . . . I went toward you . . . I saw [our love] frolic . . . I saw it grow while others envied it.' Importantly, Varda's screenplay connects these associations – pastness as marriage; newness as progress – to a larger network of signifiers relating to place. The couple refer to La Pointe Courte as a site of 'rest', a place which taught Lui to 'keep still'. Moreover, the village provides Lui the same kind of 'happiness' that he finds in their marriage. These lines connecting inertia-marriage-happiness-La Pointe Courte are contrasted by ones that frame separation in geographical terms: 'I imagine myself living somewhere else, differently.' Elle and Lui's language relating to their future as a couple symbolises Varda's feelings about the contemporaneous state of France. As the nation adopts a new way of life it abandons the unifying and restorative aspects of the old.

Discussions of *La Pointe Courte*'s ending typically turn on the question of whether Elle and Lui will stay together. In the film's final minutes, the couple are seen walking along a street of La Pointe Courte, luggage in hand, on their way to the local train station. Their conversation is friendly but opaque as it concerns their future plans, leading the viewer to wonder about the fate of their marriage – or, per my reading, the fate of France. Although this feature of the film's ending is intriguing, it seems to me that *La Pointe Courte*'s most poignant final thought is offered in the scene immediately subsequent. In this brief latter scene – the film's last, save a shot of a trio of local musicians – a group of villagers pile into a wooden boat fitted with a small motor and set off for Paris. A long shot captures the boat as it streams down the canal and under a metal bridge supporting a passing train, possibly carrying Elle and Lui. The villagers' conversation is still audible as the boat moves out of clear view: 'When do we get to Paris?' a woman's voice asks; 'Tomorrow morning', a man answers. The scene affirms *La Pointe Courte*'s principal interest in place and offers a tentative forecast for the setting's future. The train passes the upper third of the image to form a perpendicular angle with the boat below, thus encompassing the film's central conflict between tradition and modernity in a single, arresting shot. The speed at which the train moves relative to the far slower boat conveys Varda's thoughts about the rate of French modernisation and what the nation leaves behind.

The lack of scholarly attention granted to this penultimate shot leads me to believe that *La Pointe Courte* depends on the lens of film noir to bring its ideas about its context into focus. Film noir emerged as a response to the global force of modernity, thus producing a set of films that are geographically and temporally varied, and decidedly anxious. By placing Varda's enigmatic but important film under such a framework, we can appreciate it in new ways. For one, the many binary oppositions that the film entertains across multiple levels – foremost between tradition and modernity, but also past-future, content-form, realism-artifice, marriage-separation, and so forth – become legible as a reflection on the sociocultural climate of post-war France. Second, the film's strange and unsettling mood is both made intelligible and augmented through association with the film noir. To end, I would like to propose this fit as mutually enriching. By linking Varda's film to the style, we can further efforts to dispel the notion that film noir is historically contained or American. More profoundly, such an association serves to diversify this distinctly masculine cinematic category.

Notes

1. Agnès Varda and Pierre Uytterhoeven, 'Agnès Varda from 5 to 7', in *Agnès Varda: Interviews*, ed. Jefferson T. Kline (Jackson: University Press of Mississippi, 2014), p. 3.
2. Jennifer Fay and Justus Nieland, *Film Noir: Hard-Boiled Modernity and the Cultures of Globalization* (London and New York: Routledge, 2010).

3. Agnès Varda, 'Agnès Varda on *La Pointe Courte*', *La Pointe Courte*, DVD, directed by Agnès Varda (1954; USA: Criterion Collection, 2008).
4. Kelley Conway, 'Planning and Precision: La Pointe Courte', in *Agnés Varda* (Champaign: University of Illinois Press, 2015), pp. 9–25; Rebecca J. DeRoo, *Agnés Varda: Between Film, Photography, and Art* (Oakland: University of California Press, 2017); Richard Neupert, 'Testing the Water: Alexander Astruc, Agnés Varda, and Jean-Pierre Melville', in *A History of the French New Wave Cinema*, 2nd ed. (Madison: University of Wisconsin Press, 2002), pp. 45–72; Varda, 'Agnés Varda on *La Pointe Courte*'.
5. Varda quoted in Neupert, 'Testing the Water', p. 63.
6. Truffaut translated by Conway, 'Planning and Precision', p. 25.
7. Ginette Vincendeau, 'La Pointe Courte: How Agnès Varda "Invented" the New Wave', The Criterion Collection, 21 January 2008, https://www.criterion.com/current/posts/497-la-pointe-courte-how-agn-s-varda-invented-the-new-wave.
8. For more on the differing reception of *Hiroshima mon amour* and *La Pointe Courte*, see Lauren Du Graft, 'The Wild Palms in a New Wave: Adaptive Gleaning and the Birth of the Nouvelle Vague', *Adaptation* 10, no. 1 (2016), pp. 43–7.
9. DeRoo persuasively debunks this notion, suggesting that Varda wilfully cultivates 'myths of her own naiveté' to thwart ideas about her work as derivative. See DeRoo, *Agnés Varda*, p. 17.
10. André Bazin, 'La Pointe Courte: A Film Free and Pure', in *French Cinema from the Liberation to the New Wave, 1945–1958* (New Orleans: University of New Orleans Press, 2012), p. 318.
11. André Bazin, 'La Pointe Courte', p. 318.
12. Neupert, 'Testing the Water', pp. 60–1.
13. Carolyn Porter, *William Faulkner: Lives and Legacies* (Oxford: Oxford University Press, 2007), p. 188.
14. Sarah Keller argues that a cross-medial tendency is characteristic of the modernist movement at large. Keller, 'Introduction: Jean Epstein and the Revolt of Cinema', in *Jean Epstein: Critical Essays and New Translations*, ed. Keller and Jason N. Paul (Amsterdam: Amsterdam University Press, 2012), p. 28.
15. Faulkner tried his hand at a treatment of *Sutter's Gold* (James Cruze, 1936) for Paramount Studios during his time in Hollywood, an assignment that had previously been attempted by Eisenstein. Sarah Gleeson-White maps the similarities between Eisenstein's and Faulkner's treatments to convincingly argue for the significance of Eisenstein's parallel montage for Faulkner's subsequent literary practice. Sarah Gleeson-White, 'Auditory Exposures: Faulkner, Eisenstein, and Film Sound', *PMLA* 128, no. 1 (2013), pp. 87–100. See also Bruce F. Kawin, 'The Montage Element in Faulkner's Fiction', in *Selected Film Essays and Interviews*, ed. Bruce F. Kawin (London and New York: Anthem Press, 2013), pp. 131–48.
16. James Naremore, *More than Night: Film Noir in Its Contexts* (Berkeley: University of California Press, 2008), p. 45.
17. Varda, 'Agnés Varda on *La Pointe Courte*'.
18. Homer B. Pettey, 'Introduction: The Noir Turn', in *Film Noir*, eds. Homer B. Pettey and R. Barton Palmer (Edinburgh: Edinburgh University Press, 2014), p. 10.

19. Neupert, 'Testing the Waters', p. 57.
20. Interview with Agnès Varda in Jean-Andre Fieschi and Claude Ollier, 'A Secular Grace: Agnès Varda', in *Agnès Varda: Interviews*, p. 24.
21. Varda, 'A Secular Grace'.
22. Varda, 'A Secular Grace'.
23. Fay and Nieland, *Film Noir*, p. xi.
24. Fay and Nieland, *Film Noir*, p. xiii.
25. Fay and Nieland, *Film Noir*, p. xiii.
26. Fay and Nieland, *Film Noir*, p. xiii.
27. Fay and Nieland, *Film Noir*, p. ix.
28. Kristin Ross, *Fast Cars, Clean Bodies: Decolonization and the Reordering of French Culture* (Cambridge, MA: MIT Press, 1996), p. 21.
29. Ross, *Fast Cars, Clean Bodies*, p. 5.
30. Ross, *Fast Cars, Clean Bodies*, p. 4.
31. Susan Hayward links this sense of nostalgia to French decolonisation; France was thought to be an 'honourable nation' before the war. Susan Hayward, 'French Noir 1947–79: From Grunge-Noir to Noir-Hilism', in *International Noir*, ed. Homer B. Pettey and R. Barton Palmer (Edinburgh: Edinburgh University Press, 2014), p. 49.
32. The Situationist International was an avant-garde group of artists and intellectuals that criticised the economic and cultural transformation of Paris following World War II. For more on the evidence of this aspect of Varda's politics in her work, see DeRoo's chapter concerning *Daguerréotypes* (Agnés Varda, 1978): DeRoo, *Agnés Varda*, pp. 84–114.
33. Varda in Fieschi and Ollier, 'A Secular Grace', p. 23.
34. Varda, 'Agnès Varda on *La Pointe Courte*'.
35. DeRoo, *Agnés Varda*, pp. 43–4.
36. I am grateful to my colleague, Alex Davis, for pointing out that Varda also seems to exemplify this photographic practice in her 1964 short film, *Salut les Cubains*.
37. Conway, 'Planning and Precision', p. 14.
38. DeRoo, *Agnés Varda*, p. 169. Varda has also commented on this historical reference, see 'Agnés Varda Talks about the Cinema', p. 71.
39. Fay and Nieland and Ross tarry on the fact of modernisation's *uneven* development, both globally and within particular nations. See Fay and Nieland, *Film Noir*, pp. 68–9; Ross, *Fast Cars*, p. 12.

10. DOSTOYEVSKY '58: RICHARD BROOKS'S *BROTHERS KARAMAZOV* AS BAROQUE NOIR

Matthew Sorrento

INTRODUCTION

Though often dismissed as a low point for the style, noir in the 1950s remains complex and still worthy of study.[1] In this period, the documentary style of noir, introduced in the late 1940s, continued to dominate, especially with the low-budget possibilities afforded by lightweight cameras and location shooting. And yet a mix of expressionism with 'documentary noir' helped to create a vibrant experimental tone.

With such a complex style now strong for over a decade, noir has some rich examples in the late 1950s, even if the narrative ideas were running out. The common benchmark that signalled the end of the traditional noir cycle, as kind of a super-noir (in André Bazin's sense), Orson Welles's *Touch of Evil* (1958) demonstrates that there was still fresh narrative territory.[2] As a 'borderlands' noir – situated on the US/Mexico border – *Touch of Evil* employs the benefits of location shooting (in Los Angeles and Palmdale, in place of the fictionalised Mexican border town Los Robles) while achieving what James Naremore describes as a baroque treatment of noir.[3] By invoking the docu-realism trend to revise it, Welles, Stephen B. Armstrong argues, struggles to offer stylisation in this Hollywood assignment.[4]

Discussions of *Touch of Evil* as a baroque treatment of noir have not spanned beyond Naremore's comments.[5] Welles's style – employing the framework to unify the style's differing modes, in order to address border politics – reveals how noir was applicable to other genres and themes, especially with the benefits of a baroque style. His example stands out as one pathway to liminal noir.[6]

With noir regarded primarily as a style, in *Touch of Evil*, itself a reworking of Whit Masterson's 1956 novel *Badge of Evil*, we see flexibility for its use as a platform and engine for one of the most problematic modes in cinema: literary adaptation. By 1958, Richard Brooks had much experience in the practice. Preferring to adapt well-known literary properties, Brooks used a noir approach to navigate through his difficult years as a writer-director at MGM, when he did not have choice of his projects.[7] Biographer Douglass K. Daniel regards this period as a low point in Brooks's career, coming in between *Blackboard Jungle* (1955, based on the 1954 novel by Evan Hunter) and *Cat on a Hot Tin Roof* (1958, based on the 1955 play by Tennessee Williams), whose popular success enabled him to leave MGM and establish himself as an independent filmmaker with the triumphant *Elmer Gantry* (1960, based on the 1927 novel by Sinclair Lewis).[8] This reading of Brooks's filmography has left *The Brothers Karamazov* (1958, adapted by the director himself) largely ignored.[9] It is a film that critics thought could have negatively overshadowed Brooks,[10] and it has remained dismissed, up through Daniel's 2011 biography.[11]

Though a journeyman in style, Brooks already possessed extensive experience in urban crime films (what would later be described as film noir), beginning with his 1947 adaptation of Ernest Hemingway's 1927 short story 'The Killers'.[12] Brooks continued to work as a screenwriter in various noir styles. In returning to noir in the style's final stage, Brooks, again informed by the baroque style of Welles, used an experimental approach similar to *Touch of Evil* to streamline and distil Fyodor Dostoyevsky's final masterpiece. A classic thought to reflect the range of human experience, the 1879–80 serialised novel features the theme of patricide in relation to an oppressive father, especially in a Freudian reading.[13]

This chapter will discuss how in *The Brothers Karamazov* – a largely ignored and misunderstood film, due to its hybrid-genre approach that ran contrary to other 1950s literary adaptations – Brooks developed his own baroque style out of the multifaceted blended styles of noir in the late era. With Captain Hank Quinlan (Welles) serving as an oppressive father in *Touch of Evil*, Brooks simultaneously created an alternative to Welles's noir treatment of the monstrous patriarch. Thus, the film offers a counterpart to Welles's baroque style to shape Dostoyevsky into a liminal noir, one employing motifs of period chamber melodrama equally with expressionism.

Docu-realism and the Roots of Baroque Noir

The rise of the semi-documentary style of film noir in the late 1940s signalled the first major revision of the noir style, thus offering a variation that artists like Welles could blend with expressionism.[14] While expressionism and French poetic realism remained highly influential to noir, the 1940s influence of neorealism from Europe, along with the availability of lightweight cameras, offered opportunities for location shooting. Similarly, noir projects opted for true 'documentary' stories of crime in the city, including *T-Men* (Anthony Mann, 1947) and *Call Northside 777* (Henry Hathaway, 1948), two examples of docu-noir filmed at actual locations.[15] J. P. Telotte notes the influence of newsreels as an influence to 'documentary noir'.[16] The B-picture trend of noir that grew at this time shows how quality work could result out of budget constraints.[17] Eventually, a refinement of this style, which pushed for realism, inspired a complex 1950s film form, with the everyday infused with the nightmarish. Meanwhile, the 'travelogue' impulse that fuelled documentary noir would not escape manifestations of the dream factory soundstages. Stanley Kubrick's modestly budgeted *The Killing* (1956) makes use of location shooting, and various B-roll scenes, to situate the confinement and oppression of the interiors (filmed on soundstages), from the set in which a bank robbery is planned, to the apartment where the doomed result plays out, a dismal massacre of almost all the robbers.

Nicholas Christopher notes how docu-noir, like its expressionist predecessor, aims to capture the experience of the city.[18] The screen's cityscapes in the 1940s, like that of the actual American cities of the time period, were in an ever-changing state of flux. Thus, noir styles depict the city as a reflection of our tortured psyche: while early expressionist noirs present nightmares through claustrophobic, tortuous urban imagery, docu-noirs employ the actual locations to place loners in lost environs. To see the thin, but revealing boundary that Christopher discusses, we can look to Fritz Lang's *Scarlet Street* (1945), especially the famous ending in which Christopher Cross (Edward G. Robinson) cannot escape the memory of his framing an innocent man for a murder that he committed himself. The victim's haunting voice in Cross's memory becomes one with the urban *mise en scène*, lurking from the nooks all around. Informed by the famous moment of the title character's megalomaniacal madness in *Das Cabinet des Dr. Caligari* (*The Cabinet of Dr. Caligari*, Robert Wiene, 1919: 'You must become Caligari!'), *Scarlet Street* uses the expressionist conceit to conflate the urban environs with a despairing psychology. *T-Men*, in turn, finds moments of expressionist claustrophobia, but the attention to the actual city (shot on location in Los Angeles) shows that the title figures can single out and apprehend the loners of the city (in this case, counterfeiters) that have turned to crime.

While docu-noir captures realistic locations to offer verity to urban life, it also moves the style away from the dreamlike realism of classical noir, which, Naremore argues, is a product of the fusion of literary modernism and 'blood melodrama'.[19] Noir's capturing of gritty cities and its tales, the goal of the famous crime photographer Weegee and independent filmmakers alike, showed crime cinema working to reveal political corruption.[20] In this way, noir returned to the goals of the 1930s Warner Bros. social problem film.

Telotte, however, argues docu-realism noir to be faulty, as it creates another device that removes cinema away from the classical realism that is appropriate for noir. To Telotte, by inserting more devices in between the established tradition of crime cinema and its filmic delivery, 'docu-noir' distances itself from viewers. Devices of the 'noir documentary'

> threaten that style's effectiveness by implicitly showing it to be a fashioned, contrived mode, its reality not so much an extension of *our* world as of a conventional *cinematic* world (classical noir) which might or might not speak to our situation.[21]

The conventions distract viewers more than the invisible devices of classical noir, and while Telotte sees this as a 'conventional world', it nonetheless contains naturalistic truth. And yet, the industry regarded this fashioned 'docudrama' as truth on-screen. For example, the industry regarded the noir unofficial investigation *I Was a Communist for the F.B.I.* (Gordon Douglas, 1951) as documentary, insofar that the Academy of Motion Picture Arts and Sciences nominated this narrative film for an award as a documentary![22] The docu-noir devices here (specifically a newsreel-style opening, similar to those in *T-Men* and *Call Northside 777*) serve as more conventions that, in Telotte's perspective, become distancing for the viewer.[23] While docu-noir exposes crime, it does so while reassuring viewers in a safe, 'nonthreatening way'.[24] Telotte even reasons that docu-noir attempts to disguise truth (relating to desire) by making the *mise en scène* excessively real. While classical noir shapes how we see the world, docu-noir, in regulating law and order (as the earlier example from *T-Men* shows) and balancing imaginary and real, threatens the unique psychological perspective of the classical cycle by regulating threat to safety (with the police taking over the role of the unofficial investigator in classical noir). Telotte astutely notes that the 'voice of god' narration of the law, which replaces the voice-over of the doomed protagonist (see *Double Indemnity,* Billy Wilder, 1944) or beleaguered PI (*Murder, My Sweet*, Edward Dmytryk, 1944) in the classical cycle, makes docu-noir more like moral propaganda. In the end, the docu-noir reaffirms that absolute truth is elusive and widens the gap between film and reality that the approach intended to bridge.[25] While the docu-noir cycle served as an attempt to depict justice on-screen, and one that led to the tradition of the filmmaker as avenger in the contemporary crime documentary, its setbacks inspired the baroque treatment in the late 1950s, which blended elements of docu-noir and the classical cycle.[26]

BAROQUE NOIR – A STYLE REFINED: *KISS ME DEADLY* TO *TOUCH OF EVIL*

Into the 1950s, traces of docu-noir exist even in budget entries filmed on soundstages, like the Edward G. Robinson vehicles *The Glass Web* (Jack Arnold, 1953) and *Illegal* (Lewis Allen, 1955). With straightforward shooting styles, these films avoid moody visuals and expressionism, likely to combat the direct approaches of television gaining influence at the time.[27]

As a standout noir from the mid-1950s, *Kiss Me Deadly* (Robert Aldrich, 1955), like the docu-noirs of the late 1940s, moves the viewer throughout Los Angeles via exterior location shooting. With frequent use of soundstage interiors, however, the film moves towards subjectivity with baroque framing and its use of sound, which the film also aims for in many location shots.[28] The shocking contrast of this moody style with the verity viewers came to expect from docu-noir reflects the film's aim to fuse noir motifs with atomic age anxiety (like its predecessor, *White Heat* (Raoul Walsh, 1949), did with the gangster film at its conclusion), through the mysterious 'great whatsit'.[29] As Telotte notes, moody scenes of expressionism and real locations offer metaphorical truth.[30]

Aldrich's film provides an early example of a baroque style of noir that Naremore sees in *Touch of Evil*.[31] *Kiss Me Deadly* shows a complex approach, something that would challenge Welles.[32] Welles avoids movie naturalism to make a film that is 'grittily accurate and surreal' to reflect the prominent themes of racism and border politics.[33] Naremore argues that Welles uses this blend of docu-noir and expressionism to achieve 'theatrical intensity', his regular aim, and what would be a given goal for Brooks in bringing such a prominent literary work as *The Brothers Karamazov* to the screen.[34] Far from *The Brothers Karamazov*, though, is Welles's use of continual kinesis, which, putatively, moves away from classical stylisations of noir.[35] (*The Brothers Karamazov*, as we will see below, works as a chamber piece that still channels such energy in closed framing.)

Touch of Evil treats its setting as borderlands, presenting it (in a rather racist premise) as the end of 'civilization' and an area of recklessness. Naremore sees the unstable borderland as one between civilisation and the libido, a moral wasteland instead of 'right and wrong' of liberal humanism, the kind of conclusions forced upon classic noir.[36] Welles's Quinlan exploits this sense of ideological danger. As a contradictory figure – one childlike, at times, but gaining control of others – he uses sexual violence towards his own goals, as does Fyodor (Lee J. Cobb), the oppressive father of *The Brothers Karamazov*, who shatters familial unity with manipulations of sexuality.[37]

Robin Wood, who has analysed the father as monster,[38] reads *Touch of Evil* as a collapse of the monstrous father figure.[39] In line with Freud's theory of God the Father (a source of oppression and an idea that Wood used to develop his theory of the monster in the horror film),⁴⁰ Wood asserts that Quinlan usurps the power of God.⁴¹ While arguing for *Touch of Evil*'s tragic intensity (at the film's closing), Wood notes its connection to Joseph Conrad's 1899 novella *Heart of Darkness*, with Quinlan like Conrad's General Kurtz and Vargas as a form of Marlow; Conrad's text, like Dostoyevsky's longer work, is an exemplar of psychological realism.⁴² Conrad's Kurtz, an ivory trader, fashions himself a surrogate father to African natives, helping to transform himself into a godlike presence over them. While putatively seeing Quinlan as a villain, Wood notes that with his defeat, the film does not restore order (and align to the Motion Picture Production Code, still in effect in 1957–8) but reaches 'out for a tragic weight and grandeur' of this doomed figure.⁴³ The noir devices work to create a Shakespearean fall of a man of hamartia, and thus, Welles's uber-noir works in a highbrow liminal mode.⁴⁴ In *The Brothers Karamazov*, such a tragic fall will come to the doomed anti-hero (Dmitri, played by Yul Brynner), while the monstrous father, Fyodor, sees his own defeat (downplayed in comparison to Dmitri's, since Fyodor's death occurs off-screen). Brooks, as adaptor of the novel and director of the film, resituates the kind of high-tragedy seen in Welles.

Revisionist Baroque Noir: *The Brothers Karamazov*

Touch of Evil's tone of tragedy reveals the noir style's power to relate strong pathos, even if traces of such appeared at the onset of the style. The early cornerstone *Double Indemnity* takes pains to 'convict' Walter Neff (Fred MacMurray) immediately as the film opens, with him confessing to murder on a Dictaphone. The film's equally famous closing shows Barton Keyes (Edward G. Robinson) – his boss and friend – overhearing his confession. Keyes's despair at the betrayal signifies that his familial bond with Neff had weakened or, more tragically, was never actually present.⁴⁵ Though Wood and Naremore note the prominent tragedy of *Touch of Evil*, Naremore had predecessors in the style from which to draw upon.

Similarly, Brooks shaped the narrative of *The Brothers Karamazov* in dialogue with Welles,⁴⁶ just as Welles's framework in *Citizen Kane* (1941) helped fuel Brooks's shaping of *The Killers* after the film's opening vignette, a faithful adaptation of Hemingway's story (itself, casting doom like the opening confession in *Double Indemnity*).⁴⁷ Having already assigned adaptations to Brooks, producer Mark Hellinger again appointed him to 'The Killers' project to open up the short story. In the screenplay, Brooks added noir unofficial investigation (featuring an insurance investigator mirroring *Double Indemnity*'s Keyes), to build a mystery/suspense narrative. This part of the film also works as an *interpretation* to the opening event (à la *Citizen Kane*), thus delivering a deeper truth to the unofficial investigative tradition, while unveiling a bleak world view.

Brooks is often left out of auteurist discussions due to his tendency to work in a variety of styles, but *The Killers* demonstrated that he could bring a personal sensibility to his treatment of film noir.[48] Scant biographical attention on Brooks exists apart from Daniel, who regards the filmmaker as a workhorse but having a sentimental streak.[49] However, Daniel highlights Brooks's skill in adaptation, noting that the approach had given the filmmaker a framework.[50] After *The Killers*, Brooks continued working as a screenwriter on a variety of noirs: the Hellinger-produced, prison thriller *Brute Force* (Jules Dassin, 1947), late gangster-noir *Key Largo* (John Huston, 1948), scholar-as-detective in *Mystery Street* (John Sturges, 1950), and the newsroom story *Deadline – U.S.A.* (Brooks, 1952). Brooks had a rooted understanding of the hard-boiled style of fiction, as seen in his 1945 novel *The Brick Foxhole*, which screenwriter John Paxton adapted as *Crossfire* (Edward Dmytryk, 1947). A novel not directly written in the noir style – but in a stream of consciousness, modernist style – turned into a social-problem-themed noir (focusing on antisemitism, though the novel focused on homophobia), which offers an interesting example of the liminal approach. With the novel steeped in first-person subjectivity, often using flashbacks, Brooks employs language akin to cinematic expressionism on-screen, thus one ready-made for noir treatment. This source novel, along with his adaption of *The Killers*, informed Brooks in adapting 'The Doubters' by George Tabori as *Crisis* (Brooks, 1950), which would mark his directing debut and begin his tenure at MGM. In writing and directing *Deadline – U.S.A.* (his sole early original screenplay), Brooks works in the noir investigation style (featuring Humphrey Bogart) to work in the trend of docu-noir and relate a real-life case.

At MGM, Brooks realised he would not have complete control over his projects while under contract. Daniel regards Brooks's 1950s output as evidence of him biding his time until having the power to secure better prospects.[51] However, as *Blackboard Jungle* and *Cat on a Hot Tin Roof* attest, Brooks's 1950s work shows him navigating with hybrid styles, as both productions employ adaptation with film melodrama.[52] In *The Brothers Karamazov*, Brooks shapes his melodrama approach with noir motifs to achieve a successful adaptation of a literary property far more imposing than that of Tennessee Williams.

The obvious charge against Brooks's adaptation of *The Brothers Karamazov* is that it narrowed the novel's power. As a masterpiece of psychological realism, the book divides three personalities of its author into the three Karamazov brothers, though even more broadly, the work covers the range of humanity, with the story representing existence (of Russia and beyond) confronting itself.[53] To add to the charge against the endeavour, MGM presented the project as a high concept prestige production and star vehicle.[54] In the years since the film's release, this kind of highbrow promotion continued: at the onset of home video, MGM packaged the VHS version of the film in its 'Great Books on Video' series instead of a more appropriate studio classics-style presentation.

And yet, by employing noir in a liminal mode, *The Brothers Karamazov* shows how adaptation should support the literary work itself, and not just the institution of literature in academia.[55] The film moves away from the point of view of the pious monk Alexey of the novel (played by William Shatner in his feature film debut).[56] Brooks, instead, centres the narrative on Dmitri, who follows the mold of the compromised noir protagonist (in this case, inclined towards gambling under the control of an oppressive father).

The film employs expressionism familiar to noir, in one aspect, to employ sizable use of interior scenes.[57] While the classical noir style preferred expressionist interiors, by the mid-1950s it used cityscapes and street scenes to create a sense of urban strain and confinement.[58] The interiors of *The Brothers Karamazov*, like the best in the noir tradition, show psychological confinement (mirroring key scenes of confrontation and deviance in *Touch of Evil*) along with several involving Quinlan. Noir's repeated use of water/rain in the outside elements[59] reflects the internal experience of the characters in the interior, as we see in *Out of the Past* (Jacques Tourneur, 1947) and *Key Largo*.[60]

Brooks's rendition of Dostoyevsky consists of a series of confrontations on interior sets; hence, he uses the noir style's approach to filming *inside*, from the first encounter between Alexei and Fyodor (discussed below) to the final banishment of Dmitri (his noir defeat).[61]

With Dmitri at the centre of these confrontations, the film focuses on this gambler whose drives mirror the destructiveness of his father, the licentious Fyodor. In this sense, Dmitri becomes an interesting case as a noir protagonist: isolated from his family though under its control, he serves as an Everyman loner who turns to crime. In the noir tradition, this figure usually gets ensnared by a femme fatale. The family's crisis leading to its dissolution comes, in spite of Alexey's attempts to make the family work as a system.

Robin Wood has analysed this kind of monstrous father, whose influence indicates the widespread Law of the Father. While the theorist's main concept of the monstrous concerned a societal outsider, he also discusses this figure as inherent to the family, the source of terror.[62] While Hollywood horror was compelled to evolve to such a progressive conceit (away from the reactionary/conservative approach in the 1930s),[63] Dostoyevsky, in preceding Freud's and Marx's ideas that inspired Wood, already captured it in his novels.[64] The monstrous outsider also appears in noir,[65] which tends not to focus on the traditional family unit, since this factor would mean security in the classical Hollywood style (focused on 'vulnerable' loners).[66] And yet, oppressive patriarchal figures sit at the top of criminal organisations in noir, something solidified with Sydney Greenstreet's Gutman in the cornerstone noir *The Maltese Falcon* (John Huston, 1941). Similarly, oppressive lawmen defined the influence of patriarchy, especially Welles's Quinlan, who, as Wood and Armstrong note, experiences a tragic fall with his demise into muck.[67]

In the source novel, Dostoyevsky invokes the oppressive fathers of Shakespeare (*Hamlet, King Lear*)[68] to highlight the theme of patricide, as noted by Freud.[69] Brooks uses this element, which stems from the strains of incest in the narrative, to connect to the familial destruction inherent to noir.[70] To achieve this, Brooks fashions Grushenka (Maria Schell) into a femme fatale, one that is under Fyodor's influence while also tempting Dmitri. She also invokes Freud's concept of the Madonna-whore complex in her promise of purity to Dmitri and as a body for Fyodor to exploit.[71] In *Touch of Evil*, the incestuous actions of the father appear with Quinlan's arrangement with Grandi (Akim Tamiroff), whose family has attacked Susie Vargas (Janet Leigh), the wife of Ramon Vargas (Charlton Heston), with imagery that invokes gang rape: Quinlan decides to stage Susie as drugged. As an oppressive 'father figure' in law enforcement, Quinlan violates the legal code by infringing on the familial bond/budding familial unit of the Vargases. Quinlan's actions further show him exploiting hysteria over the racist miscegenation laws in the United States, as Ramon and Susie are a mixed-race couple. With Quinlan's manipulations leading to his fall, Naremore sees these causal actions as transforming the film into a Shakespearean tragedy,[72] one more sympathetic to the racial outliers regularly condemned in crime cinema.[73] By embellishing and complicating the tragic touches in the closing of a noir like *Double Indemnity*, Welles's film works as a liminal noir that is hybridised with tragedy. The film's unique mix of high and low elements shows intertextuality between this and other liminal noirs from the late 1950s.[74] With critical discourse arguing that the noir style waned by 1957, scholars have ignored the unique situation that led to a final mini-cycle, as evidenced by connectivity between Welles's final noir and Brooks's *The Brothers Karamazov*.

Though Dmitri is the main perspective, Brooks's film zeros in on the oppressive father right away. An opening scene of Fyodor channels violence and rampant extramarital sexuality, which was certainly surprisingly in a 1958 Hollywood film. The vibrant folk music inspires frenetic dancing of violinists in a dark room, one carefully lit low-key, and fuels Fyodor's actions that represent unbridled (though seemingly impotent) lechery, as he tickles the feet of a young woman on a table, after tying her down and pouring drink down her throat. Meanwhile, he imbibes carelessly, as he brings the girl to heightened titillation. Notably, the lighting highlights the girl's blonde hair to establish a colour scheme that mimics the chiaroscuro in black-and-white noirs, while the remaining shots in this and other scenes are more subdued. Here Brooks and cinematographer John Alton establish a low-key lighting scheme, which they will use continuously for interior shots. Notably, the ceilings are present in the shots to offer what Naremore describes as a noirish claustrophobia, especially considering that the set-building practice still involved absent ceilings.[75] The chaotic kinesis captured by Alton fashions sexuality into a violent image, underscoring noir's conceit of 'Kiss of Death', which was prominent in that 1947 Henry Hathaway film, along with *Kiss Me Deadly* and *Killer's Kiss* – though these elements were sublimated due to the Motion Picture Production Code. Immediately, with this opening scene, Brooks captures energy in closed framing, thus containing the 'open' movement of Welles's camera to capture multiform *mise en scène*. The girl's quasi-orgasmic joy fuels delight in Fyodor, who signifies, with the manual stimulation, as a figure of impotence, his wealth his means of satisfaction. Entering into this scene is Fyodor's pure son, Alexey, who asks for funds for Dmitri that are due to him. As Alexey attempts to right a dispute, Brooks offers a kernel of Dostoyevsky's reflection of wide humanity while hitting right on the premise that will lead to familial decay. With Fyodor's refusal, and his decision to bind Dmitri with a loan, comes the high seriousness of the source while the film positions the material into a melodramatic framework – thus, capturing the high and low elements of noir.

The frivolous Fyodor nonetheless has a firm grasp on the finances, even to the point of diminishing his late wife's influence (by withholding inheritance money). Dmitri, the dark noir protagonist, is due to receive some of these funds that Fyodor has withheld from him, thus fuelling the son's incessant gambling (in a tavern visually reflecting the location of Fyodor's orgiastic party). When Alexey arrives to the tavern to bring Dmitri 5,000 rubles from Fyodor (but under the conditions of the loan, Dmitri was promised twice as much), the scene shows kinesis, especially once a confrontation ensues, when Dmitri is accused of theft. The scene carefully mirrors the *mise en scène* of Fyodor's previous exploits. The tavern door appears on the right, to counterpoint Fyodor's left entryway, thus underscoring the claustrophobia stemming from the prominent ceilings. Dmitri sits, at a card table, one room removed from the entryway, where the production design situates Fyodor's party. Paired with similarly low-key lit, cluttered *mise en scène*, the two scenes reveal the oppressive father fuelling his son's compulsion to gamble.

Outside of the Karamazov family, another father oppresses children: here his daughter, Katya (Claire Bloom), who, in the upcoming scene, offers her body to Dmitri to pay her father's debts. Dmitri responds with an attempt to escape from patriarchy, and one to create his own familial system. He proposes to Katya, though she believes this will only degrade her more. Dmitri then gives her money, which shows his potential for grace/empathy, while resisting the chance to exploit a woman (a situation that Fyodor, judging from his opening scene, would exploit).

Brooks's narrative then breaks continuity in time (flashing forward) to reveal Dmitri in prison. Such a scripting and editing choice likely fuelled the film's detractors, as Brooks's pacing shifts right when it has found momentum. Yet, the development shows necessary condensation in adaptation. Brooks presents a dreamlike shift by placing Dmitri in another time/place while maintaining perspective. In particular with Dmitri now jailed for the fight at the tavern, the narrative shift comes in place of the disorientating traditional noir flashback. Now that Dmitri's physically imprisoned (as a result of Fyodor's influence), his situation revises the opening flashback regularly used in noir in which time is altered to reveal the doomed situation of a loner protagonist who has turned to crime (Walter Neff in *Double Indemnity*) or has become a victim (Edmond O'Brien's Frank Bigelow in *D.O.A.*, Rudolph Maté, 1950). Brooks needed to work within the parameters of the novel; thus, this shift from his imprisonment by patriarchy to actual prison invokes the noir shift.

With Dmitri imprisoned for the tavern incident, Katya visits him to accept his hand in marriage; this action only complicates Dmitri's situation, now that Katya promises them more money (from her grandmother's dowry). With Dmitri under the agency of another's finances again, he senses the same lack of control he possessed under his father, since Dmitri's previous offering to Katya saved her father from disgrace. When Katya wants him to leave the army (and intends to pay his debts), it further complicates his agency in a masculine role as an inactive male, a fragility which his father already stressed.[76]

When Dmitri's brother, Ivan (Richard Basehart), shows an attraction to Katya, the film incorporates incestuous competition, which the narrative echoes later between Fyodor and Dmitri. The film thus invokes the tradition of repressed incest in the early sound-era gangster film (see Howard Hawks's *Scarface* and William A. Wellman's *The Hatchet Man*, both 1932). Upon learning of Dmitri's marriage and new financial status, Fyodor expects repayment and attempts to retain control of Dmitri's inheritance even after his marriage (which would mean security in the noir movement, as it would remove him from his 'loner' status). To demean the security of the family further, Fyodor threatens to sue Dmitri, which would, in turn, taint Katya's family. By giving Fyodor's new intended, Grushenka, debts for her to collect, he attempts to 'buy' happiness with her, through wealth and power, at the expense of his family. By selling the debts to former army captain Snegiryov (David Opatoshu), Fyodor further complicates Dmitri's security by removing his debt from the family.

With Snegiryov now owning Dmitri's debts, non-payment can have him brought to debtor's prison. This act shows Fyodor's attempt to use the law in order to exploit his own son. As controlled by the patriarch, familial relations have become a commodity, as a means for power relations. When Snegiryov addresses Dmitri about his acquisition (of which he had little control), the latter publicly threatens the ailing Snegiryov, weakening him in front of his young son. As one of the few exterior scenes (though shot on a soundstage), Brooks frames the moment with his actors abutted to a rough building façade. This scene, like several other interiors in the film, uses the cragged production design to invoke tortured psychology, as in the liminal noir westerns by Anthony Mann (see *The Naked Spur*, 1953). Thus, Fyodor's machinations, as with Katya earlier, break down another family by extension. Benighted by his father's influence, Dmitri soon squanders Katya's money. Under the strain, Dmitri finds himself attracted to the faux-fatale Grushenka. At this point, the narrative reveals the secondary incestuous strain with this one directly in the Oedipal mould.

These complications lead to violence, with Dmitri threatening to kill Fyodor if he sees Grushenka. In noir fashion, this act results, in part, from the faux-fatale's actions (but equally from the doomed hero's anxiety over her). Grushenka forgives Dmitri his remaining debt to her in reward for his commitment (i.e. his refusal to marry Katya). And yet the fatale's actions are a mere accessory to the oppressive father's influence, as Fyodor created the power structure. Brooks, wanting to make Grushenka's noir characteristics clear, presents her planning to return to her former beloved, a Polish officer. Dmitri, learning this, sees the liminal fatale is out to dupe him, in a web spun by his father.[77]

The melodramatic effects of this act further reveal Fyodor's influence: when Ivan decides to leave for Moscow, the influence of Fyodor, and Dmitri (by extension), have thwarted a potentially healthy union between Ivan and Katya. Although still a victim and agent of oppression, Dmitri continues to 'disarm' himself (i.e. making himself impotent, in the shadow of the monstrous father), by pawning his pistols. While this action may show the doomed noir protagonist attempting to reform himself and right actions before punishment comes, he weakens under Fyodor's continual machinations.

The young son of Snegiryov, Illyusha (Miko Oscard), wants his father to refuse the money brought to him by Alexey (which he collected from Dmitri's army acquaintances who owed him), as Dmitri's actions have weakened the father publicly. If masculinist codes of pride, ones that reflect the influence of patriarchy, have already imprisoned young Illyusha, he nonetheless reflects a strong family union – one not merely invoking the crutch of a sacred theme in film noir, but a true family in its own right (though it is strained and has intensified Snegiryov's illness). The illegitimate son of Fyodor, Smerdyakov (Albert Salmi) – one removed from the family proper, but still under his influence – schemes to create confrontation between Fyodor and Dmitri. If the narrative demeans the bastard brother for fuelling confrontation, it still shows his desperation for attention and acceptance from his father. When Smerdyakov's ploy works against Dmitri, he remains inactive against the oppressive father. Dmitri confronts his father over Grushenka, out of honour but more so strained by his impotence (he cannot attack his father, even when Fyodor beats him). The feeble Fyodor has empowered himself via his procured sexuality.

The levels of deception certainly fuel Brooks's melodrama, but also create an especially bleak world view. Duped, in turn, by the Polish officer (who wants her just for the money), Grushenka returns to Dmitri, whom she flouted.

This precedes the killing of Fyodor by Smerdyakov, which appears in the narrative as a faux noir mystery. In Brooks's casual condensation of Dostoyevsky, the plot soon reveals Smerdyakov having framed Dmitri for the murder of the man who oppressed him.[78] Before the court convicts Dmitri, public opinion has already found him guilty, since 3,000 rubles has been stolen from Fyodor. The fact that the noir protagonist does not commit the crime underscores his purported guilt and banishment to come. And while Smerdyakov's suicide removes him from suspicion, Dmitri admits guilt, like a loner from the film adaptations of James M. Cain novels (*Double Indemnity* and *The Postman Always Rings Twice*, Tay Garnett, 1946). Dmitri's punishment is not execution, but instead banishment with Grushenka, a removal from the community under Fyodor's influence. While Dmitri may remain benighted, like Christopher Cross in *Scarlet Street*, due to wrongful accusation of patricide and his father's influence, the viewer also imagines him having the kind of freedom possessed by Ringo Kid (John Wayne) in *Stagecoach* (John Ford, 1939), also an outsider banished with a redeemed woman.

Right to the conclusion, *The Brothers Karamazov* continues a melodramatic chain. With continual attention to the monstrous father (as Dmitri offers apologies to Illyusha and Snegiryov before departing), Brooks fashions Welles's symbolic oppressive father in *Touch of Evil* into an actual one. This patriarchy not only ruins the spirit and drive of the sons, and the women in their lives, but, in turn, shapes their economic reality. Using a Gothic rendering of the monster in the family to cast a noir world view, *The Brothers Karamazov* works as a complex melodrama, with its hybridisation of horror, noir, and literary adaptation. It is all the more chilling and doom-laden in that the monster is within the family, and not a grotesque outsider. The latter was a mainstay of the classical noir and horror film, and with Brooks's skilled revision of hybrid genre modes, we see a 'modern' revision of genre before it became a trend in the 1960s.

Notes

1. While Robert Miklitsch cites several studies that argue noir to end by the early 1950s, he argues that there is 'more to '50s noir than meets the eye and ear'. Miklitsch, *The Red and the Black: American Noir in the 1950s* (Urbana: University of Illinois Press, 2017), p. xv.
2. Raymond Borde and Étienne Chaumeton have argued the film to be a 'point of no return' for the noir style, and thus signalling its end. Borde and Chaumeton, *A Panorama of American Film Noir: 1941–1953*, trans. Paul Hammond (San Francisco: City Lights Books, 2002), p. 155. André Bazin invokes a similar concept for another genre when he argued that *Shane* (George Stevens, 1953) was positioned to end the traditional western by outdoing it. Bazin, 'The Evolution of the Western', in *The Western Reader*, ed. Jim Kitses and Gregg Rickman (New York: Limelight Editions, 1998), p. 52.

3. James Naremore argues that Welles blends realism and expressionism by ignoring 'most of the rules of movie naturalism. His idea is to make a world that is both grittily accurate and surreal, characters that are both plausible and weirdly out of key, a film that maintains a level of serious intent even while it calls attention to itself as a grotesque joke.' Naremore, *The Magic of Orson Welles* (Dallas: Southern Methodist University Press, 1989), p. 167. Note: Naremore and Robin Wood both write about the 1958 released version of the film, before its 1998 restoration based on a 58-page memo by Welles from 1997 that outlined his creative vision. Wood, *Personal Views: Explorations in Film*, Rev. ed. (Detroit: Wayne State University Press, [1976] 2006). For a discussion of the 1998 restoration, see Jonathan Rosenbaum, *Discovering Orson Welles* (Berkeley: University of California Press, 2007), pp. 248–57.
4. '[W]ith each effort to make the film adhere to the visual and thematic conventions of film noir, Welles moved closer to professional failure.' Stephen B. Armstrong, '*Touch of Evil* and the End of the Noir Cycle', in *Film Noir Reader 4: The Crucial Films and Themes*, ed. Alain Silver and James Ursini (New York: Limelight Editions, 2004), pp. 133–43.
5. James Naremore returns to the question of baroque noir only briefly in his landmark study, *More than Night: Film Noir in Its Contexts* (Berkeley: University of California Press, [1998] 2008), p. 174.
6. This is evident in the location-shot but expressionistic *Kiss Me Deadly* (Robert Aldrich, 1955). While filmed in several Los Angeles locations to help bring to life the urban landscape, the film repeatedly delivers nightmarish *mise en scène*. The opening scene begins before the famous title credits (unrolling in reverse, like street signs approaching drivers), in which Mike Hammer (Ralph Meeker) encounters Christina Bailey (Cloris Leachman) on the pitch-black street. From here, the viewer experiences the everyday that has become a bleak nowhere. As Hammer drives Christina away, their ominous conversation (A. I. Bezzerides's reworking of Spillane's 1952 novel) sounds like an attempt to clarify the illogic of Aldrich's distinct universe. Similarly, Stanley Kubrick's self-produced noir of the same year, *Killer's Kiss*, hovers close to documentary in capturing New York of the mid-decade. And while principally a 'docu-noir', the film shows flashes of expressionist verve during the confrontations of Davey Gordon (Jamie Smith). Thirdly, while Richard Brody has described *Blast of Silence* (Allen Baron, 1961) as a film noir, it appeared in the early neo-noir cycle (coming after the common end point, 1958). The film serves as a distillation of such a baroque approach, employing New York locations with a firm grasp of expressionism (thanks to Lionel Stander's narration) to reveal the experience of disturbed hitman Frankie Bono (Baron) going after his crime boss. Richard Brody, 'Blast of Silence', *The New Yorker*, 10 June 2012, https://www.newyorker.com/culture/richard-brody/allen-barons-blast-of-silence.
7. 'Most important for [Brooks] was how adapting the Dostoyevsky novel provided him with the frame of reference – some would argue the rationalization – through which he would view the screenplays for his most significant films to come, adaptations all and often from complex works.' Douglass K. Daniel, *Tough as Nails: The Life and Films of Richard Brooks* (Madison: University of Wisconsin Press, 2011), p. 120.

8. While the Director's Guild commended Brooks for his direction on *The Brothers Karamazov* (and the Academy nominated J. Lee Cobb as Best Supporting Actor), Brooks's own *Cat on a Hot Tin Roof*, which was released by MGM in the same year as *The Brothers Karamazov*, overshadowed the latter. Daniel, *Tough as Nails*, p. 124.
9. Producer Pandro S. Berman previously assigned Julius J. and Philip G. Epstein to write an early draft of the script, which Brooks ignored when he adapted the book on his own. Daniel, *Tough as Nails*, p. 120.
10. See Albert Johnson, in which the author references *The Brothers Karamazov* as a film that makes viewers 'apprehensive' of Brooks adapting literary works in the future. Johnson, 'Review: Cat on a Hot Tin Roof', *Film Quarterly* 12, no. 2 (1958), pp. 54–5.
11. The production was the source of rumours and controversy about Marilyn Monroe starring as Grushenka, which likely affected viewer objectivity upon its release. Daniel, *Tough as Nails*, p. 120.
12. Although the script was credited to Anthony Veiller, *The Killers* was co-written by Brooks and director John Huston.
13. Sigmund Freud discusses that fear of the father leads to a repressed hatred of the figure. Freud, 'Dostoyevsky and Parricide', in *The Standard Edition of the Complete Psychological Works of Sigmund Freud: Volume XXI (1927–1931)*, ed. James Strachey (London: Hogarth, [1928] 1961), p. 184.
14. Matthew Sorrento, 'Documenting Crime: Genre, Verity, and Filmmaker as Avenger', in *Framing Law and Crime: An Interdisciplinary Anthology*, ed. Caroline Joan Picart, Michael Hviid Jacobsen, and Cecil E. Greek (Madison, NJ: Fairleigh Dickinson University Press, 2016), p. 249.
15. Sorrento, 'Documenting Crime', p. 250.
16. J. P. Telotte, *Voices in the Dark: The Narrative Patterns of Film Noir* (Urbana: University of Illinois Press, 1989), p. 135.
17. Naremore, *More than Night*, p. 142.
18. Nicholas Christopher, *Somewhere in the Night: Film Noir and the City* (New York: Henry Holt, 1997), p. 37.
19. Naremore, *More than Night*, pp. 45–6.
20. Telotte, *Voices in the Dark*, p. 140.
21. Telotte, *Voices in the Dark*, p. 155.
22. During this era, referring to fact-based narrative films as documentaries was common: Eric Rohmer and Claude Chabrol refer to Hitchcock's *The Wrong Man* (1956) as a 'documentary without embellishment'. Rohmer and Chabrol, *Hitchcock: The First Forty-Four Films*, trans. Stanley Hockman (New York: Frederick Unger, 1979), pp. 146–7, quoted in John Billheimer, *Hitchcock and the Censors* (Lexington: University of Kentucky Press, 2019), p. 218.
23. Telotte notes that classical noir best reflects psychology/despair. Telotte, *Voices in the Dark*, p. 135.
24. Telotte, *Voices in the Dark*, p. 137.
25. Telotte indicates *Boomerang!* (Elia Kazan, 1947) as an example, noting that in the film's re-enactments of events (through voice-over) it testifies to its own integrity

'while admitting the sense of doubt and anxiety to which film noirs usually spoke'. Telotte, *Voices in the Dark*, p. 141.
26. See Sorrento, 'Documenting Crime'.
27. *The Glass Web*, in fact, reflects the influence of television (as it concerns a TV script consultant for a crime series, played by Robinson, who is involved with a murder), while also filmed in 3-D in an attempt to draw home viewers back to theatres.
28. Alain Silver argues that by using locations that remain 'unspecified', *Kiss Me Deadly* 'has no clearly defined landscape'. '*Kiss Me Deadly*: Evidence of a Style', in *Film Noir Reader*, ed. Silver and James Ursini (New York: Limelight Editions, [1996] 2005), p. 211.
29. To underscore the anxiety, the film ends on a note of irresolution. William Luhr, *Film Noir* (Hoboken, NJ: Wiley-Blackwell, 2012), p. 124.
30. Telotte, *Voices in the Dark*, p. 136.
31. Naremore, *The Magic of Orson Welles*, p. 167.
32. The pair reflects an early example (what Naremore called '"hybrid thrillers" of the 1950s') of art-house crime that triumphed in the 1990s. Naremore, *More than Night*, p. 267.
33. Naremore, *The Magic of Orson Welles*, p. 167.
34. Naremore, *The Magic of Orson Welles*, p. 169.
35. Naremore, *The Magic of Orson Welles*, p. 166. Similarly, Welles, in making 'the last flowering of artful crime melodrama from the 40s' (Naremore, *The Magic of Orson Welles*, p. 170), avoids stylised imitation of noir in neo-noir just around the corner from France in the 1960s (Jean-Luc Godard's *À bout de souffle* (*Breathless*, 1959) and *Alphaville: une étrange aventure de Lemmy Caution* (*Alphaville*, 1965); François Truffaut's *Tirez sur le pianiste* (*Shoot the Piano Player*, 1960)) and reaching the US in the 1970s (Robert Altman's *The Long Goodbye*, 1973 and Roman Polanski's *Chinatown*, 1974).
36. Naremore, *The Magic of Orson Welles*, pp. 157, 155.
37. Naremore (*The Magic of Orson Welles*, p. 153) notes that Quinlan steps into an 'ironic childhood' when visiting the mother figure, the equally dualistic Madonna and whore Tanya (Marlene Dietrich), but that he also 'easily dominates the action' when undergoing detective work (p. 152).
38. The father's place in horror and control of the family suggests 'tremendous energy perverted toward repression instead of creativity'. Robin Wood, *Robin Wood on the Horror Film*, ed. Barry Keith Grant (Detroit: Wayne State University Press, 2018), p. 115.
39. In supporting an auteurist stance on Welles, Wood notes the tragic dimensions of the film and that the theme of a man 'usurp[ing] the functions of god' in *Touch of Evil* connects the work to his remaining filmography (Wood, *Personal Views*, pp. 169, 182–3). In discussing the film's tone of tragedy, Naremore argues that Welles 'forces a political melodrama into the realm of personal tragedy' (*The Magic of Orson Welles*, p. 151).
40. See Wood, *Robin Wood on the Horror Film*, pp. 57–62, 73–110, for a discussion of the horror film as a genre, in its early forms especially, containing outsiders as monstrous.

41. Wood, *Personal Views*, p. 169.
42. Wood, *Personal Views*, p. 170.
43. Wood, *Personal Views*, p. 168.
44. Sheri Chinen Biesen notes that lead figures of post-war noir had 'other lives' that removed them from outsider status. *Blackout: World War II and the Origins of Film Noir* (Baltimore: Johns Hopkins University Press, 2005), p. 217. These statuses in society led them to broader thematic dimensions and thus opened up connections to styles outside film noir.
45. Here, *Double Indemnity* touches upon tragic tones: Keyes's final match strike, to light Neff's cigarette, working as one last bond with Neff, while the extinguished light also reflects Neff's life to fade with his coming execution (originally planned for the film, but removed before release).
46. While no direct connection between Welles and Brooks is evident, *The Hollywood Reporter* reported on the Universal-International production in March and April 1957, thus likely piquing the interest of Welles-influenced Brooks, working nearby at MGM. *AFI Catalog Notes*, 'Touch of Evil', https://catalog.afi.com/Film/53683-TOUCH-OFEVIL.
47. Though, as Andrew Spicer notes, ironic to *Double Indemnity*, the Swede in *The Killers* is never 'allowed his own voice as a narrator', with the film focusing on a complex structure of eleven different flashbacks. Spicer, 'Producing Noir: Wald, Scott, Hellinger', in *Kiss the Blood off My Hands: on Classic Film Noir*, ed. Robert Miklitsch (Urbana: University of Illinois Press, 2014), p. 143.
48. Hellinger credits Siodmak for many 'adroit transitions' in the film (Spicer, 'Producing Noir', p. 143).
49. Daniel, *Tough as Nails*, p. 3.
50. Daniel, *Tough as Nails*, p. 114.
51. Brooks was also frustrated that MGM prevented him from filming overseas, in Russia, with MGM fearful of any Communist associations. The filmmaker had to settle with MGM soundstages, which forced him to focus more on interiors. Michelangelo Capua, *Yul Brynner: A Biography* (Jefferson, NC: McFarland, 2006), p. 66.
52. Naremore notes 'blood melodrama' as one of the roots of film noir (*More than Night*, p. 48).
53. Robert Bird, 'Refiguring the Russian Type: Dostoyevsky and the Limits of Realism', in *A New Word on the Brothers Karamazov*, ed. Robert Louis Jackson (Evanston, IL: Northwestern University Press, 2004), p. 23.
54. Producer Dore Schary initiated the project as a star vehicle for Marlon Brando and Marilyn Monroe (Capua, *Yul Brynner*, p. 65).
55. Thomas Leitch, *Adaptation and Its Discontents* (Baltimore: Johns Hopkins University Press, 2007), p. 2.
56. Shatner's well-known associations to overacting in a camp style is likely another reason the film is not taken more seriously.
57. Brooks and cinematographer John Alton intended their use of the colour red to signify Dmitri's death wish (Capua, *Yul Brynner*, p. 66).
58. Christopher, *Somewhere in the Night*, p. 45.

59. Paul Schrader, 'Notes on Film Noir', in *Schrader on Schrader*, Rev. ed., ed. Kevin Jackson (New York: Faber and Faber, 2004), p. 85. Originally published in a 1971 pamphlet for the Los Angeles Film Festival; reprinted in *Film Comment* 8, no. 1 (Spring 1972), pp. 8–13.
60. Though Naremore ties the noir style to modernism, such leitmotifs stem from romanticism, especially Edgar Allan Poe's reflection of the mind and body in 'The Fall of the House of Usher' (1839) and its later inclusion of his poem, 'The Haunted Palace' (1839), as a song by Roderick Usher. Poe added the poem to the story in his 1840 collection, *Tales of the Grotesque and Arabesque*.
61. In this approach, the film creates a pressurised theatricality of George Schaefer's 1978 film *of An Enemy of the People*, from Arthur Miller's 1950 adaptation of Henrik Ibsen's 1882 play. This example shows how the multifaceted noir style also borrows elements of literary naturalism.
62. Wood, *Robin Wood on the Horror Film*, p. 115.
63. See Robin Wood for a discussion of horror as either, in a progressive mould, addressing the oppression and repression of the traditional family unit, or as a reactionary form – i.e. horror stemming from the 1930s that would defeat and repress a monstrous outsider. Wood, *Hollywood from Vietnam to Reagan . . . and Beyond* (New York: Columbia University Press, 2003), pp. 63–9.
64. Freud, 'Dostoyevsky and Parricide'.
65. See Emmett Myers (William Talman), the villain of *The Hitch-Hiker* (Ida Lupino, 1953), who eerily sleeps with one eye open.
66. Robinson's role in *The Red House* (Delmer Daves, 1948) serves as an example of an actual father as oppressive monster in noir, a 'blood melodrama' (in Naremore's sense (*More than Night*, p. 48)) in the noir style.
67. Wood, *Personal Views*, p. 168 and Armstrong, '*Touch of Evil* and the End of the Noir Cycle', p. 138.
68. Brooks especially plays upon Dostoyevsky's invoking of *King Lear* by centring the narrative on a patriarch choosing an heir.
69. Freud, 'Dostoyevsky and Parricide'.
70. See Alfred Hitchcock's *Shadow of a Doubt* (1943), in which Uncle Charlie (Joseph Cotten), a murder suspect estranged from his extended family, attempts to sever familial unity when he returns. He aims to murder Young Charlie (Teresa Wright), even if family values win out in the end. For discussions of conservative values and the family place creating a sense of security but, really, a form of repression, in horror and other genres, see Wood, *Personal Views*, p. 84; Tony Williams, *Hearths of Darkness: The Family in the Horror Film*, Updated ed. (Jackson: University of Mississippi Press, 2014); Christopher Sharrett, 'The Horror Film as Social Allegory (and How It Comes Undone)', in *A Companion to the Horror Film*, ed. Harry M. Benshoff (Hoboken, NJ: Wiley-Blackwell, 2014), pp. 56–72; and John Edgar Browning, 'Classical Hollywood Horror', in *A Companion the Horror Film*, ed. Harry M. Benshoff (Hoboken, NJ: Wiley-Blackwell, 2014), p. 229.
71. Sigmund Freud, *On Sexuality* (London: Penguin, 1977), p. 251.
72. While Naremore supports the film's stance as 'personal tragedy' (*The Magic of Orson Welles*, p. 151), Armstrong sees this aim as one of 'personal failure' ('*Touch of Evil* and the End of the Noir Cycle', p. 140).

73. See the Catholic gangsters of the 1930s Warner Bros. pictures, who were regularly punished at a film's end.
74. Naremore, *More than Night*, p. 38.
75. For an example of Kubrick's noir treatment in *Dr. Strangelove or: How I Learned to Stop Worrying and Love the Bomb* (1964), see James Naremore, *On Kubrick* (London: British Film Institute, 2007), p. 129.
76. For an extended discussion of noir and gender, see Frank Krutnik, *In a Lonely Street: Film Noir, Genre, Masculinity* (New York: Routledge, 1991).
77. In line with Freud's theory, the narrative clearly delineates Katya and Grushenka as Madonna and whore, respectively.
78. In the novel, a young Smerdyakov shows promise as a precocious child but also collects stray cats to hang them.

11. MEN IN BLACK: *I CONFESS*, THE HITCHCOCK NOIR, AND THE AMERICAN GOTHIC

David Greven

Not without ongoing controversy, Alfred Hitchcock's cinema and film noir have been linked by critics such as James Naremore and John Orr. Naremore's essay 'Hitchcock at the Margins of Noir' and Orr's chapter 'Inside Out: Hitchcock, Film Noir, and David Lynch' remain the standard treatments of the director's relationship to the genre. 'The first thing to be said', Orr writes, 'is that Hitchcock is a world apart from many elements of noir style.'[1] Naremore essentially concurs though places different emphases: Hitchcock is not a noir director but his films have noirish elements. Indeed, a particular cycle of Hitchcock's films – *Stage Fright* (1950), *Strangers on a Train* (1951), and *I Confess* (1953) – contains so many noir elements that one's viewing experience runs counter to the manifest content. In other words, Hitchcock's films feel like *Hitchcock's* films rather than noir, even when they brim with typical noir elements, such as flashbacks, expressionistic lighting, the perpetration and solving of murder, a particularly vexed heterosexual relationship, and fraught connections between male characters that tread the line between the homophobic and homoerotic. Orr expands on the noir style we see in the films: 'low-key lighting and high-contrast photography in rooms with cross-hatched blinds, extreme camera angles, subjective distortion in the shot or in the ambiance of city streets with mist and rain, seedy bars and diners, glistening sidewalks and neon light'.[2]

Despite clear overlaps, critics tend to read Hitchcock's films as comprising a genre of their own. Naremore notes, 'Hitchcock became one of the great tests of the auteur theory and a kind of genre unto himself.'[3] Observes another critic:

His reputation of 'The Master of Suspense' began while he was still in England, and within a few years of his arrival in America, he himself became not only a celebrity but also a kind of genre all of his own – one would go see the 'new Hitchcock' the way you would buy tickets to 'that new horror picture'.[4]

If Hitchcock's suspense films are always 'at the margins of noir', this chapter considers *I Confess* as a film where form matches content. Just as Father Michael Logan (Montgomery Clift) forever runs the risk of exposing the guilt of Otto Keller (O. E. Hasse), the murderer who confesses to and then hounds Logan, *I Confess* forever threatens to expose the noir underpinnings of the Hitchcock thriller. The film's quasi-explicitness as noir, moreover, matches the quasi-explicitness of homosexual themes in the film, organised around a figure that recurs in Hitchcock, the tremulous brunet. As I elaborate elsewhere, the tremulous brunet, an underappreciated counterpoint to the more famous Hitchcock blonde, is a male character type marked by dark hair and eyes, great sensitivity, fearfulness, and the banked but palpable capacity for violence.[5] *I Confess* offers a pastiche of noir by choosing as its setting not the trademark noir city Los Angeles but instead the French-Canadian Québec City. Similarly, the hero, Logan, is not a typically morally compromised and suspect noir male protagonist or hard-boiled detective but a Catholic priest doing his duty and remaining bound by the strictures of the Catholic sacrament of confession, which prevents Logan from revealing Keller's crime (see Figure 11.1).

Hitchcock locates within noir a tendency to subject male identity and male-male relationships to particularly intense scrutiny. As do noirs such as *Double*

Figure 11.1   Father Logan (Montgomery Clift) anxiously hears the murderer's confession. [Creative Commons]

Indemnity (Billy Wilder, 1944), *Gilda* (Charles Vidor, 1946), *Dead Reckoning* (John Cromwell, 1947), *Desert Fury* (Lewis Allen, 1947), *The Hitch-Hiker* (Ida Lupino, 1953), and *The Big Combo* (Joseph H. Lewis, 1955), *I Confess* explores male bonds and potentially homoerotic tensions. Though various means of deflecting the homoerotic secret of Logan and Keller exist, the film makes Clift's Logan a site of compelling, impenetrable mystery to heighten the illicit nature of his sexuality. Hidden behind the veil of the confessional, Logan emerges as the ultimate noir male subject who must confess. The steps taken to eroticise Logan and render him an unattainable erotic object threaten to expose noir's comfort level. The Cold War context, policing forms of masculinity and male sexuality that fail to conform to normative standards and subjecting homosexuals and other subversives to state discipline, makes Keller's transgressive desire for Logan synonymous with the crime he could only confess to the priest. *I Confess* metatextually explores noir through its co-optation of noir's investments in destabilising norms and protocols of male gender and sexual performance.

Another context adds considerable depth to Hitchcock's depiction of male-male desire. The intertextual relationship that both Hitchcock and noir maintain with the nineteenth-century American Gothic, traditionally though not exclusively embodied by the works of Edgar Allan Poe, Nathaniel Hawthorne, and Herman Melville, allows us to see that Hitchcock continues a long-standing tradition of framing fraught male relations and gendered anxiety generally in Gothic terms linked to national identity. Like Poe, Hawthorne, and Melville before him, Hitchcock tells the story of America through a Gothic framework that emphasises bonds between men as simultaneously desirable and dangerous, as this chapter will explore.

To establish the director's Gothic lineage, we turn immediately to Poe, whose influence on him Hitchcock made explicit in several interviews. 'Whereas little is known of Hitchcock's reading of Hawthorne, the filmmaker spoke quite openly about Poe's importance for him', Carl Freedman observes.[6] Dennis R. Perry wrote a 1993 book devoted to this connection (*Hitchcock and Poe: The Legacy of Delight and Fear*). In 'Hitchcock at the Margins of Noir', Naremore also claims Poe's influence on Hitchcock as central. Beyond Hitchcock, Poe has been cited as crucial to classic film noir, especially given his status as the inventor of the modern detective story (the Dupin stories, such as 'The Murders in the Rue Morgue', foregrounding the amateur detective's formidable powers of 'ratiocination').[7]

Poe and his influence synthesise the link between film noir and the American Gothic and Hitchcock's links to both. In his essay 'Film Noir and the Gothic', David Fine writes, 'Gothic elements have been so tightly woven into American film noir that one can make the case that noir *is* a twentieth-century manifestation of the American Gothic', a statement made in an essay that focuses on the

European Gothic's, especially Germany's, influence on American noir.[8] Another critic locates the beginnings of the American Gothic tradition in film noir in the gangster films of the 1930s. American crime films of the 1930s and 1940s continue an American Gothic tradition that depicts the United States as inherently corrupt and routinely committed to mayhem. Here, 'Gothic spaces predominate: threatening dark alleys, ghetto structures that remind viewers of deserted castles, dimly lit backrooms in police stations, and filthy jail cells.' Scenes of night and fog abound because 'no one wants to be exposed to the bright light of day'. This world, noir's continuation of the American Gothic, is 'inhabited by monsters'.[9] In their hugely influential and path-breaking study *A Panorama of Film Noir*, a 1955 book expanded from their 1946 article, the French critics Raymond Borde and Étienne Chaumeton describe the world of film noir as centred in death, 'in all senses of the word'.[10] Monsters and death, the connective tissue between the American Gothic and noir, assume myriad forms in both.

This chapter discusses American Gothic writing as a key influence on Hitchcock and film noir and central to our understanding between the genres of the Hitchcock film and noir, with emphasis on the male body and male-male relationships. In particular, I consider the intertextual relationship between *I Confess* and works by Melville and Hawthorne.

Gothic City

I Confess is adapted from a turn-of-the-century French play by Paul Anthelme set in France, *Nos deux consciences* (*Our Two Consciences*) (1902), that Hitchcock saw in the 1930s. Given the prohibitive expenses of filming in France, a new location for the film's setting was sought. In an early draft, the setting was San Francisco; in the final version, the setting is Québec City. Two crucial points: first, Hitchcock had sought to make *I Confess* since the late 1940s. Elated by his release from contractual obligations to producer David O. Selznick, who had engineered the English director's transition to Hollywood and (quite overbearingly in Hitchcock's experience) produced three of the director's films, Hitchcock and producing partner Sidney Bernstein were revving up their independent production company Transatlantic Pictures. *I Confess* was slotted to be the third Transatlantic film, and in 1947 Louis Verteuil completed a first treatment that transposed the action of the French play to the San Francisco area.[11] The most noir-like Hitchcock picture, his adaptation of Patricia Highsmith's novel *Strangers on a Train*, would appear to have paved the way for *I Confess*, and no doubt it did, yet the latter was already in Hitchcock's mind and presumably shaped *Strangers on a Train*. Certainly, both make central a fraught, overly intimate, invasive male-male bond. Second, Alma Reville, the director's wife, wrote a fresh treatment for *I Confess* that transferred the setting from San Francisco to Québec. *Stage*

Fright was the last film for which Reville received a screen credit. According to Hitchcock's biographer Patrick McGilligan, the failure of *Under Capricorn* (1949), which Hitchcock adapted from a novel by Helen Simpson that his wife recommended as a property, was the basis for Reville's lack of any screen credits from this point on, though she remained an active collaborator on her husband's films.[12] It can hardly be an insignificant detail that the villain's long-suffering wife in *I Confess* is named Alma.

The film opens with a thrillingly odd credit sequence set against the looming, imposing, Gothic structure of Le Château Frontenac, a heritage urban resort located close to the St Lawrence River. As we move closer and closer to the Chateau, gliding over the river's waters, Gregorian chant suffuses Dimitri Tiomkin's score. The opening credits sequence establish the film's Gothic orientation visually and thematically, the architectural landmark signalling that we are in Québec City, filmed in a manner that Sylvie Bissonnette describes as an 'estranged representation' designed to indicate 'the oppressive effect of concealment'. We view the Chateau's tower from a 'crooked low-angle shot' that makes the structure look like 'a medieval castle on a hill', decisively establishing a 'gothic ambience'. The film's 'expressionist aesthetic' uses these visual symbols to thematise Québec City's 'dual nature' and the 'ambiguity between guilt and innocence' central to the plot (see Figure 11.2).[13]

Figure 11.2 The Hitchcock cameo: the director strides across the screen atop Quebec City's 'L'escalier Casse-cou'. [Creative Commons]

The film's post-opening credits montage brings the Hitchcock cameo in a low-angle extreme long shot. The director walks across the screen on the grounds above a vertiginously high and lengthy stairway, the singularly shaped celebrity director recognisable in the daylight even from this distance. A series of signs all labelled DIRECTION – pointedly leading in the *opposite* direction from where Hitchcock was heading as he walked across the screen – guide us to the window of an apartment, through which we see a corpse on the floor.[14] It is night, and a man wearing a long black cassock – dressed as a priest – briskly makes his way through noirishly dark and winding streets. We know that he must bear some relation to the dead man. And indeed he does. The body is that of Vilette (Ovila Légare), a lawyer. The man disguised as a priest is Otto Keller. Keller and his wife Alma (Dolly Haas) are German refugees employed by the Catholic church where the film's protagonist, Father Michael Logan, has been assigned. Seeing a light in the church later that night, Logan investigates and discovers Keller, the rectory handyman, inside. Clearly concerned by Keller's agitated state, Logan asks him what's wrong, and Keller asks the priest to hear his confession. In the confessional, Keller reveals that he has killed Vilette, for whom Keller also worked, when the lawyer discovered Keller attempting to rob him. Logan encourages Keller to give himself up, but he refuses to do so. Instead, he begins incessantly hounding Logan about his sacred order not to reveal the details of the confession, alternately reminding him of his duty and taunting him that he will buckle under the pressure and, like a coward, reveal it.

Logan, though under clear duress, never reveals the confessional's secrets. He does, however, bring a most awkward personal dilemma to the situation. In the past, Logan had a friendship, possibly a romance, with a woman named Ruth (Anne Baxter). In a flashback sequence from Ruth's point of view, Logan, not yet a priest, returns from war and encounters Ruth. Unbeknownst to him, she is now married to Pierre Grandfort, a member of Parliament. In the countryside, the couple gets caught in a terrible all-night thunderstorm and seeks shelter in a summer house. The summer house belongs to Vilette, which the pair discover in the morning when he appears to berate them for being on his property. We never hear any of this conversation, but it leads to a confrontation between Vilette and Logan, who punches him (probably for impugning Ruth's character). Seizing on her prominent social position, Vilette begins blackmailing Ruth, threatening to expose illicit behaviour (though no evidence for it exists) that will harm Ruth and Logan. So, though innocent, Father Logan emerges as the principal suspect for Vilette's murder, since he was seen meeting Ruth on the night of the crime (their opportunity to discuss the blackmail) and a man (Keller) dressed as a priest was seen leaving the lawyer's home. Father Logan's tormented silence emerges as the central drama of the film, as he undergoes a series of trials from the man in charge of the investigation, Inspector Larreau (Karl Malden), the

Crown Prosecutor (Brian Aherne), the judge in the courtroom where he is tried for murder, and, increasingly, from what would appear to be the city's populace, who violently turn on Logan even after he has been acquitted by the jury (at the judge's highly vocal displeasure).

THE CASSOCK

Asked by the reporter Gerald Pratley in 1952 why he decided to make *I Confess*, described by Pratley as an 'odd film for him to make', Hitchcock responded:

> Well, I like to make different kinds of melodramas. . . . *I Confess* is somewhat similar [to *Shadow of a Doubt* (1943)], except it is laid in the city of Quebec. First, because the original story had a French setting, but chiefly because our treatment of the script calls for the murderer, who works in a rectory, to put on a cassock as a kind of disguise. He is seen leaving the house by two little girls . . . Now, there's no other town on the North American continent . . . where priests walk around wearing their cassocks, so Quebec is the only suitable city in which to start the plot that way.[15]

Given Hitchcock's frequent construction of elaborate sequences organised around a prop of particular fascination to him rather than crucial plot points and narrative logic (think of the key in Ingrid Bergman's/Alicia Huberman's hand in *Notorious*'s (1946) dizzying high-angle crane shot), it is entirely plausible that *I Confess* found its setting because it showcased the cassock-clad bodies of male priests.

Hitchcock's Catholic themes are of crucial importance, stemming, as they do, from his religious upbringing and childhood education in London's Jesuit schools. Their urgency is keenly felt in *I Confess* and *The Wrong Man* (1956), both of which feature overt Christian symbolism. For the moment, however, I want to discuss a more irreverent, and queer, dimension of Hitchcock's religious iconography. John Orr has persuasively read *I Confess* as a homoerotic work, arguing that the film contains coded references to homosexual sex. The casting of Montgomery Clift, arguably the most significant (with a great deal of competition) gay male actor of classical Hollywood in the ways that his sexuality is inextricable from the meanings of his stardom (which I will discuss below), lends considerable depth to these concerns.

Orr broadens the point: 'Hitchcock's casting of two gay actors, Montgomery Clift and O. E. Hasse, might well intimate a hidden agenda.' He notes that Warner Bros., which eventually took over what was to have been a Transatlantic Pictures film, forced Hitchcock 'to take out those elements . . . that attracted him and were present in the early drafts of George Tabori'. Tabori and William

Archibald are credited on-screen; Barbara Keon, who is listed on-screen as production associate, also collaborated on the script.[16] Removed from the script were all references to the story that attracted Hitchcock: 'the falsely accused priest has fathered an illegitimate child after an affair with a married woman, and then is powerless to prevent a guilty verdict that results in his execution for a murder he did not commit'. The loss of these tantalising plot dynamics, Orr theorises, may have led Hitchcock to rework 'an intensely personal project' in ways that lend themselves to a queer reading. *I Confess*, with its casting of two gay male actors, continues 'the queer aesthetic inherent in *Rebecca*, *The Paradine Case*, *Rope*, and *Strangers on a Train*'.[17] Orr reads a number of moments in the film as suggestive of 'homosexual ambiance'. Ruth worries that Logan will be 'unfrocked', not 'defrocked'; Alma, Keller's wife, complains, in reference to their mutual efforts to paint a room, about the bad smell Logan and Keller's 'joint activity' produces; we never know what exactly Vilette says to or of Logan or Ruth that causes Logan to punch the lawyer, given that the story is relayed from Ruth's perspective. 'Vilette . . . acts as the signifier of an alternate circuit of desire whose full nature the film never reveals (and never can reveal) to us.'[18] Homosexual blackmail and, I would add, a network of clandestine homosexual relationships (recalling *Rope* and the relations among former schoolmates and their headmaster) might be a possibility here.

In agreement with Orr's suggestive queer reading, I want to argue that the image of Father Logan in his cassock functions as an important queer signifier. Paradoxically, the long black robe that covers the priestly male form from below the neck to above the shoes feminises and phallicises the male body at once. Given the non-standard elements of the cassock in terms of conventional male attire – that it can be viewed as a dress, to put it bluntly – it can be read as feminising and therefore threatening on gendered and sexual levels. At the same time, especially as worn by Clift, the cassock regularises and snugly encases a lithe male body, emphasising this litheness and manliness. That Keller wears a cassock to his scene of criminality – robbery and murder – adds the noirish and Weimar Gothic element of the doppelgänger, a motif given additional heft by the fact that Keller stuffs the bloodied cassock into Logan's trunk in order to frame him.

The queer aspects of cassocks are highlighted in a fascinating intertext for *I Confess*: Melville's 1851 masterpiece *Moby-Dick; or, The Whale*. Embedded within several lengthy and encyclopedic accounts of the lives and labours of whale hunters at sea, Chapter 95, 'The Cassock', irreverently likens the makeshift garb of a particular kind of sailor to the titular item of clothing. The whale's penis, a 'very strange, enigmatical object' called the 'grandissimus', is carried by 'the sailor, called the mincer', 'as if he were a grenadier carrying a dead comrade from the field'. He then 'proceeds cylindrically to remove its dark pelt, as an African hunter the pelt of a boa. This done, he turns the pelt inside out, like a pantaloon leg', stretching it out, hanging it, and leaving it to dry. The mincer then dons this whaleskin pelt – his cassock – to mince 'horse-pieces of blubber'. Lest we miss Melville's blasphemous humour (which got him into considerable trouble with contemporary reviewers), he spells it out: 'Arrayed in decent black; occupying a conspicuous pulpit; intent on bible leaves; what a candidate for an archbishoprick, what a lad for a Pope were this mincer!' As Herschel Parker, the editor of this edition, rightly notes, the archaic spelling of 'archbishoprick' 'emphasizes the phallic pun'.[19]

Perhaps because he is not associated with literary adaptation, even though quite a few of his films are precisely that, Hitchcock is not typically considered alongside literary auteurs apart from figures such as Poe and Henry James. So, one does not find many comparative treatments of Hitchcock and Melville or the director and Hawthorne, or of Hitchcock and the American Gothic generally. Sianne Ngai is the exceptional critic to compare Hitchcock and Melville as artists who thematise the Heideggerian 'thrownness' of the intellectual subject.[20]

Donald Spoto offered an early and infrequently travelled path for the comparative analysis of Hitchcock and early American literature. Discussing the script largely, though not exclusively, written for *Shadow of a Doubt* by the playwright Thornton Wilder, whose most famous 1938 work *Our Town* Hitchcock admired, Spoto finds the 'clearest parallel' for Hitchcock and Wilder's collaboration

> with that authentically American Puritan view of man and his world as flawed, weak, and susceptible to corruption and madness. This view, found in our earliest writers – Jonathan Edwards, Edward Taylor, Cotton Mather – reached its most dramatic development in the hands of Herman Melville, Nathaniel Hawthorne, and Edgar Allan Poe. . . . To put the case briefly, Hitchcock seems to me the quintessentially *American* filmmaker.[21]

Spoto's most valuable readings of Hitchcock were made in this first edition of his study, and I propose a return to consideration of the idea of Hitchcock's links to American Gothic literature and its Puritan roots.

The American Gothic tradition that Spoto associates with Hitchcock has deep interconnections with film noir as well. Charles Scruggs aptly cites Leslie Fiedler's contention, in *Love and Death in the American Novel*, that 'behind the gothic lies a theory of history, a particular sense of the past'. Scruggs locates a renewed interest in American history as a phenomenon wrought by the Great War. 'It is no accident that the Melville revival began in 1921 with Raymond Weaver's biography of Melville and his 1924 edition of Melville's last manuscript, *Billy Budd*', which was left unfinished inside the author's writing desk at his death in 1891. Scruggs identifies Melville masterworks such as his 1856 novella *Benito Cereno* as key precursors to film noir, 'frightening not only in terms of its terror but also as the banality of evil: the slave trade as everyday commerce'. He identifies several other topics of the American Gothic as germane to noir. Scruggs cites Justin D. Edwards: 'the crimes within America's past are not limited to the African presence: "gender, homosexuality, incest, genocide, rape, war, murder, religion, and class" are also "proper subjects of the nation's Gothic literature". Over time, the same has come true for film noir and neo-noir.'[22] To return to the subject of cassock-clad Father Logan with Melville in mind, the image of Logan in his cassock, a religious garment traditionally fitted with thirty-three buttons signifying the years of Christ's earthly life, is a pious one. It is also an irreverent one if we imagine Hitchcock and Melville sharing an anarchic and parodistic attitude towards authority, tradition, and the sacred. Certainly, much like Melville, Hitchcock scandalously mixes modes of sympathy and scorn, humour and vulnerability, compassion and derision, empathy and cruelty. The cassock marks Logan as a holy object, a kind of mortal god to be reverenced; certainly, Ruth seems reverential towards him, if principally as an object of sexual desire. The intensity of Ruth's attraction charges the film with some of the buried/excised original content about a *Scarlet Letter*-like illegitimate child and a clandestine, illicit affair; her passion threatens to spill over into scandalous screen content. Again, we can think of Melville: in *Moby-Dick*, he includes a reference to Queen Maachah in Judea, who worshipped a phallic idol that her son Asa destroyed when deposing her. He then 'burnt it for an abomination at the brook Kedron, as darkly set forth in the 15th chapter of the first book of Kings'.[23]

Ruth's burning, naked desire for Logan, perhaps the film's most transgressive element, is underscored and ironised by an extraordinary shot, filmed from a bizarrely canted angle in slow motion and punctuated by heavenly Gregorian chant, of Ruth descending the stairs to be greeted by Logan, who takes her in his arms. This moment occurs within her flashback narration in Larrue's office, where she is under considerable duress as she attempts, quite unsuccessfully, to clear Logan by revealing her love for him, even as her politician husband watches and listens. The stylised shot where Ruth swoons pointedly indicates that her romance-tinged recollections may not be entirely accurate – that is, may not be a true portrait of Logan's own experiences. Woman's desire is transgressive and painful as well as narratively problematic here.

Amy Lawrence argues a different point in her excellent study of Clift's star persona, though her contention dovetails with my reading.

> The flashback is usually discussed in terms of what it reveals about Ruth's subjective perception of the past, but it is constructed through frequent returns to the present. By cutting back and forth from the sexually available young soldier to the priest in his cassock, the film raises the issue of the *priest's* sexuality.[24]

The effect of all of this is to show that Ruth desires Logan no less ardently now than she did then. I would tweak Lawrence's reading to argue that the film does indeed show us that Ruth continuously desires Logan, but that the stylisation of the flashback, by representing her own memories as halcyon fantasy, calls into question how accurate she can be about Logan's feelings towards her. A different moment confirms this. Meeting clandestinely on a ferry to discuss his predicament as a suspect, Ruth tells Logan that he still loves her; rather than affirming her asseverations, he remarks, 'I've changed.'

I argue that Ruth's provocatively problematic desire is doubled by another character that deepens the provocations and the problems. Keller also desires Logan. His unceasing, hovering persecution can be read – to reference another key and famously homoerotic Melville work, *Billy Budd, Sailor* (published posthumously in 1924) – as a Claggart-like defensive and paranoid expression of conflicted desire for an unattainable, beautiful man. (In Melville's sea-fiction novella, Claggart, the master-at-arms, preys upon the beautiful and morally innocent sailor Billy Budd, whom he desires but cannot possess. Instead, he entraps Billy, falsely accusing him of mutiny, a charge that eventually leads to Billy's death sentence and to Claggart's death at Billy's hand and Billy's death sentence.) Logan in his cassock advertises his sexual unavailability and suggestive desirability at once. Logan thus signals the return of a figure from nineteenth-century American literature, the sexually inviolate male who incites desire and cannot return nor satisfy the lover's feelings.[25] As Lawrence writes:

> No matter how hard the Production Code office fought any expression of sexuality on Logan's part, Hitchcock arranged for the priest to be the object of desire. But in place of the heterosexual romance the publicity people hoped for, Hitchcock inserted a 'perverse', obsessive desire. The most taboo desire, of course, is not Ruth's adulterous lust for a priest, but Otto's treacherous, persistent demand that Logan be his 'friend'. To chart this desire, the film shifts in its final scenes from Logan's travails to Otto's desire.[26]

Antipathy and Love

As noted, the backstory of a priest's illicit affair and illegitimate child that Warner Bros. forced Hitchcock to excise recalls the most famous work of adultery in American literature, Hawthorne's 1850 novel *The Scarlet Letter*. The Puritan Hester Prynne is married to the Englishman Roger Chillingworth, a physician who is much older than her and someone she has never had the chance to love. Before the novel opens, Hester has had an illicit sexual relationship with the handsome young minister Arthur Dimmesdale and given birth to their daughter Pearl without ever revealing the father's identity, even though Hester is jailed and forced publicly to wear the titular letter that proclaims her crime of adultery. If Hawthorne's narrative echoes in *I Confess*, it does so most pointedly in its version of a crucial relationship in Hawthorne's work: that between Dimmesdale and Chillingworth, who suspects the young man of being the newborn Pearl's father. All under the deceitful guise of acting as the young man's therapeutic healer and counsellor, Chillingworth moves in with Dimmesdale, determined to find evidence of his guilt. One night, Chillingworth spies on the tremulously agitated young man splayed out in sleep; the physician seizes on his opportunity and parts the minister's vestments to expose his chest. It is a same-sex version of a typical scene from a nineteenth-century bodice-ripper. We do not, in Hawthorne's cagey manner, learn exactly what Chillingworth sees on the minister's chest, but his triumphant look suggests that Chillingworth has found the proof he seeks – the scarlet A carved into the minister's flesh by his own hand.

The insidious, poisonous intimacy between Dimmesdale and Chillingworth finds an apt complement in the relationship between Logan and Keller. Everywhere Logan goes after Keller confesses to him, he sees or is surprised by the older, feverish man, who goads him regarding the knowledge they both share. Keller ostensibly attempts to shame or terrorise Logan into silence, but he also seizes on the constrictions that force Logan to be silent – he is unable even to discuss or hint at the situation with his fellow priests, lest he break the seal of the confessional – as an opportunity to corral and even possess the agonised and beautiful priest. Clift's amazingly contained, stoic, yet deeply expressive performance suggests layers of feeling – compassion but also suppressed anger – beneath the rectitude. The tremulous brunet opposes the more famous Hitchcock figure of the cool blonde by conveying a vulnerability that threatens to destabilise male stoic gender performance, to give the secret away – the secret being that male gender identity is a performance, one forever poised on failure. Keller's heavy-handed seduction of Logan takes the form of creeping, subterranean assault, as if he were the living embodiment of that voice inside Logan's head that reminds him that he is sexual and desired.

Noir and Hitchcock films emerge as crucial cites for the expression of otherwise forbidden male-male intimacy. Hitchcock's Cold War-era thrillers such as *Strangers on a Train* and *I Confess* can only understand bonds between men as threateningly sexualised – one man's desire impinging on the sanctity of another's personal realm – and laced with an intensifying violence. For all these reasons, *I Confess* is ultimately one of Hitchcock's most moving films. *Strangers on a Train* concludes with Bruno Antony (Robert Walker) and Guy Haines (Farley Granger) battling on a berserk, out-of-control merry-go-round; even in the heaps of rubble after the merry-go-round collapses, the dying Bruno refuses to admit his guilt. Surrounded by the police who have been hounding him as a suspect in his wife's murder, which Bruno committed on Guy's 'behalf', Guy attempts to pry the secret of Bruno's guilt from him – to elicit and enact a public confession. Bruno remains intransigently uncooperative right until the end; only the lighter that Bruno tried to plant on the fairground to incriminate Guy, falling from dying Bruno's hand, exonerates the hero.

I Confess takes the climax of *Strangers on a Train* and revises its logic. Logan tries to prevent Keller from incriminating himself; he tries to circumvent the public confessional. More than this, he tries to save Keller's life. After the conclusion of the trial, Logan has been found not guilty by the jury (for insufficient evidence), but quite guilty by the frightening angry mob awaiting his departure from the courthouse. Taunted and jeered by the crowd ('Preach us a sermon, Logan!'), the priest stumbles forward, not for the first time but now most resonantly likened to Christ during the Passion. The mob seething around him masses into a brutal force that leads Logan to punch his elbow through the window of a car and shatter it. As if this expression of explosive violence frees something in her, Keller's wife cries out that Logan is innocent and attempts to name her husband as Vilette's killer; Keller shoots her. Logan tenderly comforts the dying woman as Larreau observes the scene. She cannot, in her dying moments, articulate the name of the culprit; she asks only that Logan forgive her. But a police officer makes note that Alma cried out 'He is innocent!' in reference to Logan, which Larreau registers with a significant look. In the meantime, Keller, now being chased by the police for shooting Alma, has gone mad, running into Le Château Frontenac to elude the police and shooting those in his path. Finally cornered inside an auditorium, he keeps firing at anyone who comes close and continues taunting Logan. These taunts reveal all that Keller has tried to conceal, exposing his crime as he attempts to expose Logan as a coward for having revealed it, which the priest has not. As Logan bravely and resolutely walks towards Keller, Keller does exactly what the priest insists he will not do: he attempts to shoot Logan. The police shoot Keller before he can do so, however. Before he dies, Keller asks Logan for help: 'Father, forgive me'; Logan recites the Latin prayer of absolution. While this is a highly ambivalent scene in many ways, what it signifies most importantly is a decision to accept and offer reconciliation and forgiveness. In this regard, Hitchcock's film complements Hawthorne's novel. The narrator speculates that the addled minister and the corrupt, insinuating physician, so at odds in life, find the 'golden love' of rapprochement in the afterlife. Echoing Hawthorne's vision of reconciliation between agonised and agonist men, Hitchcock's film finds redemption not from the American Gothic's terrifying entrapments but through the American Gothic's own capacity for love.

Notes

1. John Orr, *Hitchcock and Twentieth-Century Cinema* (London: Wallflower Press, 2005), p. 154.

2. Orr, *Hitchcock and Twentieth-Century Cinema*, p. 154.
3. James Naremore, 'Hitchcock at the Margins of Noir', *Alfred Hitchcock: Centenary Essays*, ed. Richard Allen and S. Ishii-Gonzalès (London: British Film Institute, 1999), p. 266.
4. Stephen Whitty, *The Alfred Hitchcock Encyclopedia* (Lanham, MD: Rowman & Littlefield, 2016), p. 176.
5. This figure recurs in Hitchcock: Ivor Novello in *The Lodger* (1927), Gregory Peck in *Spellbound* (1945), Farley Granger in *Rope* (1948) and *Strangers on a Train* (1951), and especially Anthony Perkins in *Psycho* (1960). I discuss the tremulous brunet in my book *Intimate Violence: Hitchcock, Sex, and Queer Theory* (New York: Oxford University Press, 2017), p. 82.
6. Carl Freedman, 'American Civilization and its Discontents: The Persistence of Evil in Hitchcock's *Shadow of a Doubt*', *The Cambridge Companion to Alfred Hitchcock*, ed. Jonathan Freedman (New York: Cambridge University Press, 2015), p. 102.
7. For the relationship between Poe and noir, see especially John T. Irwin, *Unless the Threat of Death Is Behind Them: Hard-Boiled Fiction and Film Noir* (Baltimore, MD: Johns Hopkins University Press, 2006).
8. David Fine, 'Film Noir and the Gothic', *A Companion to American Gothic*, ed. Charles L. Crow (New York: John Wiley & Sons), p. 475.
9. Cecil E. Greek, 'The Big City Rogue Cop as Monster: Images of NYPD and LAPD', *Monsters in and Among Us: Toward a Gothic Criminology*, eds. Caroline Joan S. Picart and Cecil E. Greek (Madison, NJ: Fairleigh Dickinson University Press, 2007), p. 166.
10. Borde and Chaumeton, *A Panorama of Film Noir, 1941–1953* (1955) (San Francisco: City Lights Books, 2002), p. 5.
11. For these production details, I am drawing on Patrick McGilligan, *Alfred Hitchcock: A Life in Darkness and Light* (London: HarperCollins, 2004), p. 415.
12. McGilligan, *Alfred Hitchcock*, pp. 439–40.
13. Sylvie Bissonnette, 'Adaptation as an act of confession in Lepage's *Le confessionnal* and Hitchcock's *I Confess*', *Camera Lens to Critical Lens: A Collection of Best Essays on Film Adaptation*, ed. Rebecca Housel (Newcastle: Cambridge Scholars Publishing, 2006), p. 84.
14. John Bruns opines, 'Hitchcock is warning us' by juxtaposing the image of himself 'walking in the wrong direction above L'Escalier Casse-cou, or breakneck stairs, a seventeenth-century stairway that connects Upper and Lower Town in Old Quebec'. Inciting a 'topographic fascination', the city nevertheless 'resists mapping . . . rational cartography'. Bruns, *Hitchcock's People, Places, and Things* (Chicago: Northwestern University Press, 2019), pp. 104–5.
15. Alfred Hitchcock, *Alfred Hitchcock: Interviews*, ed. Sidney Gottlieb (Jackson: University Press of Mississippi, 2003), p. 35.
16. 'Upwards of a dozen writers toiled on *I Confess*', 'a dispiriting record for a Hitchcock film'. McGilligan, *Alfred Hitchcock*, p. 458.
17. Orr, *Hitchcock and Twentieth-Century Cinema*, pp. 178–9.
18. Orr, *Hitchcock and Twentieth-Century Cinema*, pp. 182–3.

19. Herman Melville, *Moby-Dick: An Authoritative Text, Contexts, Criticism*, Third Norton Critical Edition, ed. Herschel Parker (New York: W.W. Norton, 2018), pp. 310–11. Parker's editorial note: p. 311n4.
20. Sianne Ngai discusses Heidegger, Hitchcock, and Melville in terms of their treatment of anxiety, 'involving fantasies of the subject as thrown or airborne entity'. Ngai, *Ugly Feelings* (Cambridge, MA: Harvard University Press, 2009), p. 212.
21. Donald Spoto, *The Art of Alfred Hitchcock: Fifty Years of His Motion Pictures* (New York: Dolphin Books, 1976), p. 134. Lincoln Konkle helpfully draws our attention to this early Spoto passage in his *Thornton Wilder and the Puritan Narrative Tradition* (Columbia: University of Missouri Press, 2006), p. 167. I discuss the distinctions between Wilder's original screenplay and the final script for *Shadow of a Doubt* in the chapter on that film in my book *Intimate Violence: Hitchcock, Sex, and Queer Theory*, considering the queer dimensions of the collaboration.
22. Charles Scruggs, 'American Film Noir', *The Cambridge Companion to the Modern Gothic*, ed. Jerrold E. Hogle (New York: Cambridge University Press, 2014), p. 135.
23. Melville, *Moby-Dick*, p. 311.
24. Amy Lawrence, *The Passion of Montgomery Clift* (Berkeley: University of California Press, 2010), p. 108. The space needed to expand on the queer meanings of Clift's stardom exceeds the scope of this chapter. Another excellent resource on this subject is Elisabetta Girelli's *Montgomery Clift, Queer Star* (Detroit: Wayne State University Press, 2013), which pays unprecedented and welcome attention to the depth of Clift's performances after the brutal car accident that impacted his face and considerably altered his famous features.
25. For a treatment of this theme, see David Greven, *Men Beyond Desire: Manhood, Sex, and Violation in American Literature* (New York: Palgrave Macmillan, 2005).
26. Lawrence, *The Passion of Montgomery Clift*, p. 134.

SELECTED BIBLIOGRAPHY

Andersen, Thom. 'Red Hollywood'. In *Literature and the Visual Arts in Contemporary Society*, edited by Suzanne Ferguson and Barbara Groseclose, pp. 141–96. Columbus: Ohio State University Press, 1985.

Barlow, John D. *German Expressionist Film*. Boston: Twayne Publishers, 1982.

Baron, Lawrence, and Joel Rosenberg. 'The Ben Urwand Controversy: Exploring the Hollywood-Hitler Relationship'. In *From Shtel to Stardom: Jews and Hollywood*, edited by Michael Renov and Vincent Brook, pp. 23–46. West Lafayette, IN: Purdue University Press, 2017.

Bazin, André. 'The Evolution of the Western'. In *The Western Reader*, edited by Jim Kitses and Gregg Rickman, pp. 49–56. New York: Limelight Editions, 1998.

Bazin, André. *French Cinema from the Liberation to the New Wave, 1945–1958*. New Orleans: University of New Orleans Press, 2012.

Bell, Melanie. 'Fatal Femininity in Post-War British Film'. In *The Femme Fatale: Images, Histories, Contexts*, edited by Helen Hanson and Catherine O'Rawe, pp. 98–112. Houndmills: Palgrave Macmillan, 2010.

Bell, Melanie. *Femininity in the Frame: Women and 1950s British Popular Cinema*. London: I. B. Tauris, 2010.

Berns, Fernando Gabriel Pagnoni. *Alegorías Televisivas del Franquismo: Narciso Ibáñez Serrador y las Historias para no Dormir (1966–1982)*. Cádiz: Universidad de Cádiz, 2020.

Berns, Fernando Gabriel Pagnoni. 'Cine de terror argentino: Historia, temas y estética de un género en el período clásico'. In *Horrofílmico: Aproximaciones al cine de terror en Latinoamérica y el Caribe*, edited by Rosana Díaz-Zambrana and Patricia Tomé, pp. 432–51. San Juan, Puerto Rico: Editorial Isla Negra, 2011.

Berns, Fernando Gabriel Pagnoni. 'Stories to Make You Think: The Horror of Daily Life under Francisco Franco's Regime in *Historias para No Dormir*'. In *Global TV*

SELECTED BIBLIOGRAPHY

Horror, edited by Stacey Abbott and Lorna Jowett, pp. 67–83. Cardiff: University of Wales Press, 2021.

Biesen, Sheri Chinen. *Blackout: World War II and the Origins of Film Noir*. Baltimore: Johns Hopkins University Press, 2005.

Biesen, Sheri Chinen. *Music in the Shadows: Noir Musical Films*. Baltimore: Johns Hopkins University Press, 2014.

Bilík, Petr. 'Kinematografie po druhé světové válce (1945–1970)'. In *Panorama českého filmu*, edited by Luboš Ptáček, pp. 85–130. Olomouc: Rubico, 2000.

Billheimer, John. *Hitchcock and the Censors*. Lexington: University of Kentucky Press, 2019.

Bird, Robert. 'Refiguring the Russian Type: Dostoyevsky and the Limits of Realism'. In *A New Word on the Brothers Karamazov*, edited by Robert Louis Jackson, pp. 17–30. Evanston, IL: Northwestern University Press, 2004.

Bissonnette, Sylvie. 'Adaptation as an Act of Confession in Lepage's *Le confessionnal* and Hitchcock's *I Confess*'. In *Camera Lens to Critical Lens: A Collection of Best Essays on Film Adaptation*, edited by Rebecca Housel, pp. 73–90. Newcastle: Cambridge Scholars Publishing, 2006.

Blottner, Gene. *Columbia Noir: A Complete Filmography, 1940–1962*. Jefferson, NC: McFarland, 2015.

Borde, Raymond, and Étienne Chaumeton. *A Panorama of American Film Noir: 1941–1953*. Translated by Paul Hammond. San Francisco: City Lights Books, 2002.

Bordwell, David. *Poetics of Cinema*. New York: Routledge, 2008.

Bordwell, David, Janet Staiger, and Kristin Thompson. *The Classical Hollywood Cinema: Film Style and Mode of Production to 1960*. New York: Columbia University Press, 1985.

Botting, Fred. *Gothic*. London: Routledge, 2007.

Bould, Mark. *Film Noir: From Berlin to Sin City*. London and New York: Wallflower Books, 2005.

Boyarin, Daniel. *Unheroic Conduct: The Rise of Heterosexuality and the Invention of the Jewish Man*. Berkeley and Los Angeles: University of California Press, 1997.

Breu, Christopher, and Elizabeth A. Hatmaker. 'Introduction: Dark Passages'. In *Noir Affect*, edited by Christopher Breu and Elizabeth A. Hatmaker, pp. 1–28. New York: Fordham University Press, 2020.

Brodkin, Janet. *How the Jews Became White Folks . . . and What That Says about Race in America*. New Brunswick, NJ: Rutgers University Press, 1998.

Broe, Dennis. *Class, Crime and International Film Noir: Globalizing America's Dark Art*. New York: Palgrave Macmillan, 2014.

Broe, Dennis. *Film Noir, American Workers, and Postwar Hollywood*. Gainesville: University Press of Florida, 2009.

Brook, Vincent. *Driven to Darkness: Jewish Émigré Directors and the Rise of Film Noir*. New Brunswick, NJ: Rutgers University Press, 2009.

Brookes, Ian. *Film Noir: A Critical Introduction*. New York: Bloomsbury Academic, 2017.

Brown, Geoff. 'Which Way to the Way Ahead?: Britain's Years of Reconstruction'. *Sight and Sound* 47 (Autumn 1978): pp. 242–7.

Browning, John Edgar. 'Classical Hollywood Horror'. In *A Companion to the Horror Film*, edited by Harry M. Benshoff, pp. 225–36. Hoboken, NJ: Wiley-Blackwell, 2014.

Bruns, John. *Hitchcock's People, Places, and Things*. Chicago: Northwestern University Press, 2019.

Buhle, Paul, and David Wagner. *Radical Hollywood: The Untold Story Behind America's Favorite Movies*. New York: New Press, 2002.

Buss, Robin. *French Film Noir*. London: Marion Boyars, 1994.

Caballero, Chamion, and Peter J. Aspinall. *Mixed Race Britain in The Twentieth Century*. London: Palgrave Macmillan, 2018.

Camus, Albert. *The Rebel: An Essay on Man in Revolt*. Translated by Anthony Bower. New York: Vintage Books, 1956.

Capua, Michelangelo. *Yul Brynner: A Biography*. Jefferson, NC: McFarland, 2006.

Casty, Alan. *Robert Rossen: The Films and Politics of a Political Idealist*. Jefferson, NC: McFarland, 2012.

Caute, David. *Joseph Losey: A Revenge on Life*. New York: Oxford University Press, 1994.

Cazorla Sánchez, Antonio. *Fear and Progress: Ordinary Lives in Franco's Spain 1939–1975*. Malden, MA: Blackwell, 2010.

Chibnall, Steve, and Robert Murphy. 'Parole Overdue: Releasing the British Crime Film into the Critical Community'. In *British Crime Cinema*, edited by Steve Chibnall and Robert Murphy, pp. 1–15. London: Routledge, 1999.

Christopher, Nicholas. *Somewhere in the Night: Film Noir and the City*. New York: Henry Holt, 1997.

Ciment, Michel. *Conversations with Losey*. London: Methuen, 1985.

Clark, Colin, and Margaret Greenfields. *Here to Stay: The Gypsies and Travellers of Britain*. Hatfield: University of Hertfordshire Press, 2006.

Cohan, Steve. *Masked Men: Masculinity and the Movies in the Fifties*. Bloomington: Indiana University Press, 1997.

Cohen, Rich. *Tough Jews: Fathers, Sons, and Gangster Dreams in Jewish America*. New York: Simon and Schuster, 1998.

Conway, Kelley. *Agnés Varda*. Champaign: University of Illinois Press, 2015.

Cook, Pam. *Fashioning the Nation: Costume and Identity in British Cinema*. London: British Film Institute, 1996.

Cook, Pam, editor. *Gainsborough Pictures*. London: Cassell, 1997.

Cook, Pam. 'Neither Here nor There: National Identity in Gainsborough Costume Drama'. In *Dissolving Views: Key Writings on British Cinema*, edited by Andrew Higson, pp. 51–65. London: Cassell, 1996.

Cressy, David. *Gypsies: An English History*. Oxford: Oxford University Press, 2018.

Daniel, Douglass K. *Tough as Nails: The Life and Films of Richard Brooks*. Madison: University of Wisconsin Press, 2011.

Davidson, Michael. 'Phantom Limbs: Film Noir and the Disabled Body'. In *The Problem Body: Projecting Disability on Film*, edited by Sally Chivers and Nicole Markotic, pp. 43–65. Columbus: Ohio State University Press, 2010.

De Rham Edith. *Joseph Losey*. London: André Deutsch, 1991.

Del Col, José Juan. *Psicoanálisis de Freud y religión*. Buenos Aires: Centro Salesiano de Estudios San Juan Bosco, 1996.

Dell'Agnese, Elena. 'The US-Mexico Border in American Movies: A Political Geography Perspective'. *Geopolitics* 10, no. 2 (2005): pp. 204–21.

DeRoo, Rebecca J. *Agnés Varda: Between Film, Photography, and Art*. Oakland: University of California Press, 2017.

Di Paolo, Osvaldo, and Nadina Olmedo. *Negrótico*. Madrid: Pliegos, 2015.

Dimendberg, Edward. *Film Noir and the Spaces of Modernity*. Cambridge, MA: Harvard University Press, 2004.

Dixon, Wheeler Winston. *Film Noir and the Cinema of Paranoia*. Edinburgh: Edinburgh University Press, 2009.

Doane, Mary Ann. *Femmes Fatales: Feminism, Film Theory, and Psychoanalysis*. New York: Routledge, 1991.

Dombrowski, Lisa, editor. *Kazan Revisited*. Middletown, CT: Wesleyan University Press, 2011.

Drazin, Charles. *The Finest Years: British Cinema of the 1940s*. London: I. B. Tauris, 2007.

Drummond, Susan Gay. *Mapping Marriage Law in Spanish Gitano Communities*. Vancouver: UBC Press, 2006.

Du Graft, Lauren. 'The Wild Palms in a New Wave: Adaptive Gleaning and the Birth of the Nouvelle Vague'. *Adaptation* 10, no. 1 (2017): pp. 34–50.

Durgnat, Raymond. *A Mirror for England: British Movies from Austerity to Affluence*. New York: Praeger Publishers, 1971.

Durgnat, Raymond. 'Some Lines of Inquiry into Post-war British Crimes'. In *The British Cinema Book*, edited by Robert Murphy, pp. 90–103. London: BFI Publishing, 1997.

Dyer, Richard. *In the Space of a Song: The Uses of Song in Film*. London: Routledge, 2012.

Dyer, Richard. *Stars*. London: British Film Institute, 1998.

España, Claudio. *Cine argentino: Industria y clasismo, 1933/1956*. Buenos Aires: Fondo Nacional de las Artes, 2000.

Etienne, Anne, Benjamin Halligan, and Christopher Weedman, editors. *Adult Themes: British Cinema and the X Certificate in the Long 1960s*. London: Bloomsbury Academic, 2023.

Everson, William K. 'British Film Noir: Part I'. *Films in Review* 38, no. 5 (May 1987): pp. 288–9.

Everson, William K. 'British Film Noir: Part II'. *Films in Review* 38, nos. 6–7 (June/July 1987): pp. 341–7.

Faison, Stephen. *Existentialism, Film Noir, and Hard-Boiled Fiction*. Amherst, NY: Cambria Press, 2008.

Falicov, Tamara. *The Cinematic Tango: Contemporary Argentine Film*. London: Wallflower Press, 2007.

Fay, Jennifer, and Justus Nieland. *Film Noir: Hard-Boiled Modernity and the Cultures of Globalization*. London and New York: Routledge, 2010.

Fine, David. 'Film Noir and the Gothic'. In *A Companion to American Gothic*, edited by Charles L. Crow, pp. 475–87. New York: John Wiley & Sons.

Fluck, Winfried. 'Crime, Guilt, and Subjectivity in "Film Noir"'. *American Studies* 46 (2001): pp. 379–408.

Freedman, Carl. 'American Civilization and its Discontents: The Persistence of Evil in Hitchcock's *Shadow of a Doubt*'. In *The Cambridge Companion to Alfred Hitchcock*, edited by Jonathan Freedman, pp. 92–105. New York: Cambridge University Press, 2015.

Freud, Sigmund. 'Dostoyevsky and Parricide'. In *The Standard Edition of the Complete Psychological Works of Sigmund Freud: Volume XXI (1927–1931)*, edited by James Strachey, pp. 173–94. London: Hogarth, 1961.

Freud, Sigmund. *On Sexuality*. London: Penguin, 1977.

Gandolfo, Elvio, and Eduardo Hojman. *El terror argentino*. Buenos Aires: Alfaguara, 2002.

Gardner, Colin. *Joseph Losey*. Manchester: Manchester University Press, 2004.

Gilman, Sander. *The Jew's Body*. New York and London: Routledge, 1991.

Girelli, Elisabetta. *Montgomery Clift, Queer Star*. Detroit: Wayne State University Press, 2013.

Gleeson-White, Sarah. 'Auditory Exposures: Faulkner, Eisenstein, and Film Sound'. *PMLA* 128, no. 1 (2013): pp. 87–100.

Goldman, Herbert. *Jolson: The Legend Comes to Life*. New York: Oxford University Press, 1988.

Gomà, Francesc. *Conocer Freud y su obra*. Barcelona: Dopesa, 1979.

Gottlieb, Sidney, editor. *Alfred Hitchcock: Interviews*. Jackson: University Press of Mississippi, 2003.

Grant, John. *A Comprehensive Encyclopedia of Film Noir: The Essential Reference Guide*. Milwaukee: Hal Leonard, 2013.

Greek, Cecil E. 'The Big City Rogue Cop as Monster: Images of NYPD and LAPD'. In *Monsters in and Among Us: Toward a Gothic Criminology*, edited by Caroline Joan S. Picart and Cecil E. Greek, pp. 164–98. Madison, NJ: Fairleigh Dickinson University Press, 2007.

Greven, David. *Intimate Violence: Hitchcock, Sex, and Queer Theory*. New York: Oxford University Press, 2017.

Greven, David. *Men Beyond Desire: Manhood, Sex, and Violation in American Literature*. New York: Palgrave Macmillan, 2005.

Grisham, Therese, and Julie Grossman. *Ida Lupino, Director: Her Art and Resilience in Times of Transition*. New Brunswick, NJ: Rutgers University Press, 2017.

Grossman, Julie. *Rethinking the Femme Fatale in Film Noir: Ready for Her Close-Up*. New York: Palgrave Macmillan, 2009.

Hain, Milan. 'Film noir znovuzrozený: Počátky neonoiru v Americe'. *Cinepur* 27, no. 118 (2018): pp. 48–52.

Hain, Milan. '"Pocit neomezené fantazie": *Housle a sen* a žánr životopisného filmu'. In *Osudová osamělost: Obrysy filmové a literární tvorby Václava Kršky*, edited by Milan Hain and Milan Cyroň, pp. 102–36. Praha: Casablanca, 2016.

Hames, Peter. *The Czechoslovak New Wave*. New York: Wallflower Press, 2005.

Harper, Sue. *Picturing the Past: The Rise and Fall of the British Costume Film*. London: BFI Publishing, 1994.

Harper, Sue. *Women in British Cinema: Mad, Bad and Dangerous to Know*. London: Continuum 2000.

Harper, Sue, and Vincent Porter. *British Cinema of the 1950s: The Decline of Deference*. Oxford: Oxford University Press, 2003.
Hirsch, Foster. *The Dark Side of the Screen: Film Noir*. Boston: Da Capo Press, 2001.
Hirsch, Foster. *Joseph Losey*. Boston: Twayne Publishers, 1980.
Hollinger, Karen. *In the Company of Women: Contemporary Female Friendship Films*. Minneapolis: University of Minnesota Press, 1998.
Horsley, Lee. *The Noir Thriller*. New York: Palgrave Macmillan, 2001.
Howe, Irving, with Kenneth Libo. *World of Our Fathers*. New York: Touchstone/Simon and Schuster, 1976.
Irwin, John T. *Unless the Threat of Death Is Behind Them: Hard-Boiled Fiction and Film Noir*. Baltimore, MD: Johns Hopkins University Press, 2006.
Kahuda, František. 'Za užší sepětí filmové výroby se životem lidu'. *Iluminace* 16, no. 4 (2004): pp. 178–84.
Kaplan, E. Ann, editor. *Women in Film Noir*. London: British Film Institute, 1998.
Kasmir, Sharryn. *The Myth of Mondragon: Cooperatives, Politics, and Working-Class Life in a Basque Town*. New York: State University of New York Press, 1996.
Kawin, Bruce F. 'The Montage Element in Faulkner's Fiction'. In *Selected Film Essays and Interviews*, edited by Bruce F. Kawin, pp. 131–48. London and New York: Anthem Press, 2013.
Keaney, Michael F. *British Film Noir Guide*. Jefferson, NC: McFarland, 2008.
Keller, Sarah. 'Introduction: Jean Epstein and the Revolt of Cinema'. In *Jean Epstein: Critical Essays and New Translations*, edited by Sarah Keller and Jason N. Paul, pp. 23–47. Amsterdam: Amsterdam University Press, 2012.
Khatri Babbar, Shilpa. 'Cinematic Categorization of Gender Identities from the Gaze of Sociological Imagination'. *IORS Journal of Humanities and Social Sciences* 23 (2018): pp. 20–5.
Kierkegaard, Søren. *The Sickness Unto Death*. Edited and translated by Howard V. Hong and Edna Hong. Princeton: Princeton University Press, 1980.
Klimeš, Ivan. 'Filmaři a komunistická moc v Československu: Vzrušený rok 1959'. *Iluminace* 16, no. 4 (2004): pp. 129–38.
Kline, T. Jefferson, editor. *Agnès Varda: Interviews*. Jackson: University Press of Mississippi, 2014.
Knapík, Jiří, Martin Franc, et al. *Průvodce kulturním děním a životním stylem v českých zemích 1948–1967*, Volume II. Praha: Academia, 2011.
Koestler, Arthur. *Darkness at Noon*. Translated by Daphne Hardy. New York: The New American Library, 1961.
Konkle, Lincoln. *Thornton Wilder and the Puritan Narrative Tradition*. Columbia: University of Missouri Press, 2006.
Krasikov, Anatoly. *From Dictatorship to Democracy: Spanish Reportage*. Oxford: Pergamon Press, 1984.
Krutnik, Frank. *In a Lonely Street: Film Noir, Genre, Masculinity*. New York: Routledge, 1991.
Kynaston, David. *Austerity Britain, 1945–51*. London: Bloomsbury Publishing, 2007.
Labanyi, Jo. 'Feminizing the Nation: Women, Subordination and Subversion in Post-Civil War Spanish Cinema'. In *Heroines without Heroes: Reconstructing Female*

and National Identities in European Cinema, 1945–1951, edited by Ulrike Sieglohr, pp. 162–82. London: Bloomsbury, 2016.

Labanyi, Jo, Antonio Lázaro-Reboll, and Vicente Rodríguez Ortega. '*Film Noir*, the Thriller, and Horror'. In *A Companion to Spanish Cinema*, edited by Jo Labanyi and Tatjana Pavlović, pp. 259–90. Malden, MA: Blackwell, 2013.

Laitila, Johanna. *Melodrama, Self, and Nation in Post-War British Popular Film*. London: Routledge, 2018.

Lamberti, Edward, editor. *Behind the Scenes at the BBFC: Film Classification from the Silver Screen to the Digital Age*. London: Palgrave Macmillan, 2012.

Lander, María Fernanda. 'El Manual de urbanidad y buenas maneras de Manuel Antonio Carreño: reglas para la construcción del ciudadano ideal'. *Arizona Journal of Hispanic Cultural Studies* 6 (2002): pp. 83–96.

Landy, Marcia. *British Genres: Cinema and Society, 1930–1960*. Princeton: Princeton University Press, 1991.

Lawrence, Amy. *The Passion of Montgomery Clift*. Berkeley: University of California Press, 2010.

Leahy, James. *The Cinema of Joseph Losey*. London: A. Zwemmer, 1967.

Leitch, Thomas. *Adaptation and Its Discontents*. Baltimore: Johns Hopkins University Press, 2007.

Lieberman, Sima. *Growth and Crisis in the Spanish Economy: 1940–1993*. New York: Routledge, 2005.

Limón, José E. *American Encounters: Greater Mexico, The United States, and the Erotics of Culture*. Boston: Beacon Press, 1998.

Lott, Eric. *Love and Theft: Blackface Minstrelsy and the American Working Class*. New York: Oxford University Press, 1993.

Lovell, Glenn. *Escape Artist: The Life and Films of John Sturges*. Madison: University of Wisconsin Press, 2008.

Luhr, William. *Film Noir*. Hoboken, NJ: Wiley-Blackwell, 2012.

Lukacs, John. *The End of the Twentieth Century and the End of the Modern Age*. New York: Ticknor and Fields, 1993.

Lukeš, Jan. *Diagnózy času: Český a slovenský poválečný film (1945–2012)*. Praha: Slovart, 2013.

McFarlane, Brian. 'Losing the Peace: Some British Films of Postwar Adjustment'. In *Screening the Past: Film and the Representation of History*, edited by Tony Barta, pp. 93–107. Westport, CT: Praeger, 1998.

McGilligan, Patrick. *Alfred Hitchcock: A Life in Darkness and Light*. London: HarperCollins, 2004.

Macnab, Geoffrey. *J. Arthur Rank and the British Film Industry*. London: Routledge, 1993.

Macnab, Geoffrey. *Searching for Stars: Stardom and Screen Acting in British Cinema*. London: Cassell, 2000.

Mailer, Norman. 'The White Negro: Superficial Reflections on the Hipster'. *Dissent* 4, no. 3 (Fall 1957): pp. 276–93.

Mangen, S. P. *Spanish Society After Franco: Regime Transition and the Welfare State*. New York: Routledge, 2001.

SELECTED BIBLIOGRAPHY

Martin, Richard. *Mean Streets and Raging Bulls: The Legacy of Film Noir in Contemporary American Cinema*. Lanham, MD: Scarecrow Press, 1999.

Medrano, Juan Díez. *Framing Europe: Attitudes to European Integration in Germany, Spain, and the United Kingdom*. Princeton, NJ: Princeton University Press, 2003.

Melnick, Jeffrey. *A Right to Sing the Blues*. Cambridge, MA: Harvard University Press, 2001.

Melville, Herman. *Moby-Dick: An Authoritative Text, Contexts, Criticism*. Third Norton Critical Edition. Edited by Herschel Parker. New York: W. W. Norton, 2018.

Menegaldo, Gilles. 'Flashbacks in Film Noir'. *Sillages critiques* (June 2004): pp. 157–75. Available online from http://journals.openedition.org/sillagescritiques/1561; DOI: https://doi.org/10.4000/sillagescritiques.1561.

Mercouri, Melina. *I Was Born Greek*. Garden City, NY: Doubleday, 1971.

Meuel, David. *The Noir Western: Darkness on the Range, 1943–1962*. Jefferson, NC: McFarland, 2015.

Miklitsch, Robert. *The Red and the Black: American Noir in the 1950s*. Urbana: University of Illinois Press, 2017.

Miller, Laurence. 'Evidence for a British Film Noir Cycle'. In *Re-Viewing British Cinema, 1990–1992: Essays and Interviews*, edited by Wheeler Winston Dixon, pp. 155–64. Albany: State University of New York Press, 1994.

Milne, Tom, editor. *Losey on Losey*. Garden City, NY: Doubleday, 1968.

Mulhall, Joe. *British Fascism After the Holocaust: From the Birth of Denial to the Notting Hill Riots 1939–1958*. London: Routledge, 2021.

Murphy, Robert. 'A Brief Studio History'. In *BFI Dossier Number 18: Gainsborough Melodrama*, edited by Sue Aspinall and Robert Murphy, pp. 3–13. London: BFI Publishing, 1983.

Murphy, Robert. *Realism and Tinsel: Cinema and Society in Britain, 1939–1948*. London: Routledge, 1989.

Murphy, Robert. 'Riff-Raff: British Cinema and the Underworld'. In *All Our Yesterdays: 90 Years of British Cinema*, edited by Charles Barr, pp. 291–304. London: BFI Publishing, 1986.

Naremore, James. *Film Noir: A Very Short Introduction*. Oxford: Oxford University Press, 2019.

Naremore, James. 'Hitchcock at the Margins of Noir'. In *Alfred Hitchcock: Centenary Essays*, edited by Richard Allen and S. Ishii-Gonzalès, pp. 263–77. London: British Film Institute, 1999.

Naremore, James. *The Magic of Orson Welles*. Dallas: Southern Methodist University Press, 1989.

Naremore, James. *More than Night: Film Noir in its Contexts*. Berkeley: University of California Press, [1998] 2008.

Naremore, James. *On Kubrick*. London: British Film Institute, 2007.

Neale, Steve. 'Masculinity as Spectacle'. *Screen* 24, no. 6 (1983): pp. 2–16.

Neale, Steve. 'Questions of Genre'. *Screen* 31, no. 1 (1990): pp. 45–66.

Nelmes, Jill. *The Screenwriter in British Cinema*. London: British Film Institute/ Palgrave Macmillan, 2014.

Neupert, Richard, editor. *A History of the French New Wave Cinema*, 2nd ed. Madison: University of Wisconsin Press, 2002.

SELECTED BIBLIOGRAPHY

Neve, Brian. 'The Hollywood Left: Robert Rossen and Postwar Hollywood'. *Film Studies* 7, no. 1 (December 2005): pp. 54–65.

Ngai, Sianne. *Ugly Feelings*. Cambridge, MA: Harvard University Press, 2009.

Nord, Deborah Epstein. *Gypsies & the British Imagination, 1807–1930*. New York: Columbia University Press, 2006

O'Brien, Charles. 'Film Noir in France: Before the Liberation'. *Iris* 21 (Spring 1996): pp. 7–20.

Okely, Judith. *The Traveller-Gypsies*. Cambridge: Cambridge University Press, 1983.

Oliver, Kelly, and Benigno Trigo. *Noir Anxiety*. Minneapolis: University of Minnesota Press, 2003.

Orr, John. *Hitchcock and Twentieth-Century Cinema*. London: Wallflower Press, 2005.

Pack, Sasha David. *Spain in the Age of Mass Tourism, Modernization, and Dictatorship, 1945–1975*. Madison: University of Wisconsin Press, 2004.

Palmer, James, and Michael Riley. *The Films of Joseph Losey*. Cambridge: Cambridge University Press, 1993.

Palmer, R. Barton. 'Film Noir Begins: Some Thoughts'. *South Atlantic Review* 86, no. 4 (2021): pp. 1–30.

Palmer, R. Barton. *Shot on Location: Postwar American Cinema and the Exploration of Real Place*. New Brunswick, NJ: Rutgers University Press, 2016.

Parker, Francine. 'Discovering Ida Lupino'. *Action* 2, no. 3 (May/June 1967): pp. 19–23.

Pavlović, Tatjana, Inmaculada Alvarez, Rosana Blanco-Cano, Anitra Grisales, Alejandra Osorio, and Alejandra Sánchez. *100 Years of Spanish Cinema*. Malden, MA: Blackwell, 2009.

Payne, Stanley. *Fascism in Spain, 1923–1977*. Madison: University of Wisconsin Press, 1999.

Petley, Julian. 'The Lost Continent'. In *All Our Yesterdays: 90 Years of British Cinema*, edited by Charles Barr, pp. 98–119. London: BFI Publishing, 1986.

Pettey, Homer B. and R. Barton Palmer, editors. *Film Noir*. Edinburgh: Edinburgh University Press, 2014.

Pettey, Homer B. and R. Barton Palmer, editors. *International Noir*. Edinburgh: Edinburgh University Press, 2014.

Phillips, Gene D. *The Movie Makers: Artists in an Industry*. Chicago: Nelson-Hall, 1973.

Pippin, Robert B. *Fatalism in Film Noir: Some Cinematic Philosophy*. Charlottesville: University of Virginia Press, 2012.

Porfirio, Robert. 'No Way Out: Existential Motifs in the *Film Noir*'. In *Film Noir Reader*, edited by Alain Silver and James Ursini, pp. 77–93. New York: Limelight Editions, 1996.

Porter, Carolyn. *William Faulkner: Lives and Legacies*. Oxford: Oxford University Press, 2007.

Pozner, Valérie. '"Socialistický realismus" a jeho využití pro dějiny sovětské kinematografie'. In *Film a dějiny 3: Politická kamera – film a stalinismus*, edited by Kristian Feigelson and Petr Kopal, pp. 17–24. Praha: Casablanca, 2012.

Pulleine, Tim. 'Spin a Dark Web'. In *British Crime Cinema*, edited by Steve Chibnall and Robert Murphy, pp. 27–36. London: Routledge, 1999.

Reyes, Xavier Aldana. 'The Curious Case of the Spanish Televisual Vampire'. *Horror Studies* 8, no. 2 (2017): pp. 241–54.

Rodríguez, Carina. *El cine de terror en Argentina: producción, distribución, exhibición y mercado*. Bernal: Universidad Nacional de Quilmes, 2014.

Rogin, Michael. *Black Face, White Noise: Jewish Immigrants in the American Melting Pot*. Berkeley: University of California Press, 1998.

Rohmer, Eric, and Claude Chabrol, *Hitchcock: The First Forty-Four Films*. Translated by Stanley Hockman. New York: Frederick Unger, 1979.

Rosenbaum, Jonathan. *Discovering Orson Welles*. Berkeley: University of California Press, 2007.

Rosenberg, Joel. 'Rogin's Noise: The Alleged Crimes of *The Jazz Singer*'. *Prooftexts: A Journal of Jewish Literary History* 22, no. 1/2 (Winter/Spring 2002): pp. 221–39.

Ross, Kristin. *Fast Cars, Clean Bodies: Decolonization and the Reordering of French Culture*. Cambridge, MA: MIT Press, 1996.

Schatz, Thomas. *The Genius of the System: Hollywood Filmmaking during the Studio Era*. Minneapolis: University of Minnesota Press, 2010.

Scheib, Ronnie. 'Ida Lupino, Auteuress'. *Film Comment* 16, no. 1 (January/February, 1980): pp. 54–64, 80.

Scheib, Ronnie. "*Never Fear*' (1950) [sic]'. In *Queen of the B's: Ida Lupino Behind the Camera*, edited by Annette Kuhn, pp. 40–56. Westport, CT: Greenwood Press, 1995.

Schickel, Richard. *Elia Kazan: A Biography*. New York: HarperCollins, 2006.

Schrader, Paul. 'Notes on Film Noir'. *Film Comment* 8, no. 1 (Spring 1972): pp. 8–13.

Scruggs, Charles. 'American Film Noir'. In *The Cambridge Companion to the Modern Gothic*, edited by Jerrold E. Hogle, pp. 123–37. New York: Cambridge University Press, 2014.

Selby, Spencer. *The Worldwide Film Noir Tradition*. Ames, IA: Sink Press, 2013.

Serrano, Carmen. *Gothic Imagination in Latin American Fiction and Film*. Albuquerque: New Mexico University Press, 2019.

Sharrett, Christopher. 'The Horror Film as Social Allegory (and How It Comes Undone)'. In *A Companion to the Horror Film*, edited by Harry M. Benshoff, pp. 56–72. Hoboken, NJ: Wiley-Blackwell, 2014.

Siegel, Dorothy Schainman. *The Glory Road: The Story of Josh White*. White Hall, VA: Shoe Tree Press, 1982.

Silone, Ignazio. *Bread and Wine*. Translated by Eric Mosbacher. New York: Signet Classic, Penguin Group, 1986.

Silver, Alain, and Elizabeth Ward, editors. *Film Noir: An Encyclopedic Reference to the American Style*, 3rd ed. Woodstock, NY: Overlook Press, 1992.

Silver, Alain, and James Ursini, editors. *Film Noir Reader*. New York: Limelight Editions, 1996.

Silver, Alain, and James Ursini, editors. *Film Noir Reader 2*. New York: Limelight Editions, 1999.

Silver, Alain, and James Ursini, editors. *Film Noir Reader 4: The Crucial Films and Themes*. New York: Limelight Editions, 2004.

Sinyard, Neil. 'Intimate Stranger: The Early British Films of Joseph Losey'. In *British Cinema of the 1950s: A Celebration*, edited by Ian Mackillop and Neil Sinyard, pp. 111–24. Manchester: Manchester University Press, 2003.

Sissons, Michael, and Philip French, editors. *Age of Austerity*. London: Hodder and Stoughton, 1963.

Slobin, Mark. 'Putting Blackface in Its Place'. In *Entertaining America: Jews, Movies, and Broadcasting*, edited by J. Hoberman and Jeffrey Shandler, pp. 93–9. New York: The Jewish Museum and Princeton University Press, 2003.
Smith, Imogen Sara. *In Lonely Places: Film Noir Beyond the City*. Jefferson, NC: McFarland, 2011.
Sobchack, Vivian. 'Lounge Time: Postwar Crises and the Chronotope of Film Noir'. In *Refiguring American Film Genres: Theory and Method*, edited by Nick Browne, pp. 129–70. Berkeley: University of California Press, 1998.
Sorrento, Matthew. 'Documenting Crime: Genre, Verity, and Filmmaker as Avenger'. In *Framing Law and Crime: An Interdisciplinary Anthology*, edited by Caroline Joan Picart, Michael Hviid Jacobsen, and Cecil E. Greek, pp. 243–66. Madison, NJ: Fairleigh Dickinson University Press, 2016.
Spicer, Andrew, editor. *European Film Noir*. Manchester: Manchester University Press, 2007.
Spicer, Andrew. *Film Noir*. Harlow: Longman-Pearson Education, 2002.
Spicer, Andrew. 'Producing Noir: Wald, Scott, Hellinger'. In *Kiss the Blood off My Hands: on Classic Film Noir*, edited by Robert Miklitsch, pp. 130–51. Urbana: University of Illinois Press, 2014.
Spoto, Donald. *The Art of Alfred Hitchcock: Fifty Years of His Motion Pictures*. New York: Dolphin Books, 1976.
Steiner, George. *In Blue Beard's Castle: Some Notes Towards the Redefinition of Culture*. New Haven, CT: Yale University Press, 1971.
Street, Sarah. *British Cinema in Documents*. London: Routledge, 2016.
Street, Sarah. *Transatlantic Crossings: British Feature Films in the USA*. New York: Continuum, 2002.
Street, Sarah, Keith M. Johnston, Paul Frith, and Carolyn Rickards. *Colour Films in Britain: The Eastmancolor Revolution*. London: British Film Institute/Bloomsbury Publishing, 2021.
Swanson, Gillian. *Drunk with the Glitter: Space, Consumption and Sexual Instability in Modern Urban Culture*. London: Routledge, 2007.
Szczepanik, Petr. '"Machři" a "diletanti": Základní jednotky filmové praxe v době reorganizací a politických zvratů 1945 až 1962'. In *Naplánovaná kinematografie: Český filmový průmysl 1945 až 1960*, edited by Pavel Skopal, pp. 27–101. Praha: Academia, 2012.
Telotte, J. P. *Voices in the Dark: The Narrative Patterns of Film Noir*. Urbana and Chicago: University of Illinois Press, 1989.
Thumim, Janet. 'The Female Audience: Mobile Women and Married Ladies'. In *Nationalising Femininity: Culture, Sexuality and British Cinema in the Second World War*, edited by Christine Gledhill and Gillian Swanson, pp. 249–52. Manchester: Manchester University Press, 1996.
Trevelyan, John. *What the Censor Saw*. London: Michael Joseph, 1973.
Trigos, Rubén Sánchez. *La Orgía de los Muertos: Historia del Cine de Zombis Español*. Madrid: Shangrila, 2019.
Vernet, Marc. 'Genre'. *Film Reader*, no. 3 (February 1978): pp. 13–17.
Wager, Jans B. *Dames in the Driver's Seat: Rereading Film Noir*. Austin: University of Texas Press, 2005.

Wald, Elijah. *Josh White: Society Blues*. Amherst: University of Massachusetts Press, 2000.

Walker, Michael. 'Robert Siodmak'. In *The Book of Film Noir*, edited by Ian Cameron, pp. 138–9. New York: Continuum, 1993.

Walker-Morrison, Deborah. *Classic French Noir: Gender and the Cinema of Fatal Desire*. London: Bloomsbury Academic, 2020.

Webb, Emily. 'An Invisible Minority: Romany Gypsies and the Question of Whiteness'. *Romani Studies: Journal of the Gypsy Lore Society* 29, no. 1 (2019): pp. 1–25.

Weber, Harold. *The Restoration Rake-Hero: Transformations in Sexual Understanding in Seventeenth-Century England*. Madison: University of Wisconsin Press, 1986.

Weber, Max. 'Religious Rejections of the World and Their Directions'. In *Max Weber: Essays in Sociology*, edited and translated by H. H. Gerth and C. Wright Mills, pp. 323–61. New York: Oxford University Press, 1978.

Webster, Jason. *The Spy with 29 Names: The Story of the Second World War's Most Audacious Double Agent*. London: Chatto & Windus, 2014.

Webster, Wendy. *Imagining Home: Gender, 'Race' and National Identity, 1945–64*. London: University College London Press, 1998.

Weedman, Christopher. 'A Dark Exilic Vision of 1960s Britain: Gothic Horror and Film Noir Pervading Losey and Pinter's *The Servant*'. *Journal of Cinema and Media Studies* 58, no. 3 (Spring 2019): pp. 93–117.

Weedman, Christopher. 'Joseph Losey'. In *Fifty Hollywood Directors*, edited by Yvonne Tasker and Suzanne Leonard, pp. 143–51. London: Routledge, 2015.

Whitty, Stephen. *The Alfred Hitchcock Encyclopedia*. Lanham, MD: Rowman & Littlefield, 2016.

Williams, Melanie. 'No Love for Johnnie'. In *The Cinema of Britain and Ireland*, edited by Brian McFarlane, pp. 123–31. London: Wallflower Press, 2005.

Williams, Tony. *Hearths of Darkness: The Family in the Horror Film*, updated edition. Jackson: University of Mississippi Press, 2014.

Williams, Tony. *Structures of Desire: British Cinema, 1939–1955*. Albany: State University of New York Press, 2000.

Wood, Robin. *Hollywood from Vietnam to Reagan . . . and Beyond*. New York: Columbia University Press, 2003.

Wood, Robin. *Personal Views: Explorations in Film*, revised edition. Detroit: Wayne State University Press, 2006.

Wood, Robin. *Robin Wood on the Horror Film*, edited by Barry Keith Grant. Detroit: Wayne State University Press, 2018.

Woolfolk, Alan. 'The Dread of Ascent: The Moral and Spiritual Topography of Hitchcock's *Vertigo*'. In *Hitchcock's Moral Gaze*, edited by R. Barton Palmer, Homer B. Pettey, and Steven Sanders, pp. 237–52. Albany: State University of New York Press, 2017.

Woolfolk, Alan. 'Hints of Modernism, Shades of Noir: Huston's *The Maltese Falcon* as Transitional Text'. In *John Huston as Adaptor*, edited by Douglas McFarland and Wesley King, pp. 181–96. Albany: State University of New York Press, 2017.

Žalman, Jan. *Umlčený film*. Praha: KMa, 2008.

INDEX

adaptation, 57, 76, 85n28, 86n29, 89, 105–6, 114, 119, 127n38, 133, 150, 162, 166, 167–8, 171, 173, 174n7, 175n9, 178n61, 183–4, 188
adultery, 83, 87–8, 139, 141, 190–1
age of austerity, 108–9
alcoholism, 87–8, 92, 94, 96, 121, 122
Aldrich, Robert, 174n6
alienation, 23, 27, 29, 98, 137–8, 153
Alton, John, 169–70, 177n57
ambiguity (moral), 46, 54, 58, 99, 132, 134, 140, 184
American dream, 26–7, 29–30, 37, 150
American Puritanism, 188, 190–1
antisemitism, 71, 77, 78, 84n1, 84n7, 85n28, 86n29, 167
Arlen, Harold, 75, 78–9, 83
Ashes and Diamonds (dir. Wajda, 1958), 11–21; *see also* Wajda, Andrzej
assassinations, 12, 14, 15, 17, 18, 20
At the Terminus (dir. Kadár and Klos, 1957), 89, 91; *see also* Kadár, Ján; Klos, Elmar
Atomic age, 12, 165

autarchy/autarky, 37, 38–41, 42, 43, 45, 46, 47–8
auteurism, 167, 176n39, 180–1, 188

Bad Day at Black Rock (dir. Sturges, 1955), 64, 66n38; *see also* Sturges, John
Baroque film style, 161–2, 164, 165–6, 174n5, 174n6
Barreto, Román Viñoly, 131–42
Berlin, Irving, 74, 75
Big Night, The (dir. Losey, 1951), 115; *see also* Losey, Joseph
Black-Jewish relations, 73–5, 78–9, 83, 85n28
Black Vampire, The (dir. Barreto, 1953), 131–42; *see also* Barreto, Román Viñoly
Blackface *see* racial representation
Blackness/Black culture, 62, 75, 79, 83, 84; *see also* racial representation
Blast of Silence (dir. Baron, 1961), 174n6
Blues in the Night (dir. Litvak, 1941), 69–84; *see also* Litvak, Anatole

borderland *see* borders
borders (national), 3–4, 53–4, 59, 161, 165
Brooks, Richard, 161–73, 174n7, 175n8, 175n9, 175n10, 177n46, 177n51, 177n57, 178n68
Brothers Karamazov, The (Dostoevsky, 1879–80 novel), 162, 166, 167, 168, 169, 171, 174n7, 179n78; *see also* Dostoevsky, Fyodor
Brothers Karamazov, The (dir. Brooks, 1958), 161–73, 175n8, 175n10; *see also* Brooks, Richard

Cabinet of Dr. Caligari, The (dir. Wiene, 1920), 163
Cahiers du Cinéma (film journal), 148–9
Camino Cortado (dir. Iquino, 1955), 37–48; *see also* Iquino, Ignacio
Capra, Frank, 72
Caravan (dir. Crabtree, 1946), 118
Casablanca (dir. Curtiz, 1942), 61
cassock, 185, 186–90
Catholicism, 14, 15, 39–40, 42, 84n1, 179n73, 181, 185, 186; *see also* Christianity
censorship, 41, 114, 128–9n55; *see also* Motion Picture Production Code
Christianity, 18, 110, 186, 189, 192
Civil Rights movement, 63, 64, 74, 84
class *see* social class
claustrophobia 14, 24, 51, 96, 163, 169–70
Clift, Montgomery, 186, 187, 189, 191, 194n24
coding
  homosexual, 77, 186; *see also* homosexuality
  ideological, 43
  Jewish, 78, 85n27
  racial, 76, 119; *see also* racial representation
Cold War, 182, 191
colonisation, 53, 133; *see also* decolonisation

Communism, 13, 15, 16–17, 19–20, 39, 75, 76, 87–8, 90–1, 98, 100, 101, 106, 177n51
Conrad, Joseph, 166

Daněk, Oldřich, 91, 92, 95, 101
Dangerous Exile (dir. Hurst, 1957), 111, 127n38, 128n43
Dassin, Jules, 120
Dearden, Basil, 113, 119
decolonisation, 118, 160n31; *see also* colonisation
desire, 28, 31, 35, 38, 43, 44, 82, 111, 113, 115, 118, 120, 134, 136, 137, 151, 182, 187, 189–90, 191; *see also* sexuality
disability, 27, 31, 32–5, 83, 139, 140
doomed male protagonist, 46, 113–14, 164, 166, 171, 172
doppelgänger, 187
Dostoevsky, Fyodor, 19, 162, 168–9, 170, 178n68
Double Indemnity (dir. Wilder, 1944), 70, 109, 120, 166, 169, 177n45; *see also* Wilder, Billy

entrapment, 41, 47, 48, 190, 192
ethnic self-loathing, 116, 121
ethnocentrism/ethnic prejudice, 52, 57, 113, 118, 120, 121; *see also* ethnic self-loathing; racism
expressionism, 3, 30, 76, 81–2, 97, 110–11, 128n43, 133, 138, 161, 162, 163, 165, 167, 168, 174n3, 174n6, 184

fascism, 12, 38–40, 44, 47, 49n36
fatalism, 11, 12, 26, 29, 30, 31, 35, 121
Faulkner, William, 149, 150, 153, 159n15
female protagonists, 24, 27, 32, 33, 84n4
femininity, 33, 38, 45–6, 110, 140; *see also* gender roles
feminisation, 33, 71, 139, 187; *see also* masculinity
feminism, 45

INDEX

femme fatale, 2, 16, 35, 37–8, 42, 43, 45, 55, 56, 81, 100, 109–10, 111–12, 116, 120, 122–3, 126n30, 126–7n32, 140, 168, 169, 172; *see also* wicked lady
film gris ('gray film'), 112
flashback (structure), 55, 62, 93, 94, 95, 99, 137, 167, 171, 185, 189–90
Ford, John, 58, 64
fragmentation, 4, 37, 131, 149
Franco, Francisco/Franco regime, 15, 37, 38–40, 41, 42, 43, 44, 45, 46, 48, 49n33, 49n36
French Poetic Realism *see* Poetic Realism
Freud, Sigmund, 136, 137, 138, 162, 165–6, 169, 175n13; *see also* psychoanalysis

Gainsborough Pictures, 107, 109, 110, 111, 118, 119, 124n5, 124–5n17, 127n34, 129n63
gangster film *see* genre
gender roles, 17, 33, 34, 35, 38, 39, 45–6, 117, 139–40, 142, 171, 182, 191
genre (film)
   'blood' melodrama, 163, 177n52, 178n66; *see also* melodrama
   chamber melodrama, 162, 165
   comedy, 72, 73, 77, 78, 81, 89, 98, 111
   costume melodrama, 105, 107, 108–11, 118, 122, 123, 129n63; *see also* melodrama
   gangster film, 72, 80, 81, 131, 165, 167, 171, 179n73, 133
   horror, 41, 49n24, 123, 128n43, 131, 133, 134, 140, 142, 166, 168, 173, 176n38, 176n40, 178n63, 178n70, 181
   melodrama, 3, 23, 24, 30, 31–2, 38, 46, 110, 114, 129n63, 141–2, 167, 170, 172, 173, 176n35, 176n39, 178n66, 186; *see also* 'blood' melodrama; costume melodrama
   musical, 61, 80–1, 98
   social problem film, 24, 25, 109, 113, 164, 167
   suspense thriller, 181, 191
   western, 51, 53, 56, 57, 59, 63, 64, 64n5, 65n19, 173n2
   see also genre hybridity
genre hybridity (film), 4, 24, 51, 56, 69, 72–3, 76, 79, 83, 107, 108, 111, 114, 131, 162, 167, 169, 173, 176n32
   comedy-drama, 114
   docu-noir, 163–5, 167
   Gothic-noir, 131–4, 135, 137, 139, 141, 142n6
   musical comedy, 73, 78–80, 82, 89
   musical noir, 72, 80–3
   western-noir, 51, 52, 53, 54, 56–7, 58, 63, 64
   see also genre
German Expressionism *see* expressionism
Gershwin, George, 74, 75, 82–3
Glass Web, The (dir. Arnold, 1953), 176n27
Gothic
   American Gothic, 182–3, 188–9, 192
   Gothic romance, 106, 107
   see also genre
Green, Janet, 105, 106, 112–13, 114, 118–19
Gypsy *see* Romani culture; Romani representation
Gypsy and the Gentleman, The (dir. Losey, 1958), 105–23, 124n5, 125n21, 127n38, 127n40; *see also* Losey, Joseph

hard-boiled (literature), 134, 139, 141, 149, 167
Hawthorne, Nathaniel, 182, 183, 188, 191, 192
Hitch-Hiker, The (dir. Lupino, 1953), 30; *see also* Lupino, Ida
Hitchcock, Alfred, 180–92, 193n5, 193n14, 193n16, 194n20
Hogarth, William, 105, 114
homosexuality *see* sexuality
horror *see* genre
House Committee on Un-American Activities, 64, 66n37, 76, 106

I Confess (dir. Hitchcock, 1953), 180–92, 193n16; *see also* Hitchcock, Alfred
imperialism, 53
independent film, 25–6, 164, 183
infidelity *see* adultery
individualism, 12, 82, 87, 90, 98, 137
Iquino, Ignacio, 37–48
Italian Neorealism *see* neorealism

Jassy (dir. Crabtree, 1947), 118
Jazz Singer, The (dir. Crossland, 1927), 74
Jewish émigré directors, 69–71, 72, 73, 75, 77, 84n1, 84n3
Jewishness *see* race, racial representation

Kadár, Ján 89, 91
Kahuda, František, 88
Kazan, Elia, 76, 85n28
Kern, Jerome, 75
Killer's Kiss (dir. Kubrick, 1955), 170, 174n6
Killers, The (dir. Siodmak, 1946), 162, 166–7, 177n47
Killing, The (dir. Kubrick, 1956), 163
Kiss Me Deadly (dir. Aldrich, 1955) 165, 170, 174n6, 176n28; *see also* Aldrich, Robert
Kiss of Death (dir. Hathaway, 1947), 170
Klos, Elmar, 89, 91
Krška, Vaclav, 87–102, 103n22

La Pointe Courte (dir. Varda, 1954), 147–58; *see also* Varda, Angés
Lang, Fritz, 69, 70, 77, 84n1, 133, 134, 163
Lawless, The (dir. Losey, 1950), 112; *see also* Losey, Joseph
Le May, Alan, 52, 57, 58
lighting, 41, 76, 78, 87, 95, 96, 112, 134, 137, 138, 150, 169, 180
Litvak, Anatole, 69–84
location shooting, 4, 25, 26, 51, 96, 128n41, 148, 150, 153, 161, 163, 165, 174n6, 176n28, 183

Losey, Joseph, 105–23, 128n41
Lupino, Ida, 23–35

M (dir. Lang, 1931), 84n1, 131, 133; *see also* Lang, Fritz
Man in Grey, The (dir. Arliss, 1943), 109, 110–11, 116
marriage, 24, 27, 45, 81, 84n1, 91, 92, 98, 99, 100, 113, 114, 115, 118, 120, 121, 134, 139, 147, 148, 150, 157–8, 171, 185, 187, 190
masculinity, 28, 32, 33, 43, 46, 70–1, 72, 77, 113, 139, 140, 142, 165, 171, 182, 187, 191; *see also* gender roles
melodrama *see* genre
Melville, Herman, 187–8, 189, 190
Mercouri, Melina, 105, 111, 119–20, 123
Metropolis (dir. Lang, 1927), 77, 133; *see also* Lang, Fritz
Mildred Pierce (dir. Curtiz, 1945), 93, 103n16, 114, 128n54
miscegenation, 107, 113, 114–15, 118–19, 169; *see also* race
Moby-Dick (Melville, 1851 novel), 187, 189; *see also* Melville, Herman
modernism
  cinematic, 13, 148, 150, 159n14, 178n60
  literary, 149–50, 163, 167
modernity, 37, 39, 40, 42, 45, 47, 132, 148, 150, 151, 152, 153, 154–5, 156–7, 158, 160n39
Motion Picture Production Code (Hollywood), 77, 83, 166, 170, 190
multi-ethnic identity, 107, 116, 121; *see also* race
Murder, My Sweet (dir. Dmytryk, 1941), 168

Naked City, The (dir. Dassin, 1948), 26; *see also* Dassin, Jules
neorealism, 4, 91, 148, 153, 154, 163
Never Fear (dir. Lupino, 1949), 23–35, 35–6n18; *see also* Lupino, Ida

New Wave cinema
  British, 107–8, 123
  Czech, 87, 90
  French, 148–9
Notorious (dir. Hitchcock, 1946), 186; see also Hitchcock, Alfred

objectification (female), 34, 55, 118, 139–40, 189
Out of the Past (dir. Tourneur, 1947), 12, 29, 71

Poe, Edgar Allan, 178n60, 182, 188
Poetic Realism (French), 3, 7n2, 77, 110–11, 163
populist fable, 72, 73, 75, 78, 80, 81
post-war era (World War II), 1, 2, 3, 23, 24, 26–7, 30, 31, 33, 35, 45, 52, 53, 64, 101, 107, 108–9, 114, 118–19, 122, 125n27, 128n54, 148, 151, 158, 160n32, 177n44; see also World War II
Production Code see Motion Picture Production Code
Prowler, The (dir. Losey, 1951), 112; see also Losey, Joseph
psychoanalysis, 137–8, 162; see also Freud, Sigmund

queerness, 77, 186, 187–8, 194n24; see also homosexuality

race, 53, 57, 59, 64, 80, 107, 115, 116, 118–19, 123, 169
racial representation, 61, 118–19
  Asian American representation, 64, 66n38
  Black/African American representation, 59–64, 65n24, 74, 79
  Blackface, 79, 85n15
  Jewish representation, 71–2, 73, 77, 78, 79, 82, 85n27
  Native American representation, 57–9
racial tension see racism
racism, 57–8, 59, 61, 64, 66n38, 86n29, 106, 113, 115, 118–19, 135, 165, 169

Rake's Progress, The (dir. Gilliat, 1945), 114, 128n54
Rank Organisation, The, 105, 106, 107, 110, 111, 112, 114, 122, 123
rape, 28, 30, 33, 169, 189
realism, 25, 26, 31, 35, 95, 128n41, 161, 163–4, 174n3; see also neorealism; Poetic Realism; socialist realism
Romani culture, 116, 123–4n3, 129n58
Romani representation, 107, 118, 120, 121, 129n63

Sapphire (dir. Dearden, 1959), 113, 118–19; see also Dearden, Basil
Scarlet Letter, The (Hawthorne, 1850 novel) 189, 190–1, 192; see also Hawthorne, Nathaniel
Scarlet Street (dir. Lang, 1945), 71, 82, 163, 173; see also Lang, Fritz
Scars of the Past (dir. Krška, 1959), 87–102, 103n16, 104n40; see also Krška, Vaclav
School for Fathers (dir. Helge, 1957), 89, 99
Searchers, The (dir. Ford, 1956), 57–8; see also Ford, John
self-destructiveness, 18, 19, 20
self-pity (female), 27, 30, 31, 33
self-sacrifice
  female, 46
  male, 32, 56, 114
Servant, The (dir Losey, 1963), 107, 111, 112, 113, 115, 117, 120, 127n40; see also Losey, Joseph
sexuality
  female, 38, 107–8, 113, 115, 116, 118, 119, 120, 123, 126n30, 130n70, 140, 189, 190; see also femininity
  homosexuality, 17, 113, 182, 187, 189; see also queerness
  male, 38, 136, 165, 169, 172, 182, 187, 189, 190, 191; see also masculinity
Shadow of a Doubt (dir. Hitchcock, 1943), 29–30, 178n70, 186, 188; see also Hitchcock, Alfred

INDEX

Siegel, Don, 76, 79–80
social class, 2, 37, 44, 53, 54, 61, 66n37, 72, 88–9, 90–1, 101, 106, 109, 111, 113, 115–16, 117, 120, 121, 122, 123, 129n63, 134, 138–9, 141, 142, 142n5, 151, 171, 189
social problem film *see* genre
socialist realism, 87, 89–90, 91, 92, 95, 97, 99, 100, 101
sound design, 30, 63, 96, 165
Spanish Civil War, 12, 13, 15, 38, 39, 40, 43, 49n36
Stagecoach (dir. Ford, 1939), 173; *see also* Ford, John
Strangers on a Train (dir. Hitchcock, 1951), 183, 191–2; *see also* Hitchcock, Alfred
Sturges, John, 51–64

Thirty Years' War, 11, 13
Three Wishes (dir. Kadár and Klos, 1958), 89, 91, 102n6; *see also* Kadár, Ján; Klos, Elmar
Touch of Evil (dir. Welles, 1958), 53–4, 161–2, 165–6, 168–9, 173, 174n4; *see also* Welles, Orson
trauma (psychological), 87, 137, 151
  female (postwar), 23, 27, 28–9
  war, 11–12, 21n4

Varda, Angés, 147–58, 159n9, 160n36
voice-over (narration), 4, 27, 93–4, 95, 137, 164, 174n6, 175n25, 177n47, 189

Wajda, Andrzej, 11–21
Walking Hills, The (dir. Sturges, 1949), 51–64; *see also* Sturges, John
Welles, Orson, 161, 162–3, 165–6, 170, 174n3, 174n4, 176n35, 176n39, 177n46; *see also Touch of Evil*
White, Josh, 52, 59–64
Whorf, Richard, 72, 76–7
wicked lady, 109–10, 111–12, 113, 119; *see also* femme fatale
Wicked Lady, The (dir. Arliss, 1945), 109–10, 111
Wild Palms, The (Faulkner, 1939 novel), 149, 153; *see also* Faulkner, William
Wilder, Billy, 70, 95, 103n16
women directors *see* Lupino, Ida; Varda, Agnés
World War I, 11, 188
World War II, 4, 12, 13, 32, 38, 39, 64, 69, 108–9, 118, 119; *see also* Postwar era

EU representative:
Easy Access System Europe
Mustamäe tee 50, 10621 Tallinn, Estonia
Gpsr.requests@easproject.com

www.ingramcontent.com/pod-product-compliance
Lightning Source LLC
Chambersburg PA
CBHW071713160426
43195CB00012B/1665